The Extraordinary Military Career of John Shipp

JOHN SHIPP

The Extraordinary Military Career of John Shipp
The Experiences of a Soldier in the Kaffir, Mahratta, Ghurka and Pindari Wars of the Early Nineteenth Century

John Shipp

The Extraordinary Military Career of John Shipp: the Experiences of a Soldier in the Kaffir, Mahratta, Ghurka and Pindari Wars of the Early Nineteenth Century
by John Shipp

Leonaur is an imprint of Oakpast Ltd

Material original to this edition and presentation of text in this form copyright © 2010 Oakpast Ltd

ISBN: 978-0-85706-226-0 (hardcover)
ISBN: 978-0-85706-225-3 (softcover)

http://www.leonaur.com

Publisher's Notes

The views expressed in this book are not necessarily those of the publisher.

Contents

Preface	7
Over the Hills & Far Away	9
See, the Conquering Hero Comes	20
The Sons of Neptune	34
To the Cape	39
We Fight the 'Caffres'	44
India	58
First Attempt on Bhurtpore	72
The Forlorn Hope—Again	85
The 24th Dragoons	99
Return to India	109
Ensign of the 'Old Fogs'	118
On Campaign to Nepaul	126
Fighting the Nepaulese	142
The End of the Ghoorka War	154
The Hattrass Campaign	166
Recovering From Wounds	180
The Pindarees	187
The Mad Rajah	198
Dhamoony	204
Against the Nagpore Rajah	217
Gurra Khootah	233
Asseerghur	245
The End of the Campaign	257
Ill Fortune	263
Comrades, Farewell	274
Continuation of the Memoir Until the Death of Mr. Shipp	283
Appendices	296

Preface

In laying before the public a familiar and unreserved detail of the incidents and adventures of my past life, I trust it will not for a moment be supposed that I am actuated by vanity, or by a desire to make an ostentatious display of my military services. That, in the course of those services, I have exercised some degree of daring, to the merit (if any) attached to which I may justly lay claim, I do not affect to deny; but it is far, very far, from my thoughts, to assume the possession of uncommon fortitude, or to arrogate to myself any degree of heroism superior to that which would be displayed, on occasions which required it, by every brave officer in his majesty's service.

Having thus, first, disclaimed all intention of boasting of my performances, or of holding myself up as a prodigy of valour, it becomes me next to declare that I do not pretend to afford the reader any important intelligence respecting our Indian possessions, either as regards statistics or politics. Information on these subjects must be sought in the works of writers of far higher pretensions than the humble author of these memoirs.

My design has been to present the public with a simple and unadorned narration of my own life, from the period of my infancy to the date of my having been, unfortunately, compelled to quit his majesty's service.

If, among the anecdotes which I have introduced, the eye of criticism may detect many which may be deemed of too trivial a nature, and devoid of that piquancy which can alone confer a value on such light and unimportant materials, I can only plead that I may have been led to over-estimate their merit, from the hearty laughter which they created when they were first noted by me; and I trust it will be recollected that it is a rough soldier who has ventured to think them worthy of publicity. So, also, if in my account of the battles and sieges in which I have had the honour to participate, my details shall appear flimsy or meagre, more especially as concerns the objects of the government of India in the various campaigns in which I have been engaged, be it remembered that I do not profess to know their designs; that my constant occupation in my professional duties afforded me no time to study them; and that it is the subaltern's duty to act, and not to reason.

My memoirs, such as they are, I leave to the indulgent consideration of a liberal public.

John Shipp
Bhurtpore Cottage
Alpha Road
Regent's Park
January, 1829

CHAPTER 1

Over the Hills & Far Away

In the ponderous mouldy register of the little market-town of Sax-mundham, in the county of Suffolk—covered with the red remnants of the old worn-out velvet pulpit-cushion of the said village church, into which the Christian religion had been beaten and enforced, both with clenched fist and pointed elbow, and which now plainly told the congregation that it had at last yielded only to Parson Brown's impressive manner and arguments—in this prodigious volume, protected by huge brass clasps, which naught but the rough hand of the man of skulls[1] could force to obedience, after the oft-wetted thumb had aroused some hundreds of gigantic leaves from their peaceful slumber, and the book had opened wide its time-worn pages, there was, and, I doubt not, is still to be discovered, a plainly-written record, setting forth, in most intelligible terms, that I, John Shipp, the humble author of these memoirs, came into this wicked and untoward generation on the 16th day of March, A.D. 1785. If this register be an authentic enrolment, which I have neither reason nor inclination to doubt, I was the second son of Thomas and Laetitia Shipp—persons of honest fame, but in indigent circumstances, who had both "drank deep" of the cup of sorrow. Of the latter of those dear parents I was bereft in my infancy; and, as my father was a soldier in a foreign clime, thus was I thrown on the world's tempestuous ocean, to buffet with the waves of care, and to encounter the breakers of want.

At the death of my poor mother I was left, with my elder brother, in utter destitution. The advantage which other children derive from the support and good counsel of an affectionate father, we had never known; and we were now suddenly bereft of a fond mother's fostering care, and with it, of our humble parental home. Where, under such circumstances, could we look for protection? Friends we had few, if any;

---

1. The sexton of the parish.

and those who might have been generously disposed to assist us were, unfortunately, incapacitated, by their own distressed circumstances, from extending a helping hand towards us. Need I feel shame, then, in avowing that there was one place of refuge, and one place only, in which two helpless orphans could obtain, at once, food, clothes, and shelter; and that that one asylum was the village poorhouse!

At the age of nine I was deprived of my brother, who was pressed on board a man-of-war. He was a remarkably fine youth of about fourteen; and, being of a wild spirited disposition, I have every reason to believe that but little *pressing* was required to induce him to go to sea; but rather, that being, like myself, homeless and dependent, he gladly availed himself of the opportunity which offered of setting his youthful heart free from bondage, by becoming a volunteer in the service of his country. Since that period—now upwards of thirty years—I have never heard of him!

To return to my own memoirs: now that my brother had left me, I was desolate indeed! His departure afflicted me most sincerely, and I felt myself alone in the wide world, a friendless isolated being. But the spirits of childhood, buoyant and elastic, though they may be depressed for a time, readily accommodate themselves to all exigencies, and rise superior to the greatest calamities. Grief, however poignant at first, will not dwell long with youth; and the ingenuity and curiosity of a boy ever on the alert to discover some new expedient with which to amuse his mind and to gratify his fickle fancy, effectually prevent him from indulging in unavailing despondency. I was naturally a wild dog, of an active unconquerable spirit; and although the miseries peculiar to my friendless situation could not but at first severely affect me, yet, after a short time, I found that, in spite of them all, I had so contrived it as to have established in the village a character for mischief infinitely superior to that possessed by any other boy of my own age. This character, however reverenced by boys of the same genius, was not, it must be acknowledged, very likely to increase the number of my real friends; and I therefore cannot speak in very rapturous terms of the comforts I enjoyed at this period of my youth. I have a recollection of sundry tricks and misdemeanours in which I was very actively concerned, and for which I was frequently as deservedly punished; and, as far as my memory serves me, my time, just at this juncture, was passed in a pretty even routine of planning and executing mischief, and receiving its reward.

This, however, was not long to last; for fickle fortune threw an incident in my way, which diverted my attention from all my former tricks and frolics, and turned my thoughts into a new channel. One autumn's morning, in the year 1794, while I was playing marbles in a lane called Love Lane, and was in the very act of having a shot at the whole ring with my blood-alley, the shrill notes of a fife, and the hollow sound of a distant drum, struck on my active ear. I stopped my shot, bagged my marbles, and scampered off to see the soldiers. On arriving at the market-place, I found them to be a recruiting party of the Royal Artillery, who had already enlisted several likely-looking fellows. The pretty little well-dressed fifer was the principal object of my notice. His finery and shrill music were of themselves sufficient attractions to my youthful fancy; but what occupied my thoughts more than either of these was the size of this musical warrior, whose height very little exceeded that of the drum by which he stood.

"Surely," thought I to myself, sidling up to him, "I must be myself as tall, if not taller, than this little blade, and should make as good a soldier!"

Reflections of this nature were crowding thick into my mind when the portly sergeant, addressing his words to the gaping rustics by whom he was surrounded, but directing his eyes to the bed-room windows in the vicinity of his station, commenced a right royal speech. I swallowed every word spoken by the royal sergeant, with as much avidity as the drum-major's wife would her morning libation. It was all about "gentlemen soldiers," "merry life," "muskets rattling," "cannons roaring," "drums beating," "colours flying," "regiments charging," and shouts of "victory! victory!" On hearing these last words, the rustic bumpkins who had enlisted exposed their flowing locks, and with their tattered hats gave three cheers to "the king—God bless him." In this I most heartily joined, to the no small amusement of the assembled multitude. "Victory!" seemed still to ring in my ears, and the sound inspired my little heart with such enthusiasm, that it was not until some minutes after the rest had left off cheering, that I became conscious, from the merriment around me, that I still held my tiny hat elevated in the air, waiting for a repetition of that spirit-stirring word.

Finding myself observed, I adjusted my hat with a knowing air, elevated my beardless chin with as much consequence as I could assume, and, raising myself on tiptoe, to appear as tall as possible, I strutted up to the sergeant, and asked him, in plain words, if he would "take I for a sodger?"

The sergeant smiled, and patted my head in so condescending a manner, that I thought I might venture to take the same liberty with the head of the drum; but in this I was mistaken, for I had no sooner touched it than I received from the drummer a pretty sharp rap on the knuckles for my presumption: his drum-head was as sacred to him as the apple of his eye. I again mounted on tiptoe and urged my question, "Will you like I for a sodger?" intimating, at the same time, that I was "bigger than that there chap," pointing to the little fifer.

Incensed at this indignity, the boy of notes was so nettled, that he commenced forthwith to impress on my face and head striking marks of his irritation in being thus degradingly referred to. This I felt that I could have returned with compound interest; but, as my antagonist had the honour of wearing his majesty's livery, I deemed it wiser to pocket the affront, with my marbles, and make the best of my way off. I accordingly made a retrograde movement towards home, full of the scene I had just witnessed, and vociferating, as I went along, "Left, right;" "Right, left;" "Heads up, soldiers;" "Eyes right;" "Eyes left," &c. In short, I had thus suddenly not only been touched by the military, but got the military touch; and from that day forth I could neither say nor do anything, but in what I thought a soldier-like style: my play consisted chiefly of evolutions and manoeuvres, and my conversation of military phrases.

Shortly after this adventure, I was sent to live with a farmer in the town, whose heart was as cold as the hoar-frost which often blighted his fairest prospects. Fortunately for me, however, his wife was of a different disposition. This good dame proved almost a second mother to me, and frequently screened me from the effects of my master's rage; but so restless and untoward (to say the truth) were my inclinations and propensities, and so imperious in his commands, and unrelenting in his anger, was my master, that in spite of my kind mistress's intercession in my favour, I seldom passed a day without being subjected to his cruel lash. This treatment was but little calculated either to conciliate my affections, or to effect a reformation in my conduct. My feelings became hardened under the lash of oppression; and my desire to leave a place so little congenial with my disposition increased daily. Meantime, all the cats and dogs in my master's house were made to go through military evolutions; the hoes and rakes were transformed into muskets, and the geese and turkeys into soldiers. Even my master's whip, which was always in requisition at the conclusion of these performances, could not eradicate my propensity for "soldiering." Every time his back was turned, my military exercises were resumed; and when I could not by possibility find time to be thus actively engaged, I solaced myself with whistling, *God Save the King*, *The British Grena-*

diers, and *See, the Conquering Hero Comes*. The first of these tunes I once commenced in the churchyard, during a funeral service; for which I got the sexton's cane over my back; "that being no place," as the said sexton judiciously remarked, "to show my loyalty in." Even the old women in the parish could not pass me without a military salute, such as "Heads up, missis!" "Eyes right, missis!" "Keep the step, missis!" &c. These pranks often brought me into disgrace and trouble, and usually ended with an application of the end of my master's whip.

In the dreary month of December, when the white snow danced along the glen, and the icicle sparkled on the hoary oak, I had transported my frozen limbs into a turnip field, close by the Great Yarmouth road, where I stood shrivelled up like a dried mushroom, plotting and planning how to escape from the truly wretched situation in which I felt myself to be then placed. I had just put my cold fingers into my mouth, for the purpose of warming them, and had given them the first puff, when I heard the distant sound of martial music. Down went my hands, and up went my heels. I made an *echelon* movement towards the place; jumped over the gate; brought up my right shoulder a little; then gave the word "Forward," and marched in double quick time. The music soon got nearer; or, at all events, I soon got so near to the music that I was glad to halt. Just at this moment the whole band struck up *Over the Hills, and Far Away*, which kindled a flame in my bosom which nothing but death can extinguish, though I have now long since had my full share of the reality of the Scotch melody.

On coming up to the party of soldiers, I gave the colonel a military salute, by first slapping my leathers, then bringing up my right hand (which, by the by, was the wrong hand) to my forehead, and extending the thumb as far as I could from my fingers. I continued in this position, keeping my elbow parallel with the top of my head, until the colonel came close up to me; and, remarking how studiously I retained the same position, condescendingly said, with a smile, "That's a fine fellow."

On this head I perfectly agreed with the gallant commandant, as may be readily supposed; and the compliment so elated me, that I felt by no means certain whether I stood on my head or my heels; but ran about, first in the front, then in the rear, until at last I ran bump up against "master," who presented himself to my astonished eyes, mounted on Corporal Dash (a horse of his I had so named), with a long hunting whip (a very old friend of mine) in his hand. The moment I recognized these old acquaintances, I saw that I had not a minute to lose; so, making up my mind that a good retreat was far better than a bad fight, I ran off at full charge, as fast as my legs would carry me, my master riding after me, and roaring out most lustily, "Stop! stop!"

If, instead of "Stop," he had said "Halt," it is more than probable that my legs would instinctively have obeyed; for, from the constant drills to which they had been subjected, they began to move quite mechanically. As it was, however, on I went, until a stile brought my master up; when, as I was quite out of breath, I thought I might as well halt too. Here I had the satisfaction of hearing my master swear roundly, that he would kill me when he caught me.

"Thank God," thought I to myself, "you have not got me yet."

The moment my persecutor rode on, I cut across a field, and again gained the head of the corps of Royal Horse Artillery, who were at this time just entering the suburbs of the village. Here I dared not venture to follow them any farther, until my master's hurricane had blown over; so I mounted a gate, where my heart yearned after them, as that of a wounded soldier does after his corps in the battle's heat. Here I again set my wits to work how to elude the chastisement I was sure to receive from the infuriated man of clods. The regiment which I had seen was, I had ascertained, on its march to Yarmouth, to embark for foreign service; and, from the condescending manner of the colonel (who returned my salute), I made no doubt whatever that he would be glad to take me for a soldier. Full of these thoughts, I loitered about all day, but dared not venture in, until, at length, my interior began to express wants respecting which I had not before reflected. These demands were of a nature not to be drilled into obedience; so, at last, overcome by fatigue and inanition, in I marched, having first seen my master march out. My mistress, who was ever ready to act the part of a kind mother towards me, soon provided me with a substantial meal. I was not long in doing justice to the repast thus kindly set before me; and, having effectually satisfied my appetite for the time present, I took the precaution of lining my pockets with a large hunch of bread and cheese, to subsist on the following day, when I intended to be in light marching order to follow the soldiers. Having thus prudently provided in some degree for the future, I betook myself to my usual occupations; but I had not commenced work more than five minutes, when I espied my master reconnoitring me from behind a hedge. Presently he crossed a stile with a large whip in his hand; and I could discern, from his artful movements, that it was his intention to come upon me unperceived. Now and then, in order that my fears might not be excited, he would stoop down and pull a turnip; but I was too good a soldier myself to be out-generalled in this manner. I stood from my work, the better to observe the enemy's movements, and kept my eye upon the fugleman. At last, I saw him make preparations to arrange his whip; so I immediately arranged my legs for a start.

"Every step that he now takes," thought I to myself, "is a step nearer to my back; whereas, now that I have ten yards' start, there is still a chance for me."

My master perceived that I was ready for a bolt, and soon broke from slow time into quick, and from quick to double quick, which put me to the charge, my master following me—swearing, threatening, and roaring out, "Stop him! stop him!" a second time.

I turned round to look who was likely to stop me, when my foot came in contact with a large clod, and I tumbled heels over head. Here the chase ended; for my tyrant caught hold of me by a smock-frock which I had on, and commenced flogging me; but, from the race I had given him, I found he was so winded, that he had not strength left to hurt me much; so I "showed fight" at once, by seizing hold of the lash of the whip. This so enraged him, that he threw me from him with such violence, that one side of the smock-frock and I parted company, and I had just sufficient time left me to get up again and make my escape, which I did, leaving my master, as a token of my unalterable affection, the one side of my upper garment. Let it be his winding-sheet, for he was a cruel monster!

The remaining half of my smock-frock I stuck in a hedge in the same field, as a further token of my regard, and as a proof of my anxiety to leave him all I could spare. I then made a movement towards the town, in the hope that I should see the colonel, but he was not to be found; and I went from public-house to public-house, in search of the soldiers, till night began to unfold her sombre mantle, which was as gloomy as my poor little friendless bosom. Go home I dared not; so, after wandering about the farmer's house, I at last got into the stable, and slept all night in the hay-loft, dreaming I was a general, and riding over the battle's plain. Here I slept as sound as a dead soldier, until I was awoke in the morning by the gruff voice of my master, inquiring if they had seen anything of me, and protesting that, whenever he caught me, he would skin me alive.

"Bob" (one of his men), he bellowed out, "saddle that there old horse, Corporal Dash, and I'll go and see where he is; and, if I catches him, I'll put him in the stocks, and see if that can't cool his courage for him. He is the most tarnationest and outdationest lad I have ever seen:

it was only the day before yesterday that I catched him riding the old sow, Polly, with a pitchfork, and singing out, 'Victory! Victory!' but I'll see if the stocks won't cool him."

The old corporal was saddled accordingly, and led out. I could distinctly see him through a small hole in the loft, and he trotted off towards the market-place. I now began to think what place was best and safest for me. Skinning alive I could not bear the thoughts of; and, as to the stocks, it is true they might have cooled me, for it was freezing hard, and as bitter a morning as ever blew from the heavens; but there was nothing soldier-like in the situation, and the thoughts of such a position were not to be endured.

As soon as Bob had left the place to go to his work, I began to form plans for my retreat. Resolved, for the present, to act on the defensive, I first reconnoitred the course, to see that the enemy was not lying in ambush for me, or lurking in the vicinity of my hiding-place. Finding all clear, I descended to the stable, and soon gained the road. Having passed through the barn-yard and orchard, I peeped in at the farmhouse, but could not catch a glimpse of my kind mistress. My bread and cheese I had eaten the preceding evening, and my stomach began now to evince symptoms of mutinous commotion; but the fear of falling again into the hands of my merciless enemy prevailed over all other considerations, and, in an adjoining field, I regaled myself very contentedly on a turnip. I had just concluded that sumptuous repast, and was beginning to reflect seriously on the situation in which I had placed myself, when the band struck up that beautiful old melody, *The Girl I Left Behind Me*. This was both meat and drink to me, and its sweet notes comforted my lately inconsolable bowels. I put myself in marching and soldier-like attitude; and, with my hands stuck close to my leathers, my fingers directed towards the earth, chin elevated, toes pointed, thus I stepped off with the left leg, keeping time with the tune, until I arrived at the toll-gate, about a quarter of a mile from the town. Here I could not help halting, to look back on the little place of my birth, the scene of my boyhood, and many a sportive hour. I found the tear trickling down my cheek. It was near the grave of my fond mother, too. I hesitated, for some time, whether to proceed or return; but my master's dreadful threat rushed upon my mind in all its terror, and this impelled me onwards; and I again joined the followers, men and boys, girls and dogs. I was but a child, but I was a child cast upon the world, parentless, and in the hands of a cruel master. I could not believe it possible to be worse off, and therefore continued my march towards Yarmouth, without a mouthful of bread to eat, or a penny in my pocket. I knew not a soul in the place to which I was going; but my truant disposition took a hop, step, and jump over all difficulties.

My worldly effects consisted of a hat, which had once been round, but which, from my continually turning and twisting it into the shape of cocked-hats, road-hats, soldiers' caps, &c., was now any shape you wished; a little fustian jacket; waistcoat of the same material; a coarse shirt, which, from a violent shaking fit, was completely in rags; a pair of leathers, intolerably fat and greasy; ribbed worsted stockings; and a thwacking pair of high-lows, nailed from heel to toe. These, with a little stick, were my only encumbrances, save a gloomy prospect. I was bitterly hungry, and sadly tired; but on I went until we arrived within a mile of Beccles, some sixteen miles from home. Here some of the soldiers branched off to their quarters in the vicinity of the town; but I followed the greater body, as the more probable means of getting something to eat. The band now again struck up, *Over the Hills, and Far Away*. I marched at the head, but began to find that my poor craving stomach could no longer feed upon delicious melody; so I now made up my mind to accost the colonel, and ask him if he could not enlist me for a soldier. The colonel seemed a kind-hearted man; so, as modesty on my part was now quite out of the question, I bent my way to the head inn, where all the officers were assembled. I inquired for the colonel, and was at last shown into a room where he was sitting, with other officers, at breakfast. I strutted up to him with my hat in my hand, and made him a most obsequious bow, with my hand and foot at the same time. I then stood straight, as if I had swallowed a sergeant's pike; when the colonel laughingly said, "Well, my fine little rustic, what's your pleasure?"

I said, making another bow, and scraping the carpet with my nailed high-lows, "Soldiering, your honour."

At this, the whole of the officers burst into a roar of laughter, in which the colonel most heartily joined. I thought it was the fashion in the army, so I joined them, which only served to increase their mirth; and many of them were obliged to hold their sides from excess of laughter. I soon found that all this merriment was at my expense; at which I began to evince some slight displeasure, and was just about to express it in words, when the colonel said, in the most affectionate manner, "My dear little child, you had better return to your fond mother's lap."

Here I could not help piping, and I replied, "Sir, my mother is dead."

"Could I even take you," continued the colonel, "I should imagine that I was robbing some fond parent of its child; besides, we are proceeding on foreign service, against the enemy."

This news only served to increase my anxiety to go, and I again entreated him to look with compassion upon an orphan. I saw him turn from me, and wipe away a falling tear; and then, addressing me with the affection of a parent, he said, "My dear little fellow, if I was going to remain in England, I would take you; but under the present circumstances, I cannot."

Here I again began to cry, and I told him that I was sixteen miles from home, and had not got a piece of bread to put in my mouth. Upon this, the whole of the officers vociferated, "Waiter! Waiter! Waiter!"

The waiter was speedily in attendance, when I was ordered breakfast by twenty persons at the same time. I was still resolved not to give up my point; but the colonel again told me, it would be impossible for him to take me, but assured me that I should be taken care of, and desired me to go downstairs and get my breakfast. I did so, and, in passing round the table for the purpose of retiring, some gave me a shilling, some sixpence, so that I had more money than I had ever before possessed in my life. I ate a hearty breakfast in the kitchen, the servants asking me a number of impertinent questions. After breakfast, I counted my riches, and found that I had ten shillings, at least, in my leathers, into the pockets of which I every moment introduced my hand, to feel if all was safe. In the afternoon I was ordered dinner, and at last placed in the charge of a sergeant, who inquired who and what I was. I slept with him, and slept most soundly too, thinking I was a soldier. Early the next morning I was awoke, when the sergeant showed me a note from the good-natured colonel to my master, whose name and address he had pumped me out of the evening before. The sergeant was proceeding to Woodbridge Barracks, and he had directions to take me over to my master, as well as to deliver the colonel's note, which was open, and contained a most earnest request that, for his sake, my master would not flog me. The generous colonel had also given the sergeant five shillings for me, which he gave me before I started from Beccles. About three o'clock in the afternoon I arrived at my master's, who was at home. The kind message of the colonel was communicated to him, and he faithfully promised the sergeant, that all should be forgiven and forgotten. I was lured, under this promise, to return to my work, resolved to do better in future; and I began to think that I really had not much reason to complain; for, on counting my money, I found I had fifteen shillings and sixpence left, after treating the sergeant on the way home. Scarcely, however, had the sun risen on the following day, when my master seized me by the neck, and dragged my clothes off my back. He had with him a double-handed whip, such as is used by colliers, and with this he lashed me so unmercifully, that I have no hesitation in saying, that, had not a man, who was labouring in an adjoining field, interfered, he would have killed me. He was the most inhuman man I ever saw; and if he was not dead, and his family in abject poverty, I should, before this, have published his name; but, not to add to their present calamities, I will bury such feelings with their father, and begin a fresh chapter, with accounts more interesting to my readers; first entreating their forgiveness for having dwelt so long on the scenes of my boyhood.

CHAPTER 2

See, the Conquering Hero Comes

About this period (1797) the three experimental regiments[1] were ordered to be formed, *viz.*, the 22nd, 34th, and 65th regiments; the former at Colchester. I was, one morning in that year, about the month of January or February, busily employed in a field close by my master's house, when, who should I see but one of the parish officers making towards me, with a large paper in his hand. I began to muster and parade my crimes, but found, on a fair review, that I had done nothing that merited the interference of an officer; so I stood up boldly till he approached me, and smilingly said, "Shipp, I have frequently heard of, and observed your great wish to go for a soldier."

He then read the paragraph, and asked me if I was willing to go; for that, if I was, the parish would rig me out decently, and that he would take me to Colchester. My little heart was in my mouth; I repeated his words, "Willing to go!" and eagerly assured him of the rapture with which I accepted his offer. The affair was soon concluded; so down went my shovel, and off I marched, whistling, *See, the Conquering Hero Comes*.

By four o'clock of the same day, to the honour and praise of the parish be it spoken, I was rigged out in my new leather tights, new coat, new hat, new shoes, new everything—of which I was not a little proud. I begged, as a particular favour, that I might sport colours in my hat; and even this was permitted to my vanity, as long as I remained in the town. I took an affectionate leave of all my old playfellows and my

---

1. The object of government in forming these "experimental regiments," as they were called, was to relieve parishes of boys, from the age of ten to sixteen, who were allowed to enlist, on the parish paying the expenses of their journey to some recruiting depot. Each of these regiments was composed of a thousand boys, who made such excellent soldiers, that it appears extraordinary no such plan was ever again adopted; the three regiments here spoken of having been the only corps formed in this way.

SAXMUNDHAM CHURCH

good mistress; and even my cruel master was not neglected by me, for I never had malice or unforgiveness in my disposition.

The next day, by seven o'clock in the morning, I was on my way to Colchester; and, when I was seated on the front seat of the coach, I would not have exchanged situations with the grand *pasha* of Egypt, or the king upon the throne of that land of which I was a native. Scarcely had I seated myself, and adjusted my feet in a safe situation, than I indulged my coach companions by whistling several martial airs; but, coming to a well-known turn of the road, from which you take the farewell peep at Saxmundham, as much as I loved my king, I stopped short in the middle of the national anthem, and my eye bent its way instinctively towards my native village, where I first saw the light of heaven, and rested on the little village spire, which reared its Gothic head over the remains of my poor mother. Towards this painfully interesting object I looked and looked, till the place of my nativity was buried from my sight by the surrounding trees. When bereft of this view, I felt pensive and sad, and could only console myself by reflecting, that I did not fly from my parental roof; nor was I deserting aged parents, or unprotected sisters, for I had no one to bewail my departure. Yet I could not help feeling that I left something behind me that hung like a magnet to my heart; with all my misfortunes, all my cares and troubles, still I could not quit, without a pang, the place of my birth, and the tomb of my beloved mother.

At last, three gentlemen on the coach, having heard my history from the person who accompanied me, cheered me up by saying, that they knew the corps I was going to, and that they were all lads like myself. This notice from strangers so enlivened me, that I began to regard myself as no small personage, and I talked as much as any of them, until we arrived at an inn in Colchester, where we dined.

Here I was marched off to the colonel of the corps in which I was to serve; from the colonel to the adjutant; from the adjutant to the sergeant-major; from the sergeant-major to the drum-major; and thence to his wife, an old drunken Irish woman, but as good a creature as ever drank whisky. In the custody of this lady, the friend who came with me left me, first giving me a hearty shake of the hand, and wishing me every happiness. I must confess I felt now quite deserted: about twenty boys gathered round me, and I soon found that my fine leathers were the subject of their ridicule and laughter; some of them crying out, "Bill, twig his leathers!"

"Smoke his new coat!"

"My eye! what a buck!"

"Some gemman's son, I suppose, run away from his daddy!"

"Never mind," said another, "we'll soon drill his leathers into hot rolls and butter."

Here my friend Maggy, the Irish woman, interposed her aid in my behalf.

"Arrah!" said she, "what are you gazing at, you set of *spalpeens*, you? Be off, you set of thaves, or I will be after breaking some of your nasty dirty mugs for you. Arrah! don't mind them; sure they are nothing at all but a set of monkeys just catched. Come here, honey, and let me see who will be after laying a finger on you."

Here she seated me by her side, rubbed my chin, patted my back, eyed my coat and breeches, and asked me if I had got any pence in my pocket, with which she should get me some hot rolls and butter, for *ta*. I gave her a shilling, and she brought two rolls and butter. The residue I suppose she spent in gin, for she began to give me some of her Irish hugs; so much so, that I wished myself at a greater distance.

One of the boys cried out, "Ask for the change—ask her for the change, or she will do you."

At this imputation Maggy got on her legs, and, seizing a large trencher, tottered, or rather staggered, towards the boy, and exclaimed, "You great big blackguard, you, do you want to rob me of my name? Take that, and bad luck to you!"

Here she hurled the trencher at him, but the effort carried old Maggy off her legs, and she exhibited her gigantic figure on the floor, to the amusement of all the barrack. I could not help laughing heartily, though I found I had got among a queer set; when the drum-major entering, and seeing his wife on the floor, vociferated, "Get up, you old drunken hag; or, by St. Patrick! and that's no small oath, but I'll pay you off."

Here Maggy made an effort to rise, but the drop had done her up; and I was obliged to give her a helping hand, and she was put to bed, clothes and all.

On the following morning I was taken to a barber's, and deprived of my curly brown locks. My hair curled beautifully, but in a minute my poor little head was nearly bald, except a small patch behind, which was reserved for a future operation. I was then paraded to the tailor's shop, and deprived of my new clothes—coat, leathers, and hat—for which I received, in exchange, red jacket, red waistcoat, red pantaloons, and red foraging-cap. The change, or metamorphosis, was so complete, that I could hardly imagine it to be the same dapper little fellow.

I was exceedingly tall for a boy of ten years of age; but, notwithstanding this, my clothes were much too large: my sleeves were two or three inches over my hands, or rather longer than my fingers; and the whole hung on me, to use a well-known expression, like a purser's shirt on a hand-spike. My pride was humbled, my spirits drooped, and I followed the drum-major, hanging my head like a felon going to the place of execution. I cut such a queer figure, that all who met me turned round and stared at me. At last, I mustered up courage enough to ask one little chap what he was staring at, when he replied, "Ask my eye, Johnny Raw;" at the same time adding his extended fingers and thumb to the length of his nose.

Passing some drummers on their way to practice, I got finely roasted. "Twig the raw-skin!"

"Smoke his pantaloons!"

"Them there trousers is what I calls a knowing cut!"

"Look at the sign of the Red Man!" &c., &c.

Under this kind of file-firing I reached my barrack, where I was doomed to undergo the same routine of quizzing, till at length I got nettled, and told one of the boys, if he did not let me alone, I should take the liberty of giving him a good threshing. This "pluck," as they termed it, silenced most of my tormentors, and I was permitted, for a time, to remain unmolested. In this interval the drum-major went out, having first put my leathers, &c., into his box, of which he took the key.

I sat myself down on a stool, which might not inaptly have been styled the stool of repentance; for here I began first to think that soldiering did not possess quite so much delight as I had pictured to myself. Still I resolved to put a good face on the matter, and so mixed with my comrades, and in an hour was as free and as much at home with them all as if I had known them for years.

The drift of my new acquaintances, in being thus easily familiar with me, was soon apparent; for one of the knowing ones among them called me aside, and asked me if I knew where to sell my coloured clothes; as, if not, he would go with me, and show me. I told him that the drum-major had them.

"Yes," replied he, "I know he has; but you see as how he has no business with them. Them there traps should be sold, and you get the money they brings; and if you don't keep your eye on the fugleman, he will do you out of half of them."

He further said, that, when he enlisted, he got more than five shillings for his things. I replied, that of course the drum-major would either sell them for my benefit, or permit me to do it; and, if the latter, that I should be thankful for his kindness. At this moment he entered, when the boy, who had just spoken to me, approached him, and said, pointing to me, "That there chap says as how he wants to sell them things of his in your box, and that I am to go with him, to show him the place where I sold my things."

To this falsehood I could not submit, and I therefore went up to the drum-major, and said, "Sir, I said nothing of the kind; all I said was, that I supposed you would either dispose of the things for my benefit, or allow me to do so."

"Yes, yes," said the drum-major, "that's all right; I will sell them for you, and you shall have the money."

The boy here turned upon his heel, muttering something like *fudge*! and the things were put into a handkerchief and carried off into the town. When the drum-major had left us, the same boy came up to me, and called me a liar, stating that he had a great mind to thresh me; and, as a proof of his inclination, he attempted to seize my nose between his finger and thumb. I got in a rage, and told him, if he ventured to touch me, I would fell him to the ground; when all the boys gathered round us, and said, "Well done, Johnny Raw!"

"Well done, old leather-breeches!"

"That's right, Johnny Wapstraw!"

Finding that I did not venture to strike the first blow, my antagonist called me a coward. This I knew I was not; so, as I could submit to his insolence no longer, I struck him, and to it we went in right earnest. After half a dozen rounds my opponent gave in. This, my first victory, established that I was neither a coward nor to be hoaxed with impunity. Eulogiums were showered down upon me, and the shouting and uproar were beyond description. I understood afterwards that he was a great bully, and always fighting.

Our boxing-match had just concluded, when the drum-major entered, and produced the proceeds of my clothes; *viz.*, £1 1s. 6d. for a new hat, coat, waistcoat, and leathers: a fair price, some said; while others thought they ought to have fetched thirty shillings; but I was very well satisfied, and stood hot rolls and butter to all around, not forgetting my antagonist, who shook hands, and said it was the first time he had ever been beaten, and that he would some day, in friendship, have another trial. I assured him that I should be at any time at his service, and thus this matter ended.

After this I went into town, to purchase a few requisites, such as a powder-bag, puff, soap, candles, grease, &c.; and, having procured what I stood in need of, I returned to my barrack, where I underwent the operation of having my hair tied for the first time, to the no small amusement of all the boys assembled. A large piece of candle-grease was applied, first to the sides of my head, then to the hind long hair; after this, the same kind of operation was performed with nasty stinking soap—sometimes the man who was dressing me applying his knuckles, instead of the soap, to the delight of the surrounding boys, who were bursting their sides with laughter, to see the tears roll down my cheeks. When this operation was over, I had to go through one of a more serious nature. A large pad, or bag filled with sand, was poked into the back of my head, round which the hair was gathered tight, and the whole tied round with a leather thong. When I was dressed for parade, I could scarcely get my eyelids to perform their office; the skin of my eyes and face was drawn so tight by the plug that was stuck in the back of my head, that I could not possibly shut my eyes; add to this, an enormous high stock was poked under my chin; so that, altogether, I felt as stiff as if I had swallowed a ramrod, or a sergeant's halberd. Shortly after I was thus equipped, dinner was served; but my poor jaws refused to act on the offensive, and when I made an attempt to eat, my pad behind went up and down like a sledge-hammer.

In the evening I went to parade, and was inspected by the colonel, who said I was a promising lad, but that my clothes did not fit, which he ordered to be altered. At this moment the master of the band came up to the colonel, and said that he should like to have me in the band, to learn the flute and to beat the triangles. This request was granted, and I was the following day removed to the band-room, and commenced my musical avocations; and in six months I had beaten the sides of the triangles nearly as thin as my own, and had also become a tolerable flute-player: but, as at that time we got several volunteers from the militia, among whom were two excellent flute-players, I was removed back to the drummer's room, and put to the fife. In a short time I was made fife-major—no small office, I assure you. I wore two stripes and a tremendous long sash, which almost touched the ground.

As the reader may suppose, I was not a little proud of my new office; I began to ride the high horse among my old comrades, and to show my authority by enforcing obedience by very powerful arguments; for I was permitted to carry a small cane, and to use it too. In the absence of the drum-major, which was frequent, I carried the silver-headed stick, some seven feet long, and when we furnished the band for general guard-mounting, I astonished the spectators with my double *demi-semi* twist of my cane, and began to think myself one of the brightest of the bright.

At this period the regiment moved to the Hythe, about a mile from Colchester, and twice a day we beat through the streets, followed by all the girls and boys in the town, some of the rosy-cheeked beauties begging me to play favourite tunes of theirs. These entreaties for particular airs were urged with such pathos, accompanied with such fascinating smiles and leers, that the fife-major occasionally vouchsafed to comply, always, however, keeping up his dignity, by making a compliance with such requests appear a great condescension. I strutted about the town with my little cane under my arm, like some great man of eminent consequence, whom the community could not do without; became a great favourite with all my officers; was happy and contented; and time passed imperceptibly and very pleasantly away.

Meantime, I grew very tall, though somewhat slender; and my red coat had been thrown off, for which was substituted a splendid white silver-laced jacket, with two small silver epaulettes, which my swagger induced to fan the evening breeze.

My days were now comparatively cloudless; yet still my youthful tricks had not entirely left me. Some of these frequently led me into scrapes and unpleasant predicaments. The following were among the frolics with which I at this time diverted myself: *viz.*, filling the pipes of my comrades with gunpowder; putting a lighted candle in their hands while asleep, then tickling their noses with a straw; tying their great toes together, then crying out fire; blacking their hands with soot, then tickling their ears and noses, to induce them to scratch themselves, and thus to black their faces all over; putting lighted paper between their toes when asleep; pulling the stools from behind them when in the act of sitting down; sewing their shirts to their bedding when asleep: all these, with fifty more, I regret to say, were in those days my constant delight and practice.

These mischievous pranks led me into many a fight, but that did not discourage me. I had a natural propensity to tease people; and, as I did not scruple to indulge it, you may be sure I did not escape without my share of tricks in return. He who plays at fives, says the old proverb, must expect rubbers; and accordingly, one day, when I was sitting upstairs, a hundred voices bawled out, "Pass the word for the fife-major; the adjutant wants him." I bounced down in an instant, and soon found that the whole barrack were in a roar of laughter at my expense; for, to the tail of my coat was attached a large sheet of paper with these words in legible characters, "The Biter Bit." To have evinced any displeasure at this hoax, would only have served to render me more ridiculous, and to increase the hooting and laughter at my expense; so I joined in the laugh, and affected to think it a remarkably good joke.

About this period a circumstance happened which, in some degree, blighted my pride, and almost cooled my military zeal. It was nutting season: I made a party to go, and we arrived at the wood, where the filberts hung as thick as laurels on a soldier's brow. We had not bagged more than a bushel, when we were pounced upon by three keepers, and taken prisoners to the barracks.

The three boys who were my companions on this excursion got two dozen stripes; I lost my two as fife-major, and was turned back to my original post as drummer, or rather as fifer. This severe punishment did not arise from the enormity of purloining the nuts, but from the fact of our being found some four miles from the cantonment. Under these circumstances we might have been taken up as deserters, and the keepers have received two pounds each man; so that, upon the whole, we had reason to be grateful that the more serious offence was not urged against us.

Shortly after this unfortunate occurrence, the regiment was ordered to proceed to the barracks at Hilsea, Portsmouth. This was soldiering in clover; and good living, fresh scenes, faces, and events, conspired to make me, in a measure, forget the stripes which I had lost. I was not long on the march, before I became as knowing as the best of them, and was soon well versed in the tricks of the road. I found that it was the practice of some of the landlords to give us fat pea-soup, and of others to regale us with greasy suet dumplings, as heavy as lead, by way of taking off the edge of our appetites. These dishes I invariably avoided, stating that they were injurious to my constitution, or that the doctors had forbidden me to eat such food. I therefore waited for the more substantial fare—the roast and the boiled—which I attacked with such zest, as could not fail to convince the landlord of the delicacy of my constitution, and of the absolute necessity of my refraining from less substantial diet. In two hours after dinner the duff and pea-soup eaters were as hungry as ever; but I kept my own counsel, and thus was enabled to go on my way with a smiling countenance that indicated good and substantial fare.

When we were treated in the scurvy way I have spoken of by the landlords on our line of march, we never failed to leave some token of our displeasure behind us. Thus, one day at Chelmsford, we were compelled to submit to dreadful bad quarters; and even the extreme delicacy of my constitution, which had so often succeeded with me before, could not, on this occasion, induce our host to give us anything but greasy puddings and fat stews, made of the offal of his house for the last month. The fat on the top of this heterogeneous mixture was an inch thick; and I, for my own part, protested that I could not and would not eat it. Finding me so positive, he privately slipped a shilling into my hand to quiet me, which I did not think it expedient to refuse. This bribe tended, in some degree, to pacify me; but my comrades, on quitting the house, evinced their disapprobation of the treatment they had met with, by writing with a lighted candle on the ceiling, "D——d bad quarters—How are you off for pea-soup?—Lead dumplings—Lousy beds—Dirty sheets."

This was the mildest description of punishment with which we visited landlords who incurred our displeasure; for, in addition to this, it did not require any very aggravated treatment to induce us to teach some of mine host's ducks and geese to march part of the way on the road with us; to wit, until we could get them dressed.

These birds would sometimes find their way into drums. I was once myself a party concerned in a pilfering of this kind—at least, indirectly so; for I was accessory to the act of stealing a fine goose—a witness of its death, or rather, what we supposed its death—and an assistant in *drumming* it. Moreover, I do not doubt that I should have willingly lent a hand towards eating it also. The goose, however, was, in our opinion at least, very snugly secured, and we commenced our march without the least fear of detection, chuckling in our sleeves how completely we had eluded the landlord's vigilance.

The bird only wanted dressing to complete the joke, and discussion was running high among us as to how that could be accomplished, when, to our astonishment, who should pass us on horseback but the landlord himself! He rode very coolly by, and, as he took no sort of notice of us, we concluded that he might very probably have other business on the road, and for a time we thought nothing more of the matter; but what were our feelings when, on halting in the marketplace, we perceived this very landlord in earnest conversation with our colonel; and, to all appearance, "laying down the law," as it is called, in a most strenuous manner.

At last, the colonel and he moved towards us; on perceiving which my knees broke into double-quick time, and my heart into a full gallop. On arriving near to the spot where our guilty party was drawn up, the colonel, addressing us, stated that, "the gentleman who stood by his side, complained that he had lost one of his geese, and had informed him he had good reason to suspect that some of the party to whom he now spoke had stolen it." For the satisfaction of "the gentleman," whom we, one and all, most heartily wished under ground, our knapsacks were ordered to be examined, and underwent the most scrupulous inspection; but no goose was to be found.

Professing his regret for the trouble he had caused, and apparently satisfied that his suspicions were ill-founded, our worthy landlord was just on the point of leaving us, and the boys around were grinning with delight at the notion of having so effectually deceived him, when, to our utter confusion and dismay, the goose, at this very juncture, gave a deep groan, and the landlord protested roundly that "that there sound was from his goose." Upon this, the investigation was renewed with redoubled ardour; our great coats were turned inside out, and, in short, almost everything belonging to us was examined with the minutest attention; but still no goose was to be found.

The officers could not refrain from smiling, and the boys began again to grin at the fun; but this merriment was doomed to be but of short duration, for the poor goose, now in its last moments, uttered another groan, more loud and mournful than the former one. In fact, the vital spark had just taken its flight; and this might be construed into the last dying speech of the ill-fated bird, and a full confession of its dreadful situation and murder. The drum, in which the now defunct goose was confined, stood close against the landlord's elbow, and his ear was, unfortunately for us, so correct in ascertaining whence the sound of woe proceeded, that he at once roared out, "Dang my buttons, if my goose bean't in that there drum!"

These words were daggers to our souls; we made sure of as many stripes on our backs as there were feathers on the goose's; and our merriment was suddenly changed into mortification and despair. The drum-head was ordered to be taken off, and sure enough there lay poor goosey, as dead as a herring. The moment the landlord perceived it, he protested that "as he was a sinner, that was his goose." This assertion there was no one among us hardy enough to deny; and the colonel desired that the goose should be given up to the publican, assuring him, at the same time, that he should cause the offenders to be severely punished for the theft which had been committed.

Fortunately for our poor backs, we now found a truly humane and kind-hearted man in the landlord whom we had offended; for, no sooner did he find that affairs were taking a more serious turn than he had contemplated, and that it was likely that he should be the cause of getting a child flogged, than he affected to doubt the identity of the goose; and, at length, utterly disclaimed it, saying to the colonel, "This is none of mine, Sir; I see it has a black spot on the back, whereas mine was pure white; besides, it has a black head: I wish you a good morning, Sir, and am very sorry for the trouble I have given you." Thus saying, he left us, muttering, as he went along, "Get a child flogged for a tarnation old goose? no, no!"

Every step he took carried a ton weight off our hearts. Notwithstanding this generous conduct in the publican, who was also, by his own acknowledgment a sinner, our colonel saw very clearly how matters stood; but, in consideration of our youth, and that this was our first offence—at least that had been discovered—he contented himself with severely admonishing us; and the business ended, shortly after, with the demolition of the goose—roasted.

We remained at Hilsea Barracks for nearly a year, where we acquired the appellation of the "Red Knights," from our clothing being all of that colour. I do not recollect anything of importance that occurred to me at that place, except that I was condemned to pass a week in the black-hole there, for what the soldiers called "eating my shoes." This punishment I brought upon myself in the following manner.

I had been out to receive my half-mounting, consisting of a pair of shoes, a shirt, two pair of stockings, and a stock; and, on my way home, as ill-luck would have it, an old woman, with whom I had frequently before had dealings, and who was well known, among us by the title of the plum-pudding woman, happened to throw herself in my way. Her pudding was smoking hot, I was exceedingly hungry, and my mouth watered so at the tempting sight, that I could not drag myself away. But, much as I longed for a slice, what was to be done? I had no money, and my friend the plum-pudding woman was by far too old a soldier to give trust till pay-day.[2] The pudding, however, it was impossible for me to dispense with; and finding, therefore, that all my promises and entreaties, with the view of obtaining credit, were fruitless, I at length, in an evil hour, incited by the savoury smell which issued from the old woman's basket, proposed to her to buy my shoes. After a good deal of bargaining, we at length came to an understanding, by which it was agreed, that in consideration of a quarter of a yard of pudding, and a shilling to be to me paid and delivered, my new shoes were to be handed over to the dealer in plum-pudding, as her own proper goods and chattels.

This contract being honourably completed on both sides, I retreated to a solitary shed to eat my *duff* (the name by which this de-

---

2. Soldiers were then paid once in each month.

scription of pudding was well known among us), where without any great exertion, I soon brought the two extremities of my quarter of a yard together. The last mouthful put me to the extremity of my wits to devise how I could possibly account for the sudden disappearance of my shoes. My first impulse was to run in search of the old woman, and endeavour, by fair promises, to coax her out of the shoes again; but I soon found that no such chance was left me, for she had made a precipitate retreat from the place where we had transacted our business together, knowing well that she was punishable for having bought such articles of me.

Nothing appeared to be now left for me but a palpable falsehood; and, although of this I had a great abhorrence, yet I really had not sufficient courage to think of avowing the literal truth. At length I thought I had hit upon a sort of compromise, and I determined to say that I had dropped my shoes on my way home; which, though not exactly the fact, yet approached nearer to the truth than anything else I could devise, likely to serve my end. As on all other occasions of the kind, however, it appeared that I might just as well have made a full confession at once—for my statement was not believed—and as I could not in any other way account satisfactorily for the elopement of my shoes, I was ordered seven days' black-hole for the purpose of refreshing my memory. Against this punishment I prayed long and loudly, but all to no purpose; so, with the remainder of my day's rations under my arm, off I was marched, not much elated with the dreary prospect before me.

When I heard the door of the cell creak upon its hinges behind me, and the huge key grate in the lock, I began to think that I had parted with my shoes too cheap, and, for some time after, I sat myself down in a corner, and brooded in melancholy mood over the misfortune which I had by my own folly brought upon myself. But I was never one of the desponding kind; and it therefore soon occurred to me, that, instead of indulging in dismal reflections, it would be far wiser, and more pleasant, to devise some means by which I might contrive to amuse myself during the period of my confinement.

Seven days and seven nights appeared to me at first to be a long time to remain encaged in darkness; and yet there was certainly something soldier-like in the situation. The mere fact of being a prisoner had a military sound with it. To be sure, I was imprisoned for having eaten my shoes; but what of that? Was it not quite as easy for me to imagine myself a prisoner of war? Certainly it was; and accordingly, with this impression strong on my mind, I dropped into a profound sleep in the midst of my meditations, and dreamed that I was deposited in this dungeon by the chance of war.

On waking I found myself extremely cold, from which I inferred that it would be necessary for me to contrive some plan by which I might comfort my body as well as my mind; and I therefore immediately set about standing on my head, walking on my hands, tumbling head over heels, and similar gymnastic exercises. In this manner, sleeping and playing by turns, I managed to pass my time in the black-hole for one whole day and night, by no means unpleasantly; when, about nine o'clock the next morning, I heard the well-known voice of the drum-major asking for me, and desiring that I might be liberated.

On hearing this order given, I presumed that, of course, my period of captivity had expired: and, although the time certainly appeared to have passed off at a wonderfully rapid rate, yet I accounted for it by considering that I had slept away the greater part of it; and, in addition to this, that it was but natural it should seem to have passed quickly, since I had been, during the whole period, exempt from parades, drills, head-soaping, &c.

When I first got into the daylight, I could scarcely open my eyes; and, no sooner had I brought my optics into a state to endure the light, than I was asked by the drum-major how I liked my new abode, and if I was ready to return to it. I perceived, from the smile which accompanied these questions, that I had little further to fear, and I soon understood that I had only spent one day and one night in the black-hole, and that the remainder of my sentence had been remitted. I was hailed by all my comrades, as if I had been cast on, and escaped from, some desolate island; and, having macadamized my inward man with six penny pies, out of the shilling I had received from the old pudding-woman—of which I was still possessed—I was soon as fit for fun again as the best of them.

But, the regiment being now about to embark for Guernsey, I will commence our voyage in a new chapter.

CHAPTER 3

The Sons of Neptune

We had received orders to hold ourselves in readiness to embark—as I then imagined, for foreign parts; and the idea made my heart bound for joy. In a few days we embarked on board a small sloop, at about four o'clock in the afternoon, and in an hour after got under weigh. When the sun had retired to his western chamber, the sky looked gloomy, and indicated wind; and, in another hour, there arose so terrific a gale, that we were obliged to put the tarpaulins over the hatches, to protect us against the large seas which broke over us.

The scene was enough to frighten a person of greater courage than I possessed. There were soldiers crying—women screaming—children squalling—sailors swearing—the storm all the while continuing to increase, until at length it blew a perfect hurricane; the rain came down in torrents, and the vivid lightning's flash exhibited the fear depicted on every countenance. At this juncture a poor frightened soldier mustered up courage enough to ask the captain or master of the sloop, if there was any danger. At this question every ear was open, and the son of Neptune gruffly replied, "Danger, shipmate! If the storm continues another hour, I would not give a rope-yarn for all your lives. When we reach that point on the larboard-bow, you must throw out your grappling-irons, and hold in, for she will be then close-hauled and go under water like a duck, and you will all be in David's locker before you can say, Luff, boy!" Then, addressing himself to one of his men, "Steady, Tom, steady; don't let her go off; don't you see the light ahead? run it down. Steady, boy, steady! luff a little, luff!"

At this moment an awful sea broke over us. My mouth was full, and I was wet to the skin; but, strange to say, I felt no alarm. Our little vessel dived like the gull after its prey. As soon as she righted, I said, "Captain, that was a wetter." He replied, "Ay, boy; you will get plenty of them before we make the port."

"Very consoling, truly," thought I to myself.

I had just squeezed myself up into a small compass, head and knees together, close to the helm, when we shipped another tremendous sea, which carried away our foresail, and made so terrific and dreadful a flapping, that an officer bellowed out from below, "Is there anything the matter?"

"Yes," replied the captain, "the devil to pay, and no pitch hot."

These words were scarcely spoken, when we shipped another awful sea, which washed three soldiers overboard. At this crisis, a sailor bellowed out, "Light ahead, sir."

"The devil there is! what does it look like?" roared the captain.

"Like a light," replied the sailor.

"A Frenchman, I suppose," vociferated the captain.

These words caught the ear of the military captain on board, who holloed out from below, "What did you say about a Frenchman?"

"Why, that if it gets clear, we may have a bit of a fight; for I see there is a Frenchman ahead," replied the sea captain.

"Then," said the soldier, "I had better get my men ready. Sergeant, get the bugler! Sound to arms! Call the drummer, and tell him to beat to arms!" But the devil a drummer, drum, bugler, or bugle was forthcoming.

All the men were busily engaged below, and by no means in a condition to come to the scratch, French or no French. Notwithstanding this, the noble soldier strutted about on deck by himself, with a cocked hat, and sword in hand, when a merciless sea washed off his gay hat, and the gallant captain lost his balance, and fell into the hold, bawling out most lustily for his three-cornered scraper, which was buffeting the raging billows.

"I say, captain, have the goodness to send down my hat. Is my hat upon deck? Have you seen my hat?"

"Your hat, sir," replied the son of Neptune, with infinite *sang-froid*, "has got under sail, and I should not be surprised if it made port before you." Here he changed the subject, by hailing the man on the forecastle. "Tom, where is the strange sail?"

"Sheered off to leeward; but she is a Frenchman, by the cut of her gib," replied the sailor.

"Steady," said our naval commander, and on we went; but by no means steadily, for I never saw a little bark more unsteady, though she really seemed to dive through the water like a duck.

Morning now began to dawn, which only threw light (as even the captain confessed) upon the heaviest sea he had ever seen. The black clouds seemed to fly, and the thunder and lightning to rend the very atmosphere asunder. Our distant haven was in sight; but the wind was foul, and it was therefore impossible to avoid making several tacks before we could get in. Our poor fellows, what from fear, cold, hunger, want of sleep, and being wet through, were completely worn out. I kept my station the whole night, more from fear than from any attachment to it; although I certainly did not feel the great alarm that was so visibly depicted on the countenances of most of my comrades. From extreme cold, and being quite wet through, I cut but a sorry figure by the time we began to near the land.

The prospect, from about three or four miles off, was extremely beautiful. Some little cottages studded the high and lofty rocks, and, here and there, small bays and little villages enlivened the scene, and consoled us with the idea that we were not going to be landed on a barren rock. We soon after saw the extensive town of Guernsey. Part of it seemed hanging on an eminence, and the view of the old castle, which is built of stone, and calculated to buffet with many a wintry storm, was extremely picturesque. In the distance we could see Fort George; and, in ten minutes after, we ran into the bay, which, being sheltered and protected by surrounding high lands, was tranquil indeed, when compared with the main ocean. Boats were in attendance, and we soon set our wet limbs on *terra firma*.

Having landed, I could not help viewing my person, of which I at all times had a good opinion. I looked, for all the world, like a squeezed lemon, or the bag of a Scotch pipe; and I should have been glad to have taken the edge off my appetite, and the dirt off my clothes, instead of dancing through the town; but I was, of course, obliged to obey orders, and when I struck up my tune—for I still led the fifers—I tipped *monsieur The Downfall of Paris*. I found the march did me a great deal of good; and, by the time I reached the barracks, I was in prime order for my breakfast.

We were stationed in Fort George, in exceedingly good quarters, though I could not bring myself to be reconciled to the ponderous drawbridges in use there, which foreboded no great stretch of liberty. I was particularly fond of rural and pensive wanderings, to muse on nature's beauties; and the sight of an orchard, in particular, was at all times hailed by me with great delight, for I could feast upon its beauties for hours together, to the gratification of more faculties than my vision. The drawbridges seemed to cut off these delightful prospects. It was true, I could see them from the fort; but then the prospect was too far, and I lost all relish in the distance; and, being in consequence compelled to steal out, I was apprehensive that some of my solitary rambles would get me into disgrace. My doubts and forebodings on this head were soon verified; for, in less than a week, I saw my name posted up at the gate—*John Shipp, confined to his barracks for one week.*

A week was to me an age. Confinement was to me intolerable; deprived of the pure air, of the delightful ramble along an orchard's edge, and of the salubrious smell of the orange groves. Oft have I, from the rampart-top, sighed at the distant prospect, and, while my longing eye lingered on the golden produce of the orchard within sight, my heart panted to be at liberty, to take a nearer view, and taste again of nature's beauties. The word *confinement* haunted me from one bastion to another, and I saw no refuge for the future but a more circumspect line of conduct, on which I firmly resolved.

When three long days of my week had been numbered with the dead, the drum-major was taken seriously ill, and on the morning parade the colonel inspected the drummers. I was always remarkably clean—that was my pride: the colonel eyed me from head to foot, and at last told the adjutant that I was to act as drum-major. I was nearly shouting "Liberty" in the colonel's face, but I checked myself just in time. He at the same time gave me a ticket for a play, which was to be acted in the town; and, in the evening, several boys were committed to my care, to accompany me to the theatre.

Thus, for a brief interval, I was restored to favour; but, whenever fickle fortune deigned to smile upon me, some untoward circumstance was sure to happen, and nip the fair promise in its bud. I had scarcely got the stick of office into my hands, before I cut so many capers with it, that I soon capered myself back to the dignity and full rank of fifer, was deprived of my staff of office, and, of what I considered even much worse, my liberty. My name was again exhibited to public gaze at the drawbridge-gate, for seven long days, during which I was obliged to kick my heels along the ramparts, contenting myself with contemplating the distant prospect.

One day I effaced my name from the list of the confined, unobserved by the sentinel; but in this I was detected by the sergeant, for which I had the felicity of attending drill three times a-day with my musket reversed and my coat turned inside out;[1] and, in this manner, for several hours each day I was obliged to comply with the mandates

---

1. Wearing the coat turned inside out (whence "turncoat"), an old military punishment now long since forgotten. It survived as a punishment for drunkenness among Chelsea and Greenwich in-pensioners for years after it had been discontinued in the service.

of a little bandy-legged drill-sergeant, who did not fail to enforce his authority and dignity in a manner by no means agreeable to my feelings, especially to those of my back. This I could bear well enough: indeed, I was obliged to bear it; but my turned coat seemed to hang upon me like some badge of ignominy, and I imagined that every eye was upon me.

Had I been a depraved and callous-hearted youth, this method of disgracing me would have only served to harden me in vice; and I cannot deny, that at this treatment I felt the seeds of disobedience rankling in my heart, and had almost resolved within my mind, that the next time I was doomed to wear this garb of infamy, it should be for a crime worthy of such disgrace. I found my disposition soured, and the spark of revenge kindling in my bosom; and I am persuaded that this method of disgracing youth, instead of eradicating vice, serves only to nurture those rancorous feelings which irritation, arising from a sense of degradation, is sure to excite, and which, in the young mind, might, by a more judicious and conciliatory treatment, be either totally repressed in their birth, or at least easily extinguished.

Our regiment being now ordered to prepare for embarkation for Portsmouth, my garb of disgrace was thrown off, and I embarked as sprightly as any, having been disgraced in this way for a misdemeanour that would scarcely have disgraced a schoolboy. We reached our old barracks at Portsmouth, without any other occurrence save a little casting-up of accounts, and a few distorted faces from sea-sickness.

CHAPTER 4

To the Cape

We had not been long at Portsmouth, when the headquarters of the regiment were ordered to embark on board of the *Surat Castle* East Indiaman, a fifteen-hundred-ton ship, then lying off Spithead, and the remainder of the corps on board of other ships at the same place. Our destination was the Cape of Good Hope.

The *Surat Castle* in which I was doomed to sail, was most dreadfully crowded; men literally slept upon one another, and in the orlop-deck the standing beds were three tiers high, besides those slinging. Added to this, the seeds of a pestilential disease had already been sown. An immense number of Lascars, who had been picked up in every sink of poverty, and most of whom had been living in England in a state of the most abject want and wretchedness, had been shipped on board this vessel. Many of these poor creatures had been deprived of their toes and fingers by the inclemency of winter, and others had accumulated diseases from filth, many of them having subsisted for a considerable time upon what they picked up in the streets.

The pestilential smell between decks was beyond the power of description; and it was truly appalling to see these poor wretches, with tremendous and frightful sores, and covered with vermin from head to foot, many of them unable to assist themselves, left to die unaided, unfriended, and without one who could perform the last sad office. The moment the breath was out of their bodies, they were, like dogs, thrown overboard as food for sharks. To alleviate their sufferings by personal aid was impossible, for we had scarcely men enough to work the ship.

These circumstances were, I suppose, reported to the proper authority; but, whether this was the case or not, in three or four days we weighed anchor, with about sixty other ships for all parts of the world. The splendid sight but little accorded with the aching hearts, lacerated bodies, and wounded minds of the poor creatures below.

It was about four o'clock in the afternoon when the signal was fired to weigh. Immediately every sail was waving in the wind, and in a quarter of an hour after we stood out from land, each proud bark dipping her majestic head in the silvery deep, and manoeuvring her sails in seeming competition, to catch the favouring breeze.

Such firing, such signals, such tacking and running across each other now prevailed, that our captain resolved to run from it; and the evening had scarcely spread her sombre curtains over the western ocean, and the golden clouds begun to change their brilliant robes of day for those of murky night, when our crew "up helm," and stole away from the motley fleet, plying every sail, and scudding through the blue waters like some aerial car or phantom-ship, smoothly gliding over the silvery deep.

In three or four hours we had entirely lost sight of our convoy. We were running at the rate of eleven knots an hour, and, as it seemed, into the very jaws of danger. The clouds began to assume a pitchy and awful darkness, the distant thunder rolled angrily, and the vivid lightning's flash struck each watching eye dim, and, for a moment, hid the rolling and gigantic wave from the sight of fear. The wind whistled terrifically, and the shattered sails fanned the flying clouds. All was consternation; every eye betrayed fear. Sail was taken in, masts lowered and yards stayed—preparations which bespoke no good tidings to the inquiring and terrified landsman.

I was seated on the poop, alone, holding by a hen-coop, and viewing the mountainous and angry billows, with my hand partly covering my eyes, to protect them against the lightning. It was a moment of the most poignant sorrow to me: my heart still lingered on the white cliffs of Albion; nor could I wean it from the sorrowful reflection that I was, perhaps, leaving that dear and beloved country for ever. During this struggle of my feelings, our vessel shipped a tremendous sea over her poop, and then angrily shook her head, and seemed resolved to buffet the raging elements with all her might and main. The ship was shortly after this "hove to," and lay comparatively quiet; and, in about a couple of hours, the wind slackened, and we again stood on our way, the masts cracking under her three topsails, and fore storm-staysail. However, she rode much easier, and the storm still continued to abate.

I was dreadfully wet and cold, and my teeth chattered most woefully; so I made towards the gun-deck, some portion of which was allotted for the soldiers. There the heat was suffocating, and the stench intolerable. The scene in the orlop-deck was truly distressing: soldiers, their wives and children, all lying together in a state of the most dreadful sea-sickness, groaning in concert, and calling for a drop of water to cool their parched tongues. I screwed myself up behind a butt, and soon fell into that stupor which sea-sickness will create. In this state I continued until morning; and, when I awoke, I found that the hurricane had returned with redoubled fury, and that we were standing towards land.

The captain came ahead to look out, and, after some consideration, he at last told the officer to stand out to sea. The following morning was ushered in by the sun's bright beams diffusing their lustre on the dejected features of frightened and helpless mortals. The dark clouds of sad despair were in mercy driven from our minds, and the bright beams of munificent love from above took their place. The before downcast eye was seen to sparkle with delight, and the haggard cheek of despondency resumed its wonted serenity. The tempestuous bosom of the main was now smooth as a mirror, and all seemed grateful and cheerful, directing the eye of hope towards the far-distant haven to which we were bound.

A great number of the fleet were the same morning to be seen emerging from their shelter, or hiding-place, from the terrific hurricane of the day before; but our captain was resolved to be alone; so the same night he crowded sail, and, by the following morning's dawn, we were so much ahead that not a sail was visible, save one solitary sloop, that seemed bending her way towards England.

Some three weeks after this we were again visited by a most dreadful storm, that far exceeded the former one, and from which we suffered much external injury, our main top-mast, and other smaller masts, being carried away. But the interior of our poor bark exhibited a scene of far greater desolation. We were then far from land, and a pestilential disease was raging among us in all its terrific forms. Nought could be seen but the pallid cheek of disease, or the sunken eye of despair. The sea-gulls soared over the ship, and huge sharks hovered around it, watching for their prey. These creatures are sure indications of ships having some pestilential disease on board, and they have been known to follow a vessel so circumstanced to the most distant climes—to countries far from their native element.

To add to our distresses, some ten barrels of ship's paint, or colour, got loose from their lashings, and rolled from side to side, and from head to stern, carrying everything before them by their enormous weight. From our inability to stop them in their destructive progress, they one and all were staved in, and the gun-deck soon became one mass of colours, in which lay the dead and the dying, both white and black.

It would be difficult for the reader to picture to himself a set of men more deplorably situated that we now were; but our distresses were not yet at their height: for, as though our miseries still required aggravation, the scurvy broke out among us in a most frightful manner. Scarcely a single individual on board escaped this melancholy disorder, and the swollen legs, and gums protruding beyond the lips, attested the malignancy of the visitation. The dying were burying the dead, and the features of all on board wore the garb of mourning.

Every assistance and attention that humanity or generosity could dictate, was freely and liberally bestowed by the officers on board, who cheerfully gave up their fresh meat and many other comforts, for the benefit of the distressed; but the pestilence baffled the aid of medicine and the skill of the medical attendants. My poor legs were as big as drums; my gums swollen to an enormous size; my tongue too big for my mouth; and all I could eat was raw potatoes and vinegar. But my kind and affectionate officers sometimes brought me some tea and coffee, at which the languid eye would brighten, and the tear of gratitude would intuitively fall, in spite of my efforts to repress what was thought unmanly. Our spirits were so subdued by suffering, and our frames so much reduced and emaciated, that I have seen poor men weep bitterly, they knew not why.

Thus passed the time; men dying in dozens, and, ere their blood was cold, hurled into the briny deep, there to become a prey to sharks. It was a dreadful sight to see the bodies of our comrades the bone of disputation with these voracious natives of the dreary deep; and the reflection that such might soon be our own fate would crush our best feelings, and with horror drive the eye from such a sight. Our muster-rolls were dreadfully thinned: indeed, almost every fourth man amongst the Europeans, and more than two-thirds of the natives, had fallen victims to the diseases on board; and it was by the mercy of Providence only, that the ship ever reached its destination, for we had scarcely a seaman fit for duty to work her.

Never shall I forget the morning I saw the land. In the moment of joy I forgot all my miseries, and cast them into the deep, in the hope of future happiness. This is mortal man's career. Past scenes are drowned and forgotten, in the anticipation of happier events to come; and, by a cherished delusion, we allow ourselves to be transported into the fairy land of imagination, in quest of future joys—never, perhaps, to be realized, but the contemplation of which, in the distance, serves at least to soothe us under present suffering.

When the view of land first blessed our sight, the morning was foggy and dreary. We were close under the land, and were in the very act of standing from it, when the fog dispersed, the wind shifted fair, and we ran in close to the mouth of Simon's Bay. The now agreeable breeze ravished our sickened souls, and the surrounding view delighted our dim and desponding eyes. Every one who could crawl was upon deck, to welcome the sight of land, and inhale the salubrious air. Every soul on board seemed elated with joy; and, when the anchor was let go, it was indeed an anchor to the broken hearts of poor creatures then stretched on the bed of sickness, who had not, during the whole voyage, seen the bright sun rising and setting—sights at sea that beggar the power of description. For myself, I jumped and danced about like a merry-andrew, and I found, or fancied I found, myself already a convalescent.

The anchor had not been down long, when a boat came off from shore, on board of which were several medical gentlemen, who questioned us as to whence we came, whither we were bound, the state of the ship, the nature of the disease, and the number of men that had died during the passage. The number of men was a finishing blow to our present hopes, and we were ordered to ride at quarantine; but every comfort that humanity or liberality could dictate was immediately sent on board: fresh meats, bread, tea, sugar, coffee, and fruits of all kinds; and, in a few days, our legs began to re-assume their original shapes, and the disease died away.

The quarantine was very soon taken off, and the troops landed, and were marched, or rather carried, to the barracks that stand on the brow of the hill, at the back of Simon's Town. Here our treatment was that of children of distress; every comfort was afforded us, and every means adopted by our kind officers, which could contribute towards our recovery. For the first fortnight drills were out of the question, instead of which we were kindly nursed, until the disease was completely eradicated; and by this careful treatment we were all soon restored to the enjoyment of health. But few men died of those that were landed; and, if I recollect right, our total loss was seventy-two men. Notwithstanding all our troubles and misfortunes, we arrived before the other divisions of the regiment; but they had not suffered from disease: their loss was two men only.[1]

---

1. According to Barrow, the ships bringing the other "experimental" boy-regiments to the Cape, suffered in like manner from "ship-fever." It affords a suggestive commentary on the transport-service of that time that the same ships, after they had been properly disinfected at the Cape, carried troops to Egypt without sickness.

CHAPTER 5

We Fight the 'Caffres'

Simon's Town is situated on the bay which bears the same name, and contains many well-built houses. Here we were stationed for a short time; and, as the regiment was not restricted from going out, I soon commenced reconnoitring the localities of the neighbourhood, and was glad to find that there were a number of well-stocked gardens close to the barracks. A pound of meat (and that of the worst) and three-quarters of a pound of bread *per diem*, was but a scanty allowance for a growing lad. Indeed, I frequently managed to get through my three days' bread in one; but as we could get fish for a mere song, and as the gardens of our neighbours, the Dutchmen, supplied us with potatoes, we continued, one way or another, to fare tolerably well at this station.

We were soon after moved to the station of Muisenberg, seven miles nearer to Cape Town, a post defended by a small battery, and the beach, in places of easy access, guarded by a few guns. The road from Simon's Town to Muisenberg sometimes runs along the beach, which is very flat, and on which the sea flows with gentle undulations; and, at others, winds round the feet of craggy hills, covered with masses of stone, which have the appearance of being merely suspended in the air, ready to be rolled down upon you by the slightest touch. On these hills whole regiments of baboons assemble, for which this station is particularly famous. They stand six feet high, and in features and manners approach nearer to the human species than any other quadruped I have ever seen. These rascals, who are most abominable thieves, used to annoy us exceedingly. Our barracks were under the hills, and when we went to parade, we were invariably obliged to leave armed men for the protection of our property; and, even in spite of this, they have frequently stolen our blankets and great-coats, or anything else they could lay their claws on. A poor woman, a soldier's wife, had washed her blanket and hung it out to dry, when some of these miscreants, who were ever on the watch, stole it, and ran off with it into the hills, which are high and woody. This drew upon them the indignation of the regiment, and we formed a strong party, armed with sticks and stones, to attack them, with the view of recovering the property, and inflicting such chastisement as might be a warning to them for the future. I was on the advance, with about twenty men, and I made a detour to cut them off from caverns to which they always flew for shelter. They observed my movement, and immediately detached about fifty to guard the entrance, while the others kept their post, and we could distinctly see them collecting large stones and other missiles. One old grey-headed one, in particular, who often paid us a visit to the barracks, and was known by the name of Father Murphy, was seen distributing his orders, and planning the attack, with the judgment of one of our best generals. Finding that my design was defeated, I joined the main body, and rushed on to the attack, when a scream from Father Murphy was the signal for a general encounter, and the host of baboons under his command rolled down enormous stones upon us, so that we were obliged to give up the contest, or some of us must inevitably have been killed. They actually followed us to our very doors, shouting an indication of victory; and, during the whole night, we heard dreadful yells and screaming; so much so, that we expected a night attack. In the morning, however, we found that all this rioting had been created by disputes about the division of the blanket, for we saw eight or ten of them with pieces of it on their backs, as old women wear their cloaks. Amongst the number strutted Father Murphy. These rascals annoyed us day and night, and we dared not venture out unless a party of five or six went together.

One morning, Father Murphy had the consummate impudence to walk straight into the Grenadier barracks, and he was in the very act of purloining a sergeant's regimental coat, when a corporal's guard, which had just been relieved, took the liberty of stopping the gentleman at the door, and secured him. He was a most powerful brute, and, I am persuaded, too much for any single man. Notwithstanding his frequent misdemeanours, we did not like to kill the poor creature; so, having first taken the precaution of muzzling him, we determined on shaving his head and face, and then turning him loose. To this ceremony, strange to say, he submitted very quietly, and, when shaved, he was really an exceedingly good-looking fellow; and I have seen many a "blood" in Bond Street not half so prepossessing in his appearance. We then started him up the hill, though he seemed rather reluctant to leave us. Some of his companions came down to meet him; but, from the alteration which shaving his head and face had made in him, they did not know him again, and, accordingly, pelted him with stones, and beat him with sticks, in so unmerciful a manner, that poor Father Murphy actually sought protection from his enemies, and he in time became quite domesticated and tame.

We soon bade farewell to Muisenberg, and marched to Wynberg, and were in camp for several months. Here we suffered dreadfully from the inclemency of the weather, and from lying on damp ground, in small bell tents; added to which, our very lives were drilled out by brigade field-days, from three and four o'clock in the morning, until seven and eight o'clock at night. At this period the Caffres were committing the most terrific murders and robberies amongst the Dutch Boers up the country. To stop these devastations, a rifle company was formed from the several corps of the 8th Dragoons, and the 22nd, 34th, 65th, 81st, and 91st regiments, and placed under the command of Captain Effingham Lindsay, one of the bravest soldiers in his majesty's army. We were dressed in green, and our pieces were browned to prevent their being seen in the woods where the Caffres congregated. About three months after the formation of the company, we were sent up the country, in conjunction with the light company of the 91st regiment and a corps of Hottentots. We embarked on board the *Diamond* frigate, and reached Algoa Bay in fourteen days, having experienced bad weather.[1] From thence we marched to Graaf-Reynett, about five or six hundred miles in the interior, and fifteen hundred miles from Cape Town, and took up our quarters in a Dutch church. The road from Algoa Bay to Graaf-Reynett is hill and dale, and infested with lions, tigers, hyenas, wolves, and elephants; and we frequently saw eight or ten a-day, at a place called Rovee Bank, a day's march on this side of the great pass. One day I went out shooting wild ducks here with another person. We came to a pool of water, surrounded with very high grass—some of it ten feet high—which abounded with wild ducks and geese. I took aim and fired, and had just time to see, that at least one bird had fallen a victim to number four, when I heard a most tremendous roar, and the whole pool was in a moment in a state of commotion. I was in the act of plunging into the water

---

1. Previous to the arrival of the British in 1795, an agreement between the Dutch and Caffres had recognized the line of the Sunday's River, between Graaf-Reynett and Algoa Bay, as the colonial boundary. The reader may be reminded that the British occupied the Cape Colony in 1795; restored it to the Dutch at the Peace of Amiens; and retook it in 1806.

after my butchered duck, when, imagine my astonishment and alarm, on seeing an enormous white elephant rush out from the high grass, roaring loudly, and striking the grass aside with his trunk. Neither myself nor my companion had ever seen one before, and we had now no inclination for a second peep; so, leaving the ducks to their fate, we took to our heels, and never stopped till we arrived safe in camp.

At every farmer's house on our line of march, we found sad vestiges of murder and desolation. Whole families had been wantonly massacred by this wild and misguided race of people, whose devastations it was now our duty to check, and whose ignorance is so extraordinary, that I am persuaded they are insensible that murder is a crime. Beautiful farmhouses were to be still seen smoking; the families either murdered, or run away to seek refuge elsewhere. Not a living creature was to be seen, unless, perchance, a poor dog might be discovered howling over the dead body of his master; or some wounded horse or ox, groaning with the stab of a spear or other mutilation. The savage Caffre exults in these appalling sights; gaping wounds, and the pangs of the dying, are to his dark and infatuated mind the very acme of enjoyment. This barbarous race, when they have succeeded in any of their murderous exploits, appear to be so excited to ecstasy, that they will jump about in a sort of frenzy, hurling their spears in all directions, and in the most reckless manner, either at man or beast. They are quite insensible to the value of money, which they would accept on account of its glitter only; while a more shining gilt button would be prized by them as of inestimable value. In short, they seem scarcely to possess a rational idea beyond what may tend to the gratification of the appetite; and I have myself seen them with women's gowns, petticoats, shawls, &c, tied round their legs, and between their toes, and in this manner they would run wildly into the woods, shouting in exultation. These people had got information that we were their avowed enemies, and come to destroy them and take from them their enormous herds of cattle; they were, therefore, driven far into the interior of almost inaccessible parts of the country, where we could not follow them. Some few stragglers were left in the neighbourhood, to watch our movements, with whom we had some slight skirmishes; but, from the extreme intricacy of the woods, we could do but little with them.

The Caffres may unquestionably be considered as a formidable enemy. They are inured to war and plunder, and most of them are such famous marksmen with their darts, that they will make sure of their aim at sixty or eighty paces' distance. When you fire upon them they will throw themselves flat upon their faces, and thus avoid the ball; and, even if you hit them, it is doubtful whether the ball would take effect, the skins worn by them being considered to be ball-proof. Added to this, as they reside in woods, in the most inaccessible parts of which they take refuge on being hard pressed by their enemies, an offensive warfare against them is inconceivably arduous.

Before they deliver the darts with which they are armed, they run sideways; the left shoulder projected forward, and the right considerably lowered, with the right hand extended behind them, the dart lying flat in the palm of the hand, the point near the right eye. When discharged from the grasp, it flies with such velocity that you can scarcely see it, and when in the air it looks like a shuttlecock violently struck. They carry, slung on their backs, about a dozen of these weapons, with which single men have been known to kill lions and tigers.

From this harassing warfare, travelling through almost impenetrable woods, over tremendous hills, and through rivers, we were soon in a terribly ragged condition. Our shoes we managed to replace from the raw hides of buffaloes, in the following manner: the foot was placed on the hide, which was then cut to the shape of the sole, and fastened to the foot by thongs made of the same material, sewed to the sole instead of upper-leathers. In two or three days this dried, and formed to the shape of the foot, and was sure to be a fit. When we had remained at this station about two years, it was truly laughable to see the metamorphosis of the once white regimental trousers. Here and there pieces had been sewn in to patch up holes, and, these pieces being of materials of other texture as well as other colours, we looked, at a distance, like spotted leopards. During these two years I had sprung up some six inches, outgrowing, of course, both my jacket and trousers; and, when I was in full case for parade, my figure must have been exceedingly ludicrous. My jacket was literally a strait jacket; for, from its extreme tightness, I could scarcely raise my hand to my head. My pantaloons or trousers had been, during the whole period, continually rising in the world, and now they would scarcely condescend to protect my protruding knees. I was but a novice at the needle, so that the patches I put on were either too small or too large. In this predicament I had to march nearly fifteen hundred miles through Africa. The rest of the men were but little better off; and we might well have been compared to Falstaff's ragged recruits, with whom he swore he would not march through Coventry.

Having continued on this duty for upwards of two years, to very little purpose, the Cape of Good Hope was ordered, by the British

Government, in 1801, to be given up to the Dutch. To remove the rifle company, and the light company of the 91st Foot, a small vessel was dispatched from Cape Town to Algoa Bay, for their conveyance to the capital, preparatory to embarking for India. I was dispatched over land with a Dutch Boer's family, then about to leave the station for Cape Town. The whole of the officers' baggage was committed to my care, which was a very serious charge and responsibility, through such a wild and desolate country. On this trip I had to pass along the margin of the country inhabited by the Caffres; and, although the Dutch family with whom I travelled had muskets and four wagons, these sojourners in the woods and hills neither feared them nor their guns. After laying in a good stock of powder and shot, we commenced our march in regular battle array. I was mounted on a horse, with my rifle slung over my back, always loaded, and a pistol in my holster-pipe; on each side rode the Dutchman's two sons; after us, four Hottentots, armed with muskets; then the old boss (the master); and, following him, the four wagons, containing the families and property of all. The rear-guard consisted of two head servants (Hottentots) armed, on bullocks; then four on foot, with their families, many of the women carrying two children. Thus we would accomplish twenty miles a day over the most enormous hills; and, if we could not reach a farmhouse by the setting sun, which was the time we generally halted, we selected the most open spot we could find for our encampment, forming a square with the four wagons, keeping our cattle inside, where they were fed. Six men out of the twelve kept watch the whole night, and were relieved every four hours, in which duty I always took a part. In fact, we were so often disturbed, either by the Caffres, or some beast of prey prowling about our little fortified encampment, that we might be said to be always watching. The Caffre possesses a great deal of cunning and craft. Their system of attack is this: under the garb of night, when all is still save the roaring lion, the hungry tiger, or the screeching owl, they will crawl on their hands and knees, imitating the cries of any animal of the woods, or any bird of the air. At the smallest noise they will turn themselves flat on the ground, so that you may walk close by, and not observe them; and the first indication given you of having such dangerous neighbours, is by the incision of a spear, or the blow of a club. These imitations of the cries of animals, and chirping of birds, are well understood amongst themselves. No wonder, then, that we should watch. It was no unusual thing in the morning to see their spears lodged in the top of our wagons, and close by where we kept watch; but we never attempted to leave our possessions, and resolved not to throw away our precious powder and ball on slight occasions. To narrate the numerous trials, watchings, privations, perils, and escapes of this trip, would of itself fill a larger space than I can devote to such a detail. Suffice it for the present, that we at last reached Cape Town in safety.

The Dutchman with whom I was travelling had two daughters; the younger of whom, Sabina by name, was a most lovely creature. She was tall, and rather slim; of symmetrical form; in complexion a brunette; with black eyes and hair; her foot extremely small; and her waist scarcely a span. Her manners were vivacious and interesting, and her education had been by no means neglected. As we proceeded on our perilous journey, this charming girl would single me out as her companion, and seek consolation in my society and conversation, from the coarseness of her father, who was a very gross man. It need scarcely be confessed by me, that I was nothing loth to be thus distinguished; neither can it reasonably be expected that I was long insensible to the charms of my amiable companion. I would walk by her side, while she rode my horse the whole march; and in this manner, day after day passed away like so many hours, and our attachment grew stronger and stronger, and at length settled into a deep-rooted affection, and was cemented by an interchange of protestations of mutual love. She was a year younger than I; my age being then sixteen, and hers fifteen; but the appearance of both was far beyond that tender age.

Convinced of the reciprocity of our attachment, thus we journeyed on, indulging in visions of bliss; and it was not until we had approached within a short distance of our destination, that the idea first crossed my mind that we must soon part. Until this moment all my faculties had yielded to the fascinations of my enslaver, from the contemplation of whose beauty it had seemed treason to steal a thought; but, now that the time approached when my duty must tear me from her, and when I reflected, that from that duty there was no possibility of shrinking, without disgrace, the absolute necessity of separation from my beloved Sabina rushed upon my senses, and almost drove me to despair. These bitter thoughts having thus suddenly and painfully intruded, I revolved within my mind, in all ways, the possibilities of extricating myself from my perplexing situation; and the more I reflected, the more was I distressed and embarrassed. Marriage would not have been consented to by my commanding officer, on account of my extreme youth; the thought of any less honourable proposal I could not myself encourage for a moment; and, in short, it soon became clear to me, that there was but one road of escape from the heart-rending necessity of parting at once, and for ever, from my lovely brunette—desertion. The idea of being compelled to resort to such an alternative startled me; I knew the enormity of the offence, and the consequences of such a step; but the recollection that it was my only resource, haunted me day and night. As often as it intruded upon my distracted mind, I endeavoured to drive it from me; but it stuck to me like ivy on the crumbling tower. What to do I could not resolve. I at last mentioned the subject to Sabina, and it seemed that the thought of our approaching separation had been by her also forgotten in our mutual love. The moment I hinted at the possibility of parting, she turned as pale as death; I saw the crystal tear steal down her beautiful cheek; she trembled; and at last swooned away. It was then the dark fiend again urged me on, and I promised, in the moment of grief and excitement, that I would desert, and follow her wherever she might go. Her sweet eye beamed ineffable pleasure; she seized my hand; kissed it a hundred times; and she said, in a most pathetic manner, "Will you really return with me to my home?" I declared I would, whatever might be the result. She said, "Swear it, and I shall live; deny me, and I shall die." The concluding part of this appeal was urged with such a searching anguish, that it drew from me a solemn promise of desertion. This resolution was communicated to her family; and one and all urged me to go, or rather return with them to their homes—pointing out the happiness I should enjoy with their beautiful sister. These were arguments too cogent to be resisted, and I again promised to return with them. Scarcely had the fatal promise been repeated, when the recollection of my native country, my home, my country's glory, my regiment, and the disgrace attaching to the committal of so bad a crime, all rushed in quick succession upon my bewildered mind. I thought—I paused; but a single glance from the eye of my beloved Sabina plainly told me that the first whisper of love would suffice to confirm me in my fatal resolution.

We were now within sight of Cape Town; and here again my feelings, distressed at the thought of deserting, goaded me beyond description. I sometimes gave up the idea, and resolved to fly from temptation, and seek protection with my regiment; but the melodious voice of Sabina calling me by name, would at once dissipate my better resolutions, until I at last abandoned all idea of the possibility of parting. I contented myself with praying most devoutly that the regiment might have sailed ere I arrived, which would have saved me from the stigma of desertion. In the event of the regiment being still at Cape Town, I had sworn to my betrothed and her family to return to them:

thus we parted. My arrival was hailed by my comrades with delight, as they feared I had been murdered by the Caffres; and I received every kind of congratulation, and several very handsome presents, from all those officers whose things I had in charge. Some hundred miles before I had reached Cape Town, the old Dutchman had tried hard to persuade me to remain behind, with all the property, till he and his family returned. This I resolutely refused: desertion was of itself bad enough, without adding to it the crimes of breach of trust and theft. I had not, in our long and arduous march, lost or injured a single thing, but delivered them all safe into the custody of their rightful owners, and in the evening went to see my Sabina at her friend's house, where I was informed that the family proposed leaving Cape Town for their home on the following Monday. After a severe struggle, I consented to accompany them; for which purpose I stole out of the barracks after hours, and joined them at the appointed place outside the town. I need not say my arrival was hailed with delight, for I had kept them waiting an hour beyond the appointed time; Sabina locked her arm in mine; the procession moved on; and in my excessive love I forgot my crime. Reader, judge me not too harshly; consider my youth, and the temptation I had to contend against; and, before you utterly condemn me, place yourself under the same combination of circumstances, and tell me how you would have acted in my place.

We had proceeded about thirty miles from Cape Town, and were busily engaged building castles of future bliss, when—oh, short-sighted mortals!—the provost-marshal thrust his head into the wagon, and pointed a pistol at me, saying, if I attempted to move, he would shoot me. This mandate was too pointed to be disobeyed; and, in ten minutes after, I was on my way back to Cape Town, having been dragged from the embraces of her for whom I had sacrificed my all. From that moment I never saw or heard of the fair Sabina or her family, who would also undoubtedly have been seized, but that I took all the blame upon my own shoulders. I was tried by a regimental court-martial for being absent from morning parade, and for desertion, and sentenced to receive 999 lashes, being more than fifty lashes for every year I was old; but my commanding officer was a kind and affectionate man, and had known me from the day I entered his regiment; he could not consent that I should receive a single lash, but sent for me, and admonished me like a parent, painted the crime of desertion in all its enormities, and dismissed me, with the assurance of his full forgiveness and friendship; adding, that he was assured I had been deluded away by the Dutchman and his family. This I never would acknowledge, until some months afterward, when, knowing that they must be far out of our reach, I related the whole transaction.

Some of the Dutch troops, to whom we were to resign the Cape, had already arrived from Java and Batavia, and other Dutch settlements, many of whom flocked to the wharf to see us embark, and, where they dared, to offer insults. A huge brute sidled up to me, with his greasy moustaches, which he began to curl and twist between his forefinger and thumb, at the same time chucking me under the chin, and calling me a pretty boy. For this I took the liberty of saluting him with a kick on the shins, for which he attempted to seize my ears; but I fixed my bayonet—a weapon the Dutch have a great aversion to; so he marched off. The following morning we embarked for India, on board a small American vessel that had been lying a considerable time at the Cape.

When the land was buried in distance, I could not help reviewing the many providential escapes I had already experienced during my short career, and the mercies that had been extended to me in the most perilous situations. Did men but oftener attribute them to that great source from whence all our mercies are derived, we should think less of our often fancied hardships, and feel grateful for the blessings we enjoy. In my case, it was impossible to look back upon the last four years of my life, without trembling at the scenes I had been carried through in safety, and addressing a prayer of thanksgiving to the fountain of all love, for the unmerited protection that had been extended towards me.

We had scarcely got to sea a day, when we found that it was a difficult matter to determine which was the more cranky, the vessel or the captain. She took in water in large quantities—he grog; she would not go steady—neither would he; she rolled and pitched—so did he; she shook her head—so did he; she was often sea-sick—so was he: in fact, they were a cranky pair. She had lain so long at the Cape, that her bottom had become foul, and she would not go more than four knots an hour, if it blew a hurricane, and then she seemed to tear the very water asunder. We prowled about the deep like the wandering Jew on earth, until at last our water began to evince symptoms of decline, and it was justly feared we should soon suffer much under a hot sun, for want of that great essential; but, about a week after, we stumbled upon land, which, after a great deal of reconnoitring, our wise captain pronounced to be some part of Sumatra. However this might be, it was a welcome sight to us; but, as it was late in the evening when we discovered it, we were obliged to steer about the whole night. About ten o'clock the clouds began to thicken, and the wind blew from shore; about twelve it blew a smart gale, and we hove to; our vessel lay like a log of wood, scarcely moving, till the morning dawned, when the storm had subsided in a great degree, and we stood in for land. The hills looked woody, and the valleys fertile. We at last got into a small bay, or basin, where the surrounding scenery was beautiful in the extreme. Several canoes were to be seen steering up the creeks, and men and women running into the woods, in seeming alarm and consternation. We anchored about three hundred yards from the shore. The movements of the natives did not evince any friendly inclination towards us, but the contrary; and it was fortunate that we had the means of taking by compulsion what we should willingly have purchased—wood and water, those two essentials to man's existence. To convince them, if possible, that our appearance in this basin was not of a hostile nature, a small boat was dispatched, with six or seven men, four of them armed. I was one, and we approached the shore with great caution. We could plainly see people hiding behind trees, and carrying away their moveables from some huts which stood about two hundred yards from shore, where we could also discover fishing-nets, canoes that had been dragged ashore, a few domestic fowls, and one or two goats and kids. We beckoned them to approach, but they seemed shy, and would not come near us. The captain's servant was a native of Ceylon, and could speak several languages. We landed him, but he was justly afraid to venture far from the boat. He soon, however, made them understand the object for which we put into this port, and informed them that we were willing to purchase both wood and water at a reasonable price. This they would not consent to, but requested us immediately to weigh anchor and leave the bay, or dread the displeasure of their king, whom they had apprised of our intrusion into their country. It appeared from this that we had no alternative but to take what we required by force; we therefore disregarded the threats of the subjects of his black majesty, and the following morning got out the long-boat, with implements for getting in water and cutting wood. The latter was already cut to our hands, as the surrounding country was one mass of fuel, that had decayed, and been blown down by the tempest. The water was close by—a most beautiful crystal stream; but the moment we had commenced work, we saw an enormous number of people, with swords, spears, and daggers, approaching towards us. We formed a line, primed and loaded, and prepared for a fight; but, resolved not to be the aggressors, we again dispatched the native servant to endeavour to reason them into compliance; for which purpose, a small safeguard went with him. After a great deal of threatening and blustering, they consented to sell the water for five dollars per butt, and the wood in proportion. This exorbitant claim was of course rejected with indignation; but, still wishing to keep friendly with them, we offered one dollar per butt. This was refused by them, and the servant returned. Meantime, we continued filling our water utensils and collecting firewood, with the greatest industry, keeping our eyes on them all the while. There appeared to be a deal of consultation among the natives, and a number of messengers going and coming; at last an arrow was fired, which fell close to where I was standing. Another soon followed it; and the officer in command of our party then ordered two or three men to fire in the air. This alarmed them so, that they took to their heels and ran shouting into the woods, and we went hard to work. In about an hour, the inhabitants, encouraged by our pacific appearance, sent a man to inform us, that "his majesty had been pleased to permit the strangers to tread upon the margin of his country, and drink his water of mercy" (so interpreted by the native servant), and that "his majesty would come and hold communion of friendship with the strangers on the following day, if the day was auspicious; that we might drink as much water of his mercy as we pleased, and cut as much wood; but his majesty begged we would not attempt to make incursions into his country, as he could not be held responsible, if his elephants and bull-dogs got loose, and destroyed the strangers; and further, that he would, in his most gracious mercy, send us all sorts of fruits, &c., at a moderate price." To this message we returned a very gracious answer; and about ten the following morning a great number of boats were seen coming down the several creeks, which, concentrating at the bottom of a small village a little way up the largest creek, at last came on their way towards the ship, in number about thirty, with about four men in each boat. It had been before understood that not one person would be admitted with arms, and only ten people at a time. His majesty did not choose to make his appearance, but had instructed those that did come to say, that he had consulted his diviners, and they had pronounced the day an inauspicious one. We were, therefore, deprived of his royal presence; but, if he was as big a thief as those he sent to represent him, his majesty was qualified for a more exalted sphere—the gallows: such a set of rogues I have never seen in the whole course of my life. They brought oranges, plantains, &c., and some few ducks, chickens, and eggs, for barter; but they were such thieves that you could not trust them even to handle the article you wished to barter. If you trusted it out of your own hand, it was handed by them from one to another, and ultimately to their canoes, and then you might "fish for it," to use a soldier's term. A ludicrous scene took place between a tar and one of these fellows. Jack offered his blanket for sale, as he had now got into a warm climate, and it was of no further use to him. Jack, in good, sound, and intelligible English, particularized the length, breadth, and quality of his blanket, qualifying his description with many an oath, not one syllable of which did the purchaser understand. During the examination of the said blanket, Jack kept hold of one end, pledging his tarry honour to the authenticity of his assertion that it was a real Witney. Some one at this moment took off Jack's attention, and he withdrew his hand from the blanket, which soon found its way to the canoe. The tar uttered sundry imprecations touching his "day-lights" and "grappling-irons," and was up on deck and down into the canoe in a moment, overhauling everything; but neither the blanket nor the purchaser was to be found. At this the sailor ran about like a madman, until, at last, he espied the fellow moving down the fore-hatchway. Being certain of his man, he took one hop, skip, and jump, and fastened on the fellow's neck, vociferating, "Halloa, shipmate, where have you stowed my blanket? Come, skull it over, or I shall board you before you can say luff." The fellow did not, of course, understand one word he said; but Jack soon brought him to his bearings, as he called it, by mooring him on the deck, and swearing that, if he did not "skull over the Witney," he would tear him into rope-yarns. Thus roughly treated, poor blacky bellowed out lustily for mercy, which brought down the first officer, who asked Jack Carter (for that was his name) what was the matter. He replied, "This here black rascal has grappled my blanket, so I am just after boarding him, and, if he don't shore it out, I'll sink him, or Jack Carter is no sailor."

Here he commenced hammering his head against the deck, until the knave said something to one of his countrymen, who ran forward where his canoe was, and put an end to the dispute by producing the Witney.

The following day we again bent our way towards India, with light hearts and cheerful countenances. We soon reached the Pilot, cruising off the sand-heads of Saugar, and steered our way up the river Hoogley. This river is wide, and its current powerful. The views on each side, when you get as far as Fultah, are romantic, and we gratified our eyes in feasting on nature's beauties. On rounding the corner, or protruding neck of land, on which stand the company's botanical gardens, Fort William first appears; then Calcutta, with its innumerable shipping, bursts upon the view, and the beholder gazes on the beautiful fortification of the fort, and the city of palaces, with astonishment and delight. We passed the fort in full sail, and were hailed from its ramparts by the artillery, and part of the 10th regiment of Foot, then in garrison there. We returned the welcome greeting with three loud cheers, and in five minutes after came to anchor off Esplanade Ghaut, after a voyage of more than five months.

CHAPTER 6

India

The instant the anchor was gone, boats were alongside, for the purpose of conveying the two companies ashore; and, in a couple of hours, we were safely lodged in our quarters at Fort William. Here the five companies of his majesty's 10th regiment of Foot joined our lads, with bottles of rum, and a scene ensued that was beyond description; drinking, singing, dancing, shouting, fighting, and bottles flying in all directions. The sight was terrific; so I marched off to the bazaar, to get out of the bustle; went round the fort, and visited everything worth seeing. On my return to the barracks, I found the men lying in a state of the most disgusting drunkenness; some on the floor, others on cots, trunks, and boxes. In those days, I knew not the taste of spirituous liquors; and, indeed, for years after: consequently, instead of joining those scenes of revelry and discord, they were to me offensive and disgusting in the extreme. The very smell of arrack would at any time drive me from the barrack, and many a night have I slept in the open air, to avoid the fumes arising from its use, as well as the drunken jargon of those who drank it to excess.

I had now attained the age of eighteen years; was healthy and active; a zealous, though very humble member of the profession I had chosen; and an ardent aspirant to share in my country's glory. With these feelings and qualifications, assuring myself that, now I was in India, I was in the wide field of promise, I began to revolve in my mind if I could not better my situation. I was then fifer and bugler in the light company, the kind captain of which, seeing my anxious spirit, generously undertook to improve me in reading and writing, of which I at that time knew but little. In the course of one year's close application, I so much improved as to keep his books of the company and his own private accounts. I then begged of him that I might be removed from the drummers to the ranks. I did not like the appellation drum-*boy*.

As I have seen many a man riding post, who was at least sixty years old, still called a post-boy, so, if a drummer had attained the age of Methuselah, he would never acquire any other title than drum-boy. Indeed, there were many other things I could never bring myself to relish in any eminent degree: such as flogging—to say nothing of being flogged—and dancing attendance on a capricious sergeant-major, or his more consequential spouse, who is queen of the soldiers' wives, and mother of tipplers, and an invitation-card from whom to tea and cards is considered a ponderous obligation.

In about a week after having made this request, I was transferred from the drummers' room, and promoted to the rank of corporal. This was promotion indeed—three steps in one day! From drum-boy to private; from a battalion company to the Light Bobs; and from private to corporal. I was not long before I paraded myself in the tailor's shop, and tipped the master-snip a *rupee* to give me a good and neat cut, such as became a full corporal. By evening parade my blushing honours came thick upon me. The captain came upon parade, and read aloud the regimental orders of the day, laying great stress upon, "to the rank of corporal, and to be obeyed accordingly." I was on the right of the company, being the tallest man on parade, when I was desired by the captain to fall out, and give the time. I did so, and never did a fugleman cut more capers; but here an awkward accident happened. In shouldering arms, I elevated my left hand high in the air; extended my leg in an oblique direction, with the point of my toe just touching the ground; but in throwing the musket up in a fugle-like manner, the cock caught the bottom of my jacket, and down came brown Bess flat upon my toes, to the great amusement of the tittering company. I must confess, I felt queer; but I soon recovered my piece and my gravity, and all went on smoothly, till I got into the barracks, where a quick hedge-firing commenced from all quarters; such as, "Shoulder *hems!*"

"Shoulder *hems!*"

"Twig the fugleman!" This file-firing increased to volleys, till I was obliged to exert my authority by threatening them with the guard-house, for riotous conduct; but this only increased the merriment, so I pocketed the affront, as the easiest and most good-natured mode of escape; my persecutors ceased, and thus ended my first parade as a non-commissioned officer.

In my new sphere of life I now felt that there was, unquestionably, some satisfaction derivable from being *"Clothed in a little brief authority."*

A corporal has to take command of small guards; is privileged to visit the sentinels whenever he pleases; his suggestions are frequently attended to by his superiors; and his orders must be promptly obeyed by those below him. There is certainly a pleasure in all this, and a man rises proportionately in his own esteem. In short, to confess the truth I now looked upon a drum-boy as little better than his drum.

Full of the importance of my situation and duties, thus passed the time for nearly six months, at the end of which I was advanced to the rank of sergeant, and, shortly afterwards, to that of pay-sergeant, in the same regiment. The post of pay-sergeant is certainly one of importance, and he who holds it a personage of no small consideration. He feeds and clothes the men; lends them money at *moderate* interest and on good security; and sells them watches and seals, on credit, at a price *somewhat* above what they cost, to be sure, but the mere sight of which, dangling from a man's fob, has been known to gain him the character of a sober steady fellow, and one that should be set down for promotion. Thus, at least, good may sometimes be educed from evil; and, as it is not my intention to enter into a detail of the chicanery practised among the minor ranks in the army, let it suffice that I never served in a company in which every individual could not buy, sell, exchange, lend, and borrow, on terms peculiar to themselves.

Shortly after my promotion, an order arrived for the two flank companies of the regiment to proceed to join the army then in the field, with all possible speed. We were to proceed by land, the distance about twelve hundred miles, and the season winter. Every hand was busily engaged in making the necessary preparations for the journey, equipping ourselves as lightly as possible; when an unfortunate misunderstanding occurred, which was but too likely, not only to prevent our journey, but to put an end to some of our lives.

On the arrival of troops at Fort William, it had been the custom to stop from each soldier of his majesty's army, eight *rupees*; but for what purpose, strange to say, they were never told. This deduction had been made from the pay of our two companies without any explanation; and, as the men were now proceeding on active service, it was but right and natural that they should desire to know (as we had been accustomed in the regiment) why any part of this pay was withheld from them. They called upon their officers for explanation, who were as much in the dark as themselves. The greater part of the two companies then marched, in a sober deliberate manner, towards Major-General Sir Hughen Bailey's quarters, to seek redress. Here they were given to understand that the sum of eight *rupees* was customary to be stopped from each soldier, to insure him a decent burial. This explanation only added fuel to flame, and excited in the hearts of the men—few of whom, poor fellows! ever wanted burial, as will be seen in the sequel of this narrative—the most bitter rancour against such a custom. The men returned to the barracks: liquor was resorted to to feed the spark already kindled in their bosoms; till at length they became bent upon open rebellion and mutiny. This spirit, of disaffection was manifested most strongly in the grenadier company. Both companies were dotingly fond of their officers, who took great pains to explain to them that violent measures, and taking the law into their own hands, would never be likely to get their wrongs redressed; but that, on the contrary, those very acts deprived them of the power of interceding for them, and explaining to the proper authorities the grounds of their complaints. This timely explanation had its due effect, and *we* one and all (I mean the light company) said, "March us before the enemy, that we may wipe away this our first disobedience;" but those who had drank deeper of the poisonous cup of rebellion, in the grenadier company, were still unappeased, and spreading wide the infectious sparks of mutiny; so much so, that the officers were again called in to quell them.

Their colonel they loved dearly—he was a father to his men; the adjutant they hated. On the arrival of the former, the men became passive, and the tumult was hushed; but, when the latter appeared, the shouting of, "Kick him out!"

"Turn him out!" resounded through the barracks, and he had a narrow escape for his life. When he had left, the tumult again ceased; the men retired to their cots; and, in an hour, all was silent as the grave. The next morning the eight *rupees* were refunded; and, on the morning following, we left the fort, with the band of the regiment playing us through Calcutta, where we were met and hailed by all assembled. Every face smiled with joy; every breast beat high for glory. The country through which we passed was fertile and well inhabited; plenty smiled around, and all seemed peace and contentment. Here presided English justice; the Pariah cottager was protected in his reed-thatched hovel, and the ploughman was seen smiling over his nodding crops. We lived like fighting-cocks; thought nothing of five or six and twenty miles a day; every face wore the smile of contentment; all were healthy; and the merry song and story beguiled some of our more dreary night-marches. Thus merrily we reached the army, our marches averaging twenty-six miles a day. We were met some miles from camp by his excellency Lord Lake, the Commander-in-chief, who said that he was delighted to see us. At this flattering greeting of the commander-in-chief, we gave three cheers, in which his lordship and staff heartily joined us. I must confess I felt at this moment sensations I was a stranger to before—a kind of elevation of soul indescribable, accompanied by a consciousness that I could either have laughed heartily or cried bitterly. Nearer camp we were met and greeted by nearly the whole European army. Such shouting and huzzaing I never heard; nor could I have imagined that the mind of man could be worked up to such a height of feeling. For myself, I could not help dropping a tear— for what, I cannot tell; but so it was. On reaching the general hospital, we saw many men without legs, some without arms, others with their heads tied up; and it was a most affecting sight to behold these poor wounded creatures waving their shattered stumps, and exerting their feeble frames, to greet us warmly as we passed along. The scene that followed would beggar description—drinking, dancing, shouting, that made the Byannah Pass echo again! Reader, believe me when I assure you that in those days I knew not, as I said before, the taste of spirituous liquors; consequently, I did not join in these bacchanalian orgies, but reconnoitred the camp, which, to my spirits, was far more exhilarating than the jovial cup. Three days restored us to some kind of order and discipline, and all went on smoothly.

Holkar, a Mahratta chieftain, was at this time in full force, with about sixty thousand horse, and twenty-five thousand infantry, encamped a short distance from us, ever on the alert to watch our movements, and supported by Ameer-Khan and other self-created rajahs. From the very nature of this service, against a flying enemy, thoroughly acquainted with the localities of the country, we had but little chance of coming up with them. Anything like a general engagement they studiously avoid; plunder only is their aim. In this way they pay themselves, giving their chiefs any great article of value that may fall into their hands; that is to say, if they are known to have it. Their wives are excellent horse-women, and many of them good shots with the matchlocks, and active swords-women. They are always mounted on the best horse, and it is not an unusual thing for them to carry one child before them and another behind, at full speed. The Pindaree horsemen, and indeed all horsemen in India, have a decided advantage over the English. Their horses are so taught that they can turn them right round for fifty times, without the horse's moving his hind legs from the same circle, or pull them up at full speed instantaneously. Our horses are heavy, fat, and quite unmanageable with the bit; it takes them as long to get round as a ship; and you cannot pull them up under ten or twenty yards. Some of their horsemen have spears seventeen feet in length, which they handle in so masterly a style that singly they are dangerous persons to have anything to say to: but I have frequently seen Lord Lake charge, with his body-guard, a whole column of them, and put them to the rout.

A few days after our arrival, we moved on towards Jeypore, these plundering rascals riding close by us, manoeuvring on our flanks, and giving us a shot now and then, to let us know they wished to be neighbourly. On one of these occasions it nearly cost me my life. We were in column on one side of a field, near some high corn, called *juwar*, about half a mile from our column on the other side of the field. I had at this time the fastest pony in India, called "Apple," on which I rode on ahead to the extreme end of the field, to have a shot at the head of their line of march; for which imprudence my own life was nearly the forfeit, for round the corner I came almost in contact with about a hundred of the enemy. I soon wheeled round, and galloped back again as fast as my pony could carry me: they fired at me fifty or sixty shots, not one of which touched me. Ever after, I kept a little more within bounds.

We had frequent skirmishes with detached parties, killing numbers with our six-pounders; but we could not come up with them. We therefore made our way towards Muttra, a great haunt of the Pindarees, where we lay for some time, trying to surprise them; but they were ever on the watch, as the rattling of our swords might be heard a mile off. Tired of this service, we took possession of the town of Muttra, driving them out. Here we had glorious plunder—shawls, silks, satins, *khemkaubs*, money, &c.; and some of the men made a good thing of it. I was not idle; but an untoward circumstance for a time delayed my exertions. I was quartered in a large square or *rajah*'s palace, and had to ascend several flights of steps to get at anything worth notice. All the way up this staircase were little iron plated doors, locked with several locks. As Paul Pry says, I thought this "rather mysterious"; I therefore commenced locksmith, and knocked off the locks, when I found the rooms full of bales of silk and shawls. I had just removed one of the largest bales from the top, and was in the very act of walking off with it, when, on turning round, a most brilliant eye met mine, set in one of the most hideous heads I had ever beheld. What monster this could be I could not at first imagine; nor did I stop very long to consider, but marched off rather precipitately with my prize; being at the moment more frightened than I was willing to confess, even to myself. On reflection, I was ashamed of my fears; so, having "screwed my courage to the sticking-post," in I marched again, with a drawn sword in my hand, and, having convinced myself, by a second peep, that my friend with the glaring eyes was no other personage than one of the gods Mahadooh, I saluted him with a cut across his face for taking up his quarters in that solitary place, and took the liberty of making free with all the silks and shawls under his protection. A short time after, we returned to quarters at Cawnpore, to spend the produce of our short campaign, Holkar having retired to a distant part of India, to his winter quarters.

Early in the following spring, our active enemy was again in the field, and approaching the city of Delhi, where the inhabitants were not very well disposed towards us, and in which we had but a small force of native troops. We immediately marched, by forced marches, to their relief, and found Mr. Holkar had been besieging that place, but that, some two or three days before our arrival, he had raised the siege and crossed the river Jumna; a necessary precaution on his part, for our cavalry were lightly equipped. Colonel Burn, to his praise be it spoken, was marching from the opposite direction towards Delhi, for the succour of that place, with five companies of native infantry, when he unfortunately fell in with the whole body of Holkar's cavalry; and, wonderful to say, he made his retreat good to Shamlee, a large town, fighting every inch of his way. There he took possession of a small *gurry*, or mud fort, for the space of six days, defending himself against an immense body of the enemy, suffering most dreadful privations, and worn out by continual watching. The grand army crossed the Jumna, to the rescue of Colonel Burn and his little band of native heroes, and in two days afforded him the succour he so much wanted, having, with this view, performed a distance of eighty-four miles in forty-eight hours. Never shall I forget the cheering of the handful of men on the ramparts of this little asylum. His lordship, to whom I was close, dropped the tear of sympathy when waving his hat to them. I had that morning preceded the army for the purpose of taking up the encampment; and, on the approach of our advance-guard, some of the straggling enemy were seen loitering behind the main body, who had marched early that morning. We had two six-pounders with us, five troops of his majesty's 8th Light Dragoons, five troops of his majesty's 24th Dragoons, with a regiment of native cavalry; and we succeeded in killing a few of these marauders, who were plundering and laying waste the whole country. We could always trace their line of march by the dreadful destruction they had committed. Some few *sepoys* were killed from the tops of the houses of Shamlee, many of which were higher than the little fort. For this breach of good faith his lordship gave up the town to plunder. The scene that followed would take an abler pen than mine to describe:—breaking open houses and boxes; tearing open bales of shawls, silks, and satins; and fighting hand to hand: the tumult is inconceivable to any one who has not witnessed such a scene. We marched the following morning, treading upon the heels of the enemy: but, as they had a day's start of us, and their horses will go from fifty to sixty miles a day, it was impossible for us to come up with them.

On our road we passed several villages that had been burned to the ground; poor, naked, and plundered creatures, men, women, and children; burning corn-fields; dead elephants, camels, horses, and bullocks; and the road was strewed with *moah*-berry, on which they feed their horses for the purpose of making them drunk, in which state it is incredible the astonishing distance they will go, though you can count their ribs a mile off. The rear-guard of the enemy generally kept their eye on our advance-guard, detaching parties on each of our flanks, and, by way of amusement, giving us occasionally a shot. I recollect, on one of these day's marches, a most impudent fellow, mounted on a beautiful horse, and finely bedizened, came within two hundred yards of our column, passing upon us some unpleasant epithets, and once or twice firing his matchlock. He at last wounded a man of the native cavalry. This so annoyed me that I asked his lordship if he would permit me to attack him. His answer was, "Oh, never mind him, Shipp: we will catch him before he is a week older." I never in my life felt more inclined to disobey orders, for he was still capering close by us. An officer commanding one of the six-pounders came up at the same time, and told his lordship that, if he would permit him, he would knock him over, the first shot, or lose his commission. His lordship said, "Well, try." At this moment the fellow fired his matchlock again, and immediately commenced reloading his piece. Our gun was unlimbered, laid, and fired; the ball striking the horse's rump, passed through the man's back, and the poor animal's neck, and we said, "So much for the Pin."

We marched, on the average, about twenty-five miles a day; but we were obliged to push our poor horses on even faster than this, for Holkar was making his way to Futtyghur, a small military station. This is a rich city; and, no doubt, his inclination was to plunder and burn it. He arrived at Furrackabad, about three or four miles from the above station, the day before us, for the purpose of exacting money from the *rajah* there. The little force at the station was withdrawn from the barracks, and placed for the protection of the mint, which had a short time before been established there. In the evening they arrived, and on the morning of the same day we marched upwards of twenty miles, halted till eight o'clock at night, then made ourselves as light as possible, and again moved on, intending to surprise them before daylight the following morning. We had twenty-eight miles to accomplish before that time, and there is no doubt, from the judicious arrangement made for this attack, by his excellency the commander-in-chief, that scarcely a man would have escaped us, had not a most unfortunate circumstance occurred, which was near destroying all our plans. An ammunition-tumbrel belonging to one of our six-pounders, from the rapid rate at which we were moving, blew up within half a mile of the enemy; who were buried in the arms of sleep, they having made a forced march, so as to prevent the possibility of our reaching them. This alarmed a few of those who happened to be awake; but they supposed it the station-gun at Futtyghur. This station-gun was really fired about ten minutes after, and some of them got on the move; but thousands of them were still asleep. I would recommend all officers who serve in India, to attack the enemy, if possible, in the night. At this time it often happens that not a single sentinel is to be found on the watch. This want of vigilance is to be attributed to their eating and smoking too much opium, a practice carried by them to such an excess as completely to deaden their faculties; from which, their stupor in sleep is so extraordinary, that if a gun were fired under a man's nose, he would scarcely have the power to awake.

When the day dawned they were surrounded, and a general attack commenced on all sides. Some were cut to pieces in their sleep, others in endeavouring to escape. The carnage became terrific; his majesty's 8th, 24th, and 25th Dragoons, two regiments of native cavalry, and a corps of horse-artillery, mowing them down with grape-shot in hundreds. About two thousand were left dead on the field, and amongst the number several poor tradespeople from Furrackabad, who had come to the spot to sell their commodities. We pursued them many miles from the scene of action; they, in their flight, burning the barracks and adjacent villages. The same evening, or the following morning, the enemy reached the station of Mainporee, a distance of seventy-two miles. At this station we had one native corps only; but they were prepared to receive them. This little band took possession of the house of the judge (Mr. Cunningham), and defended themselves against Holkar's immense body of horse.

The battle of Furrackabad was on the 16th or 17th day of November, 1804; after which the enemy shifted their course towards the fort of Deig, the property of the Bhurtpore *rajah*. In the neighbourhood were his infantry, about twenty-five thousand men, with upwards of a hundred pieces of cannon. Holkar little dreamt that, on the 13th of the same month, his infantry had met with a similar defeat to that which his cavalry had experienced on the 16th. Major-General Frazer, with a small force, had completely routed and defeated them, taking all their guns and stores. This action was at several intervals extremely doubtful, our force being so inadequate to that of the enemy. We had no European regiment there, except the Company's European regiment, and the 76th Foot, both corps not more than six or seven hundred men. The enemy sought protection under the walls of the fort; and, although our ally, the governor of the fort of Deig, fired on our army, General Frazer, seeing the danger of a defeat, charged at the head of the 76th, supported by the European regiment and native troops, and succeeded in driving them from their guns, and from the protection of the fort; but, in the heat of the action, the gallant general received a ball in the foot, and was obliged to retire from the field. He died a short time afterwards. Colonel the Honourable W. Monson, on whom the command devolved, completed his work, and a decisive victory was the result. Holkar, being informed of the disaster of his infantry, then shifted his course towards Bhurtpore, demanding immense sums of money from the *rajah*, under threats of laying waste his country, which at that time might be called the garden of India. His encampment was close under the walls of the fort, leaving a body of about two thousand men to harass and annoy us.

About the 18th of December we took up a position before the fort of Deig, and in two days after broke ground against it. The two companies to which I belonged led the column, carrying tools for working. The night was as dark as pitch, and bitterly cold. Secrecy was the great object of our mission, and we slowly approached the vicinity of the fort, steering our course towards a small village about eight hundred yards from the spot, where we halted under shelter from their guns. This village had been set on fire two days before, and its inmates compelled to take shelter in the fort. Small parties were dispatched in search of eligible ground for trenches, and within breaking distance. I was dispatched alone through the desolate village, to see what was on the other side. I was yet but a novice in soldiering; and, believe me, reader, I had no great fancy for this job; but an order could not be disobeyed; so off I marched, my ears extended wide to catch the most distant sound. I struck into a wide street, and, marching on tiptoe, passed two or three poor solitary bullocks, who were dying for want of food. These, startled me for the moment; but not another creature could I see. I at one time thought I heard voices, and that I could see a blue light burning on the fort, from which I inferred that I was getting pretty close to it. Just as I had made up my mind that this must be the case, I distinctly heard a voice calling out, "*Khon hie?*" in English, "Who is there?" I was riveted to the spot, and could not move till the words were repeated; when I stole behind one of the wings of a hut close on my right. Soon after I heard the same man say, "*Quoi tah mea ne deckah;*" which is, "I am sure I saw somebody." Another voice answered, "*Guddah, hogah;*" which signifies, "A jackass, I suppose;" for there were several wandering about. I fully agreed with the gentleman who spoke last, but was determined to throw off the appellation as quickly as possible, by endeavouring to find my way back. In attempting to make my retreat with as little noise as possible, I put my foot into some fire. This compelled me to withdraw rather precipitately, and they heard me, when one of them said, "*Hi quoi;*" which is, "There certainly is somebody." The other replied, "*Kis wastah nay tuckeet currah?*"

"Why don't you ascertain it, then?" Hearing this, I dashed into another hut, and squatted myself down close, resolved at least to have a fight for it. A man passed the door of the hut twice; but, at last, crying out, "*Cally ek lungrah bile hie,*" which signifies, "There is only one lame bullock," he rejoined his party. The attempt to steal away in so dark a night would have been impracticable; I must infallibly have been heard. I resolved, therefore, to have a run for it, and off I bolted, up the same street through which I had come, when a whole volley of matchlocks was sent after me, but they did not attempt to follow—at least, as far as I know, for I did not stop to look behind me. I arrived safe at the division, not a little frightened; and I can venture to say that, the elephant affair excepted, I never ran so fast before in my life. This afterwards proved to be a strong cavalry piquet.

We at last took possession of the village, and established a depot there; and a rising ground about two or three hundred yards from it was the spot selected for our batteries. We were at first heard, when the fort commenced a heavy firing, but in the wrong direction. Every man was employed in digging a sufficient space to lie down in; and, in the course of a couple of hours, we were covered and protected from their shot. We then erected batteries; and, by daylight in the morning, everything was finished, and we were so close to the enemy that we could distinctly hear English spoken,[1] and the reveille beaten.

---

1. The English, which we were confident we heard spoken on this occasion, was, no doubt, by a drummer who had deserted from the 76th regiment, and who was afterwards found dead in the fort.

On Christmas eve, as dark and cold a night as ever blew from the heavens, the breach was reported practicable, and the rising of the moon was a signal for marching to the storm. She did rise, in splendid effulgence, over one of the highest bastions of the fort we were about to storm; and we could see by her light, spears on the ramparts as thick as plants in a new-set forest. We were now and then saluted with a solitary gun from the fort, to let us know they were not asleep; blue lights were seen burning on their ramparts, and they occasionally indulged us with a rocket or two, which played beautifully in the air.

The soldiers, seeing I was a spirited youth, and a competitor with them for glory, gave me a few salutary hints, especially an old veteran of the 76th Foot, who had been then fighting about twenty years in the East. Among the hints he gave me were these: 1st. Never to pass a man lying down, or supposed to be dead, without giving him the point of the bayonet or sword; for it was a common trick of theirs to lay themselves down on your approach, and then to watch the opportunity of cutting you down. 2nd. Whenever I saw a rocket or shell fall near me, to get as close to it as possible, and lay myself flat on my face. This was undoubtedly very excellent advice; but I soon got tired of killing dead men, and lying down every time I saw a rocket; the having neglected to do which, on one occasion, however, nearly cost me my life, which I shall mention in its proper place.

The storming party consisted of about seven hundred men, composed of two companies of his majesty's 22nd regiment, two of the Company's European regiments, and the rest native troops, the whole under the command of Colonel Ball, a brave old hero, but so feeble, that he was obliged to be pushed up the track of glory. The two flank companies to which I belonged led the column. Sergeant Bury, of the Grenadier company, headed the foremost; but being wounded at the moment, he was compelled to leave the battery. I volunteered to take his place. The enemy had a strong entrenchment between our batteries and the breach, with innumerable guns, so placed as to have a cross fire on the storming party. However, we soon fought our way through their entrenchments, our gallant captain (Lindsay) cheering, and boldly leading us on. Crossing these trenches, this brave officer was cut with a spear in the arm, and also received a severe wound from a sabre; but his gallantry and zeal were so great, that he could not be prevailed upon to retire from the scene of action. A little on our right I saw some of the enemy point a gun at us. Immediately, with three or four comrades, I rushed out to spike it; for which purpose, I was in the act of searching for the touchhole, to put a nail in it, when one of the enemy's *golundauze* (artillery-men) fired the gun off, and I was thrown on my back in the trench, and the same man was in the act of cutting me to pieces, when a grenadier of our company, named Shears, shot him, and I once more escaped. Fortunately for us, the whole of the enemy's great guns were elevated too much, owing to which the shots passed over our heads. If they had been properly directed, we must have been annihilated to a man. Within fifty or sixty paces from the breach, I received a matchlock ball in the head, which dropped me to the ground, the blood flowing profusely. When I came a little to myself from the stun, I found myself impelled onward by one of our companies, who were close together, and running stooping, to avoid the shots, which, being near the breach, were uncomfortably thick; but we reached, and soon planted the British flag on the summit of the bastion which was breached. Our opponents fought hard to resist our entrance, throwing immense stones, pieces of trees, stink-pots, bundles of straw set on fire, spears, large shots, &c.; but resistance was in vain: we were determined to conquer. In spite of this laudable resolution, however, we found some hard work cut out for us on making good our ascent. The streets in the fort were narrow, running across each other, and every ten yards guns were placed, for the purpose of raking the whole streets. Added to this, many of the enemy had got into high houses, in which there were loop-holes, from which they could fire down upon us, without the possibility of our getting at them. Near the corner of a street, in a kind of nook, I saw our dear Captain Lindsay attacked by five or six of the enemy. He was on one knee, and quite exhausted, having lost much blood from his former wounds; but, to our great joy, we were just in time to save him, and punish some of his assailants. From the intricacy of the place, we were afraid of shooting our own men, and were therefore obliged to keep pretty close together. At midnight I again met Captain Lindsay, clearing one of the streets, when he asked me how I felt myself. I complained of a wound in my side, but said that I could find no hole; but this was not a time for talking. In turning sharp down a street rather larger than those we had cleared, we met a column of the enemy, with a person of rank in a palanquin. We soon stopped his black highness; and, to ascertain who was inside the palanquin, which was an open one, I, with several others, probed our way with our bayonets, when a tremendous fat *zemindar* (an officer) roared out most lustily, and began to show fight. He fired a matchlock at me, which went through the wing of my coat, but did not touch my person. Before I could retaliate, my comrades had finished him, and we then commenced at the column; but I took from the palanquin the gun which had nearly robbed me of life. It was like the barrel of a gun, about two feet long, with a round handle; at the handle end was a sharp hatchet; at the other extremity a sharp hook. This extraordinary instrument I presented to the commander-in-chief; but he refused the present, saying it was my trophy. His lordship was afterwards prevailed on to purchase it, at the price of two hundred *rupees*. We at this time got information that the five companies which had deserted from the Honourable Colonel Monson, in his masterly retreat from Jeypore, were standing, dressed in the full uniform they deserted in, outside the principal gate of the fort, with their arms ordered, without apparently making any resistance, and frequently crying out, "Englishmen, Englishmen, pray do not kill us; for God's sake, do not kill us." As these supplications proceeded rather from fear than from penitence for the crime they had been guilty of—that of deserting to an enemy—these men could expect no mercy. We had positive orders to give them no quarter, and they were most of them shot.

About three o'clock, when I was completely tired and done up, I took my station under the gable end of a brick building, and began to examine the extent of my wounds. The one on the head was a bad one, having touched the skull; it was about two inches long, and one broad, and I was a little alarmed for the consequences. The wound which I supposed I had received in the side, was nothing more than the wind of a cannon-ball, which it was thought must have passed between my arm and side. It was quite black, and much swollen, and on its margin there appeared red streaks, which convinced the doctors that it was caused as before stated. I felt it for months afterwards. The wound in my head had been so long exposed to the night air, that, on examination by the medical gentlemen, it was pronounced to be a dangerous one; but, with an excellent constitution, and youth on my side, I soon recovered.

The killed found next morning exceeded the number of our storming party. We had but few killed, but a great number wounded. Poor Sergeant Bury found his way in, wounded as he was, before the whole company had entered, and fought hard the whole night. Early in the morning he was looking over the parapet of the fort, when a cannon-ball struck him on the back, and killed him on the spot; otherwise he would have been rewarded with a commission; but such is the fate of war! The taking of this small redoubt was but a preparatory and necessary step before we commenced a regular siege against the strong fort, and equally strong town, both of which, however, they gave up, being fully satisfied of the impossibility of holding either.

CHAPTER 7

First Attempt on Bhurtpore

I was obliged to nurse myself a little, as the strong fortress of Bhurtpore was, we understood, to be our next job.[1] Having but in part led the last party in, I became a volunteer to lead the Forlorn Hope at Bhurtpore. This offer his excellency, Lord Lake, accepted, with encomiums on my zeal, and a promise that, if I escaped, I should have a commission. We arrived before this place about the 29th day of December, encamped about two miles from it, and immediately commenced our operations against it. Holkar was lying under its walls, with his immense body of cavalry, who committed every kind of cruelty on the camp-followers that fell into their hands, such as cutting off their hands from the first joint of the wrist, cutting off their noses, ears, &c.; but seldom killing them outright.

During the preparation for the siege, when off duty I amused myself with going out to the advanced piquets, where there were continual skirmishes with Holkar's cavalry, who were always loitering about, day and night. On one of these occasions I nearly paid dear for my imprudence. I ventured far beyond the piquet, in hopes of picking off a fellow who was showing off his horsemanship. As I was mounted on a good horse, and was well armed, I rode after him, gaining ground

---

1. Runjeet Singh, *rajah* of Bhurtpore, in Rajpootana—not the famous Sikh adventurer and ruler of the same name—had concluded a treaty with the British in 1803, and a contingent of his cavalry fought bravely under Lake, at the battle of Laswarree against the Mahrattas. But, on the approach of Holkar, Runjeet Singh wanted to evade his engagements with the British, whereupon Lake attacked and captured Deig and laid siege to Bhurtpore. The total loss in Lake's army at Bhurtpore is given by the historian Mill as 388 killed and 1,894 wounded. The causes of failure were, undoubtedly, those suggested by Shipp, p. 125. When disputes as to the Bhurtpore succession led the British to attack the fortress again in 1825, Lord Combermere had 25,000 men, and a strong battering-train, but had to resort to mining to render the breaches practicable.

fast; but, on looking behind, I found myself a considerable distance from the piquet, and that several horsemen had got between us, to prevent my return. To have run away would have given them encouragement: no other remedy was left but to dash through them. Our piquet, seeing my situation, got a six-pounder, and fired a long shot at them. During the consternation caused by the ball striking near them, and smothering them in dust, I made the best use of my horse's legs, got safe to the piquet, and never ventured so far from home again.

On the 1st day of January, 1805, we broke ground against this strong fortress and town. I was again on the working party, my wound being nearly closed. We halted near a wood; and, a party having been sent on to reconnoitre, we at last pitched upon a place, and commenced our nocturnal labours. We had not been at work ten minutes, when they heard our working tools, and commenced a most terrific cannonade. We were ordered to desist, and to lie down behind the earth we had thrown up, which, fortunately for us, was of a sufficient thickness to be musket-ball proof, or we must have suffered dreadfully; for their little rough iron balls flew about as thick as bees. The cannon-shot were generally high: some that fell short rolled, and were brought up by our little mound of defence. They kept it up gloriously for half an hour, conceiving that we intended to take them by surprise; but, from the reports of this fortress containing 100,000 soldiers, and the enormous sum of nineteen *crore* of *rupees*, our orders were to approach it by regular siege. I fear I shall be thought rather tedious in relating the disastrous events at this place; but we must take the gall with the honey. The firing having ceased, except at intervals, we recommenced our labours; and glad indeed were we to set blood again on the move. The night was bitterly cold, and the ground damp; but we kept ourselves in exercise with our work, and by daylight we had completed our trenches, and four-gun breaching battery, within five hundred yards of the town wall. The moment the day dawned, our night's work was observed. The fort was again in a blaze; flags were hoisted; the parapet of the town wall was one general mass of spears and little flags, as far as the eye could reach; and the heads of soldiers studded the ramparts with variegated colours—their turbans being generally of the most prominent dyes—red, yellow, and pink. Such shouting, roaring of cannon, whistling of shot, grumbling of rockets, and waving of flags and spears, made me reflect for a moment on the folly of having ever sold my "leathers," to participate in such a scene; but this thought was soon buried in the shouts of defiance from our trenches. We did not show hands, as we had none to spare; but as we

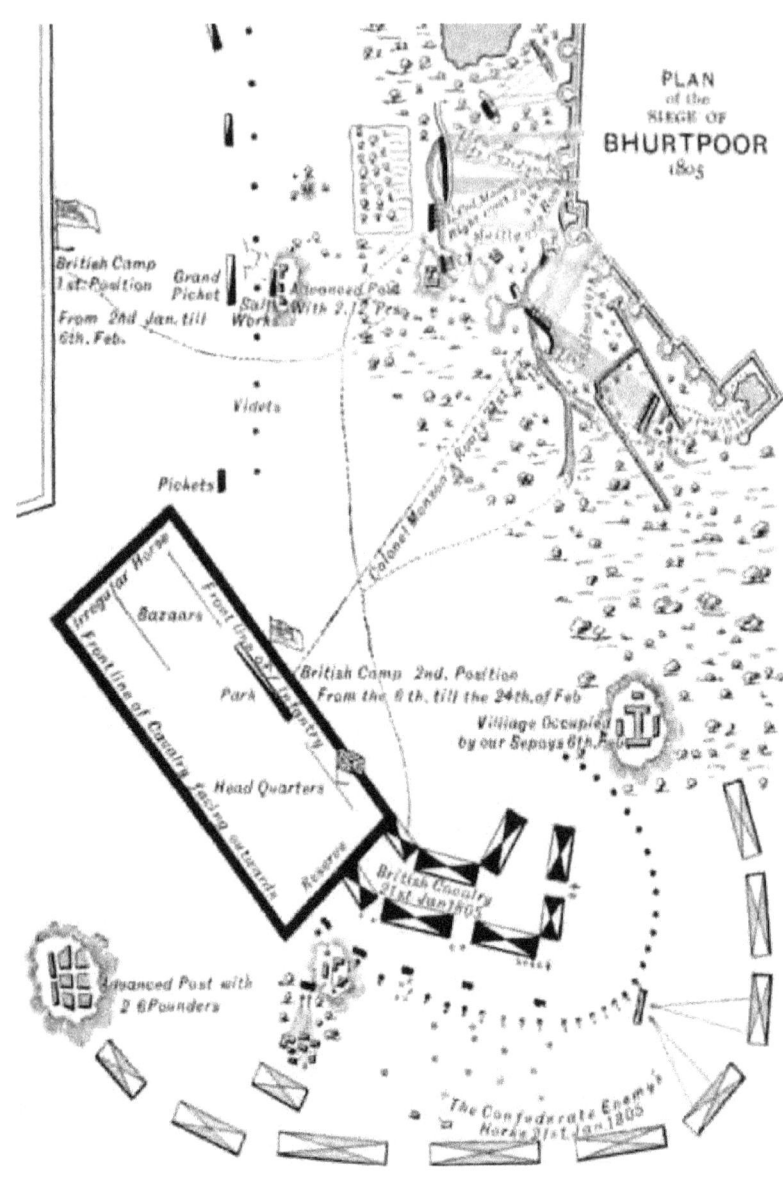

were, of course, anxious to see what kind of a place this said Bhurtpore was, we took every opportunity of peeping, whenever we saw a gun fired, crying out, "Shot," which was a signal to bob our heads. On the firing subsiding in the slightest degree, we continued our work, and at length completed our batteries and magazines, and widened our trenches to seven feet, leaving just sufficient room to pass and repass, so as to communicate with our principal depot under shelter. During the whole of this day, the enemy kept up an almost incessant fire, both with great guns and small arms, and we had some few men wounded. A soldier of the light company, named Murphy, stood upon the bank, exposing himself, and drawing upon us the fire from the fort. Some of us remonstrated with him on his imprudence, when Paddy coolly replied, "Never fear, honey; sure I have got my eye on them; and, if they kill me, bad luck to me if I don't be after paying them for it when I get into that same fort." In the course of the day he was shot in the finger, for his disregard of our advice, which, he said, was "just because he was looking another way at the time."

In the evening we got our guns into battery, erecting two small batteries of twelves and sixes. A constant fire was kept up by the enemy during the night, and blue lights were to be seen at intervals, as though to inform us that they were on the watch. From the debauched habits of the Mussulmans, in any situation in life, they seldom retire to rest till very late; and then, indeed, so stupefied with eating and smoking *auffeem* (opium), that they are incapable of being roused to any active duty. From their constant use of this intoxicating drug, they are dull companions when the spirit is absorbed and dead within them; but, when revived, I know no set of people more talkative, communicative, and jovial. Often have I listened with delight to an old Mussulman soldier's relation of his campaigns and stories. We heard drums and music the whole night, now and then accompanied by the inharmonious roar of their guns. The guns used in India by the natives are of cast iron; but, from their using ball beat out instead of cast, the guns labour and roar dreadfully, and the rough surface of their balls tears the muzzles to pieces.

When the morning bestrewed its bright rays abroad, we threw a little further light upon the subject, by opening our breaching-battery with a salvo, accompanied with such terrific cheering and shouting, as seemed to startle the new-risen sun, which at that identical moment peeped from behind its golden curtains to see what was the matter. The enemy, after a moment's pause, were seen in a tremendous bustle, mustering their full force; and their heads were so thick, that, had our shelling-battery been ready, we might have made dreadful havoc among the motley group. They shouted, yelled, screamed, groaned; small arms whistled, cannons, roared; and, in an instant, the fort was enveloped in smoke. It was altogether a most terrific scene. At this moment a soldier called out, "Shipp, have you made your will?" I said "Yes; which is, that I will lead you into that fort undaunted, for all their smoke and rattle."

"Well done, Jack!" said one; "That's a hearty!" said another; and many a joke followed; but, to confess the truth, I thought it no joking matter, but wished most earnestly that I could say, with Macbeth, "I have *done* the deed." Notwithstanding this, I saw no cause for fretting. Without parents, or ties of any other kind, I felt that I was fully justified in acting

"As if a man were author of himself, And knew no other kin."

My ambition was to signalize myself in the field of honour; and, if it was to be my fate to fall, I consoled myself with the reflection, that I could not die in a better cause than fighting for my king and country. These were my real feelings; but the business that was going on during the whole of this day, afforded me but little time for reflection. Towards evening, however, we were relieved from the trenches, and obtained some rest.

The next day I took another peep at the Pins, who were in immense numbers in front of our piquets. My fingers itched to be among them, but my last escape withheld me. It was truly tantalizing to see these fellows chuckering their horses not more than a quarter of a mile from our post; but what irritated us still more was, that these miscreants, that evening, sent into our camp about twenty grass-cutters, belonging to the 8th Dragoons, some with their right arms cut off at the wrist-joint, and others with the loss of their noses and ears. These poor creatures paid dearly for their disobedience of general orders, which forbade any grass-cutter from going out alone; but, for the love of plunder, they will at all times risk their lives. It will appear scarcely credible to the general reader, when he is informed, that to every fighting-man in an Indian army, there are at least ten camp-followers. The majority of these live by plundering the adjacent villages round the camp and on the march; robbing every hut and field within ten miles round. There is no possibility of checking them, or preventing these abuses. Amongst these fellows are thieves of every description, and the most notorious are jugglers. They commence their nocturnal pilferings in a state of nudity, oiling themselves all over to prevent their being held if caught; they then creep on their hands and feet like dogs, and frequently imitate them in barking and howling, as well as most other animals, more particularly goats, sheep, and asses. In the course of my narrative, I shall have occasion to mention several instances of this nature that happened to myself.

On the following morning, I went again on duty in the trenches. We retired into the wood before mentioned, which had a path of communication with the trenches, though it was a considerable distance from the grand breaching-battery. Our operations against the fort continued active and resolute; but our balls made but little impression upon the mud bastions and curtains. Many of them scarcely buried themselves, and others rolled down into the underworks of the enemy, and were kindly sent back to us. It is almost folly to attempt to effect a practicable breach in a fort built of such materials. The crust you knock off the face of a bastion or curtain, forms a great barrier to your approach to a solid footing. Young engineers are too apt to judge, from the appearance of the fallen mud, that the breach is practicable; when, the first step the storming-party takes, they find they sink up to their necks in light earth. A woeful instance of this nature I shall have to advert to more particularly in the course of my narrative; and, if it prove a timely hint to the inexperienced, I shall be rewarded. Stone forts are soon demolished; when undermined well at the bottom, the top will soon follow, and they cannot easily be repaired; but mud forts defy human power.

We this day erected howitzer and mortar-batteries; and, when they first opened, they struck terror and consternation into the enemy, who fled in every direction, to avoid those destructive engines; but, in a few hours, they dug holes in the ramparts, which they got into whenever they saw those unwelcome visitors on the wing; and, unless the shell happened actually to fall on them, they escaped in this way. But our shelling in those days was a mere bagatelle to what it is now. A shell in five minutes was then enormous; now, twenty in one minute is by no means extraordinary, and these twice as big as in the times of which I speak.

This day the enemy was pretty passive; no doubt, making places of refuge. Our shells, if thrown further into the town, must have been most destructive, for the population was evidently prodigious, from the number of fighting men. The houses frequently appeared on fire, and several small explosions took place daily; no doubt small magazines. These little incidents generally created cheering by the besiegers, and redoubled firing by the enemy. In the course of the day we saw the *rajah* for the first time: he was on the *shabroodge*, or royal bastion, with his suite, reconnoitring with a spy-glass. The officer commanding the howitzer battery laid a shell for the *shabroodge*, which struck the very top of it, and soon dislodged his highness and suite. In a moment not a soul was to be seen. On this bastion was an enormous gun, about a seventy-two-pounder, which before had been laid up in embryo, but which, as a mark of revenge for our having disturbed his highness, was now got ready. From its gigantic size they could not depress it sufficiently to bear upon our batteries, or it must have torn them to pieces. At last off it went; the report was like that of an earthquake, but the ball went a good quarter of a mile over us. Several other shots were, in the course of the day, fired from it, but the balls never came nearer. Our soldiers, finding it did no harm, christened it *Civil Tom*; but, from the enormous dust it kicked up, the enemy thought it did wonders for some time; until, at last, finding out their mistake, they turned its gigantic muzzle towards camp, and actually threw a ball close to the flag opposite Lord Lake's tent, more than two miles from the fort. The only real mischief Civil Tom ever did (which, by the by, was rather uncivil) was killing a poor water-carrier's bullock, and carrying away the poor man's right arm. This was more than a mile from camp.

The night passed away without anything of moment, we still keeping up a regular and constant fire, to prevent the enemy from rebuilding what we had had so much trouble in knocking down, and at times indulging them with a few whistling shells to keep them awake.

We now began to grow impatient to see what was inside this boasting fort, for we had pretty well seen what was outside. The breach soon began to wear a stormable appearance, when we discovered that they had thrown out two small guns for the purpose of a cross fire and cutting off our storming party, and to annoy and rake our breaching-battery. For removing this evil we threw out two six-pounders, and we had not fired many shots and given them more than a dozen shrapnells, when a tremendous explosion took place, which finally removed the annoyance.

In the evening I heard the engineer say to Captain Nelley, commanding the breaching-battery, that he imagined we should, on the following evening, put a stop to their vaunting. "The next evening!" I muttered to myself. I was standing close to Captain Nelley, who turned round to me and said, "Shipp, how do you like that information?" I replied, "I wish it was this night, Sir." This I did wish most sincerely, for I felt that, having once resolved to undertake the desperate service in which I had volunteered, the sooner I was in action the better.

> *Between the acting of a dreadful thing,*
> *And the first motion, all the interim is*
> *Like a phantasma, or a hideous dream;*
> *The genius and the mortal instruments*
> *Are then in council; and the state of man,*
> *Like to a little kingdom, suffers then*
> *The nature of an insurrection.*

I have heard some men say that they would as soon fight as eat their breakfasts; and others, that they "dearly loved fighting." If this were true, what bloodthirsty dogs they must be! But I should be almost illiberal enough to suspect these boasters of not possessing even ordinary courage. I will not, however, go so far as positively to assert this, but will content myself by asking these terrific soldiers to account to me why, some hours previously to storming a fort, or fighting a battle, are men pensive, thoughtful, heavy, restless, weighed down with apparent solicitude and care? Why do men, on these occasions, more fervently beseech the divine protection and guidance, to save them in the approaching conflict? Are not all these feelings the result of reflection, and of man's regard for his dearest care—his life, which no mortal will part with if he can avoid it? There are periods in war which put man's courage to a severe test: if, for instance, as was my case, I knew I was to lead a forlorn hope on the following evening, innumerable ideas will rush in quick succession on the mind; such as, "For aught my poor and narrow comprehension can tell, I may to-morrow be summoned before my Maker?"

"How have I spent the life he has been pleased to preserve to this period? Can I meet that just tribunal?" A man, situated as I have supposed, who did not, even amid the cannon's roar and the din of war, experience anxieties approaching to what I have described, may, by possibility, have the courage of a lion, but he cannot possess the feelings of a man. In action man is quite another being: the softer feelings of the roused heart are absorbed in the vortex of danger, and the necessity for self-preservation, and give place to others more adapted to the occasion. In these moments there is an indescribable elation of spirits; the soul rises above its wonted serenity into a kind of frenzied apathy to the scene before you—a heroism bordering on ferocity; the nerves become tight and contracted; the eye full and open, moving quickly in its socket, with almost maniac wildness: the head is in constant motion; the nostril extended wide, and the mouth apparently gasping. If an artist could truly delineate the features of a soldier in the battle's heat, and compare them with the lineaments of the same man in the peaceful calm of domestic life, they would be found to be two different portraits; but a sketch of this kind is not within the power of art, for in action the countenance varies with the battle: as the battle brightens, so does the countenance; and, as it lowers, so the countenance becomes gloomy. I have known some men drink enormous quantities of spirituous liquors when going into action, to drive away little intruding thoughts, and to create false spirits; but these are as short-lived as the ephemera that struggles but a moment on the crystal stream, then dies. If a man have not natural courage, he may rest assured that liquor will deaden and destroy the little he may possess.

Our two companies were relieved for the night, for the purpose of resting ourselves and preparing for the ensuing evening's attack. On this occasion one of our poor fellows was killed by a shot from the fort, and he was ordered to be immediately buried. When we were about to leave the trenches we found him still lying there, when the sergeant was called, and asked by his officer, why he had not been buried, according to orders. The sergeant, an Irishman, answered, "Faith! your honour, he has grown so mighty stiff since he went dead, that he would neither ride nor walk; he threw himself off my back twice; but I am just after ordering a fatigue-party to march him there, whether he will or not."

The same sergeant was chided a short time before for shooting an unarmed man. His officer told him it was a cowardly act to shoot a poor fellow without arms. "Arms! your honour, I beg your honour's pardon, he had two; ay, faith, and fists at the end of them; and he was just after going to be mighty saucy besides. Besides, your honour, did not a *spalpeen* shoot at and hit me at Deig, without so much as bidding me the time of the morning, or by your lave, or with your lave? Fait! they must expect no palaveration or blarney from Dennis Gaffen." To relate the anecdotes of this man would fill a volume; but, as the two little ones mentioned may bear the reading, I will insert a few more in their proper places.

I slept soundly, and early in the morning commenced cleaning and new-flinting my musket, and pointing my bayonet, that it might find its way through the thick cotton-stuffed coats of our enemies. All Mussulman soldiers wear these coats during winter. The cotton is about two inches thick, and the coats are worn rather loose, so that you can with difficulty cut through them; and I am persuaded that many of them are ball-proof, and that bayonets and spears are the only weapons against them. In the course of the day I walked down to the batteries, to well ascertain the road I had to take to the breaches. Our batteries continued, with unabated exertions, to knock off the defences; and everything, from appearances, seemed calculated to insure complete success. My heart was all alive this day, and I wished for the sombre garments of night. This was the 9th day of January, 1805. The greatest secrecy was observed as to the storming party; no general orders were issued, nor was there any stir or bustle till the hour appointed—nine o'clock. Orders and arrangements were communicated to officers commanding regiments and companies, and in the same private manner conveyed to us. The gun fired as usual at eight o'clock. This was the signal to move out. I kissed and took leave of my favourite pony, Apple, and dog, Wolf, and I went to my post at the head of the column, with my little band of heroes, twelve volunteers from the different corps of the army. Reader, you may believe me when I assure you, that at this critical juncture everything else was forgotten in the enthusiasm of the moment, except the contemplation of the honourable post confided to me. "What!" thought I, "I, a youth, at the head of an Indian army!" I began to think it presumption, when so many more experienced soldiers filled the ranks behind. I thought that every eye was upon me, and I did not regret the pitchy darkness of the night, which hid my blushing countenance. All was still as the grave, when I distinctly heard somebody call, "Sergeant Shipp!" This was Lieutenant-Colonel Salkeld, adjutant-general of the army, who brought with him a *golundauze*, who had deserted from the fort, and who, for filthy lucre, was willing to betray his countrymen. This man was handed over to me, he having undertaken to lead me to the breach. If he attempted to deceive me, or to run from me, I had positive orders to shoot him; consequently, I kept a sharp look-out on him. We then, in solemn silence, marched down to the trenches, and remained there about half an hour, when we marched to the attack in open columns of sections, the two flank companies of the 22nd leading, supported by the 75th and 76th European regiments, and other native infantry. I took the precaution of tying a rope round the wrist of my guide, that he might not escape; for, firing at him at that moment would have alarmed the fort. Not a word was to be heard; but the cannon's rattling drowned many a deep-drawn sigh, from many as brave a heart.

    I was well supported, having my own two companies behind me. Colonel Maitland, of his majesty's 76th regiment, commanded this storming-party, and brave little Major Archibald Campbell his corps. The former officer came in front to me, and pointed out the road to glory; but, observing the native whom I had in charge, he asked who he was; and, on being informed, said, "We can find the way without him; let him go about his business." I remonstrated, and repeated to him the instructions I had received; but his answer was, "I don't care; if you don't obey my orders, I will send you to the rear." I did obey, and on we moved to the attack. Immediately behind me were pioneers, carrying gabions and fascines to fill up any cavities we might meet with. The enemy did not discover our approach till within fifty paces of the ditch, when a tremendous cannonade and peals of musketry commenced: rockets were flying in all directions; blue lights were hoisted; and the fort seemed convulsed to its very foundation. Its ramparts seemed like some great volcano vomiting tremendous volumes of fiery matter; the roaring of the great guns shook the earth beneath our feet; their small arms seemed like the rolling of ten thousand drums; and their war trumpets rent the air asunder. Men were seen skipping along the lighted ramparts, as busy as *emmets* collecting stores for the dreary days of winter. The scene was awfully grand, and must have been sublimely beautiful to the distant spectator.

We pushed on at speed, but were soon obliged to halt. A ditch, about twenty yards wide, and four or five deep, branched off from the main trench. This ditch formed a small island, on which were posted a strong party of the enemy, with two guns. Their fire was well directed, and the front of our column suffered severely. The fascines and gabions were thrown in; but they were as a drop of water in the mighty deep: the fire became hotter, and my little band of heroes plunged into the water, followed by our two companies, and part of the 75th regiment. The middle of the column broke off, and got too far down to the left; but we soon cleared the little island. At this time Colonel Maitland and Major Campbell joined me, with our brave officers of the two companies, and many of the other corps. I proposed following the fugitives; but our duty was to gain the breach, our orders being confined to that object. We did gain it; but, imagine our surprise and consternation, when we found a perpendicular curtain going down to the water's edge, and no footing, except on pieces of trees and stones that had fallen from above. This could not bear more than three men a-breast, and if they slipped—which many did—a watery grave awaited them, for the water was extremely deep here. Close on our right was a large bastion, which the enemy had judiciously hung with dead underwood. This was fired, and it threw such a light upon the breach, that it was as clear as noonday. They soon got guns to bear on us, and the first shot (which was grape) shot Colonel Maitland dead, wounded Major Campbell in the hip or leg, me in the right shoulder, and completely cleared the remaining few of my little party. We had at that moment reached the top of the breach, not more, as I before stated, than three a-breast, when we found that the enemy had completely repaired that, by driving in large pieces of wood, stakes, stones, bushes, and pointed bamboos, through the crevices of which was a mass of spears jobbing diagonally, which seemed to move by mechanism. Such was the footing we had, that it was utterly impossible to approach these formidable weapons; meantime, small spears or darts were hurled at us; and stones, lumps of wood, stink-pots, and bundles of lighted straw, thrown upon us. In the midst of this tumult, I got one of my legs through a hole, so that I could see into the interior of the fort. The people were like a swarm of bees. In a moment I felt something seize my foot; I pulled with all my might, and at last succeeded in disengaging my leg, but leaving my boot behind me. Our establishing ourselves on this breach in sufficient force to dislodge this mass of spearsmen, was physically impossible. Our poor fellows were mowed down like corn-fields, without the slightest hope of success. The rear of the column suffered much, as they were within range of the enemy's shot. A retreat was ordered, and we were again obliged to take to the water; and many a poor wounded soldier lost his life in this attempt. Not one of our officers escaped without being wounded, and Lieutenant Creswell was almost cut to pieces. We, as may be supposed, returned almost broken-hearted at this our first failure in India. Our loss was a melancholy one; and the conviction that the poor wounded fellows we were compelled to leave behind would be barbarously massacred, incited our brave boys to beg a second attempt. This was denied: had it been granted, it must infallibly have proved abortive; for there was, literally, no breach. The disastrous issue of our attack caused the enemy to exult exceedingly; and the shouting and roaring that followed our retreat, were daggers in the souls of our wounded and disappointed soldiers, who were with difficulty restrained from again rushing to the breach. I found that I had received a spear-wound in the right finger, and several little scratches from the combustibles they fired at us. Pieces of copper coin, as well as of iron, stone, and glass, were extracted from the wounds of those who were fortunate enough to escape. We were, in the course of the night, relieved, and went to our lines to brood over our misfortunes.

I found, the next morning, to add to my feelings of distress, that the old wound in my head had opened afresh; the wound on my shoulder, having injured the bone, was also extremely painful; but that on my finger, being a flesh-wound, did not trouble me much. The general orders of the day following were highly flattering to us all, placing the blame, if any, where it ought to be. Our engineer, finding the spot we had attempted strong and impracticable, changed his position more to the eastward, where the difficulties were not so formidable. During these new operations, our breaching-guns, four in number, were sent to the park to be re-bushed, their bushes having been injured from the constant firing and heat.

Thus ended our first attempt to take the strong fortress of Bhurtpore by storm.

Chapter 8

The Forlorn Hope—Again

Having abundance of spare time while preparations were making for a second attack on the fort, Lord Lake determined to disturb Holkar in his hiding-place; for which purpose a party of infantry was dispatched with about four six-pounders. We soon came within sight of him, sheltered a good deal from his view by high trees and jungle. The fort, observing our manoeuvres, commenced a heavy cannonade. Holkar, alarmed, got on the move and made towards Futtypore Seccrah, one of his old haunts. Once from under the walls of the fort, our cavalry soon put his troops to flight; immense numbers were killed, and elephants, horses, camels, spears, matchlocks, colours, &c., were brought into camp. Holkar's best elephant was that day taken, and some little treasure was found on camels. Notwithstanding this routing, however, they took up their old ground, and we returned to camp, with some few men killed and wounded. This skirmish, instead of decreasing their impudence, seemed only to increase it; for they were day and night hovering round our piquets, the object of which was to take our attention from their main body, who had been dispatched to intercept a small detachment that was on the way to join us, from Muttra. Our spies soon brought intelligence of this, and, in little more than ten minutes after, three regiments of dragoons were on the move to rescue them, and arrived just in time to save our stores and the lives of the little party. Holkar commanded in person on this occasion; and it was reported that he was killed, though this proved afterwards to be false. A reward was offered for his head, and a great number were tendered, but none belonged to one-eyed Holkar. It is true, heads were produced without an eye, but the phiz of that notorious Pin was too well known to Chiggram (our best spy) to admit of our being imposed on.

My wounds at this time were nearly well; and, having been unsuccessful in the first forlorn hope which I led, I volunteered to lead the second. One night, previous to the time appointed for the second attack, I sauntered to a retired spot, far from the observation of my comrades, to muse over the prospect then immediately before me, and to ask His aid who alone has the power to protect us. Scarcely had I entered a wood about one hundred yards from the trenches, when my attention was arrested by a soldier on his knees, fervently supplicating the aid of Almighty God in the coming storm. The moment he heard my footstep, he suddenly arose, and, seeming ashamed of the way in which he was engaged, he said, "Who's that?" I answered, "Sergeant Shipp; who are you?"

He replied, "Private Murphy."

"Murphy!" I repeated; "is it possible that such a blasphemer as you, who, day after day, and hour after hour, boast your own infamy in a wanton disbelief and contempt of every quality that can constitute the man and the Christian, and who, no later than yesternight, solemnly protested before your comrades, that you firmly believed there was no place of punishment save a man's own conscience, and that hell was merely a name to frighten and intimidate schoolboys—can it be possible," continued I, "that you have at this late hour retired to this lonely place, and are found in the act of prayer?"

"Shipp," he replied, in a softer tone, and in nearly the following words, "whatever men may boast or say in their deluded and more irrational moments, there is a period when all those blasphemous expressions rush across the human mind, and the recollection of having uttered them leaves an inconceivable pressure on the humbled heart; but I pray you, do not expose me to my comrades, or I shall become their jeer and ridicule. I beg this as a favour."

"What!" said I, "more afraid of the derision of men, than the wrath of an offended God?"

"No, no," replied he; "but you know how religious soldiers are held in derision by some of our comrades."

"Well," I said, "I shall keep your secret, and you may confidently trust me on this subject; I will promise you most solemnly that I will never join in the laugh against you, and, if you have not finished, I shall be gratified in joining you in prayer, as I have rebuked you for your profligacy." He affectionately seized my hand, and pulled me toward the earth.

On the following day this poor fellow was summoned to his last account; and who knows but this single act of faith and devotion might have saved his immortal soul?

Two o'clock in the afternoon of the 20th of January, 1805, was arranged for the second storming of Bhurtpore. To prevent any obstruction by the trench, which was supposed to be at this part deep and wide, a bridge of bamboos was made, that would admit of three file a-breast. This bridge could be thrown a considerable distance by a hundred men, and was supported by *ghee dubbahs* (skins) in which the natives keep oil and butter for exportation; which, when dried, are light, and will bear a considerable weight before you can sink them. Elephants and camels were also laden with tents, and *hackeries*, or carts drawn by bullocks, with bales of cotton, all to fill up the ditch, to enable us to cross to the breach.

I once more took my station with my twelve volunteers, supported by my two companies as before. A shell from one of the howitzers was a signal to move. On this signal being given, the shell, bursting in the muzzle of the gun or mortar, killed two of our grenadiers—a sad beginning. The bridge followed the forlorn hope, carried on men's shoulders, and must have appeared some extraordinary monster to those who were not acquainted with its intended use. We moved on; and, before I got half way down to the fort, six of my men were killed or wounded. The enemy, no doubt encouraged by our late defeat, had redoubled their fire, both in guns and men; and on the right side of the breach they had thrown out an underwork, which was filled with matchlock-men, and in which they had several guns. My men kept falling off one by one; and when I arrived at the edge of the ditch, which appeared wide and deep, and was assisting the men with the bridge, I received a matchlock ball, which entered over the right eye, and passed out over the left. This tumbled me, my forehead literally hanging over my nose, and the wound bleeding profusely. I was at this time close to our gallant Captain Lindsay, who, at the same moment, received a *ginjall* ball[1] in the right knee, which shattered the bone to pieces. I recovered a little from the stun of my wound, when, the first thing that met my eye—for I could only see with one—was the bamboo bridge quietly gliding down the stream, being some yards too short. Nothing but killed and wounded could be seen, and there was not the most distant chance of getting in. To have attempted crossing the ditch would have been an act of madness. In descending we must have plunged over our heads in water; and they had two small guns bearing on the spot. At last a retreat was ordered. Previous to this, our poor fellows stood like sheep to be shot at, without the remotest hope

---

1. This is a long matchlock, which moves on a pivot, and carries about a two-pound ball.

of success. The camels and elephants, alarmed by the tremendous firing and shouting, could not be induced to approach the fort, many of them throwing their loads and running back to camp, and wild into the woods. Seven hundred men were killed and wounded on this occasion. Our brave Captain Lindsay's wound was so bad that his leg was amputated in the battery. My wound was a dangerous one, having touched the bone. I was immediately sent home to camp, where I lay completely blind for several days. This, added to our disastrous defeat, threw me into a fever, and nearly cost me my life; but, with the aid of a kind Providence, and the advantage of a strong and unimpaired constitution, I soon recovered.

Our engineer now gave up this side of the fort as perfectly hopeless, and we went more to the eastward, breaching a prominent bastion; but the whole fort was so constructed that one part protected the others; and therefore, wherever we breached we were sure of a destructive cross-fire. From our melancholy failures, our poor fellows became disheartened; scarcely a man had escaped without being wounded, and the sad recollection of their poor comrades that were left behind in a mutilated state, was the constant topic of conversation. Our mortification was greatly increased by seeing our men's clothing paraded on the ramparts, and worn by the miscreants in the fort. However, we still lived in the fond hope that our next effort would prove more successful.

I could again go abroad, although my wound was by no means healed. It was now truly distressing to enter our men's tents, where, but a month before, the merry joke went round, and mirth and hilarity prevailed. Naught but gloomy faces, and even them but few, were to be seen: some had lost brothers; others, dear comrades; Captain Lindsay had lost his leg; Lieutenant Creswell had been cut to pieces; and every other officer was wounded. Our loss in killed and wounded in the two assaults, in our two companies alone, was nearly the one half of the total number.

After the storm, our breaching-guns were again sent to the park to be re-bushed. This was a seasonable pause to enable us to recruit our shattered frames and spirits; but it also gave the enemy an opportunity of repairing and reinforcing every point of attack.

On the 18th of February things began to wear a more enlivening appearance. The breached bastion seemed to bow its haughty head to our roaring guns, and the 20th was talked of as the day for storming it. Our last disastrous repulse was scarcely eradicated from our minds; the massacre of our brave comrades was still alive in our memories;

but the fond hope of retaliation—I do not mean in cutting up a poor defenceless creature, not a single instance of which can, in the long course of our wars, be brought against the Company's army—spirited us up, and we looked forward to the time when we might drag the garments of our murdered comrades from the backs of the vaunting foe. They were now daily and hourly exhibiting to our view the number of muskets they had taken; our ammunition which had fallen into their hands was now turned against ourselves; as also our cannon-shot, which they had picked out of the two old breaches. We again possessed our wonted spirits and cheerfulness, and made preparation to retrieve the British character. The patient conduct and intrepid gallantry of our officers and soldiers when in the hour of their utmost distress, from repeated defeats, did not pass unnoticed by the enemy; and it is not improbable that the resolution and heroism then displayed by the troops were the means of facilitating that long friendship which afterwards subsisted between the *rajah* of Bhurtpore and the Company.

The day appointed (20th of February) arrived, and was ushered in with a new and unexpected scene. About four hundred men from the fort, emboldened, no doubt, by our tardiness, and the repeated defeats which our troops had experienced, rushed out upon us just as we were relieving trenches, and actually reached and had possession of our batteries and trenches before we could return. Every one of these men was in a state of intoxication, and fought desperately; but we soon drove them from the batteries; then, turning our guns against them, dreadful was the carnage. The fort fired indiscriminately at the whole party. These fellows were, no doubt, a set of vagabonds they wished to get rid of; and, if this was the case, their wish was fully realized, for a very few returned to tell the tale. This was the kind of retaliation we sighed for; but we lost a considerable number of men, killed and wounded, in this affray; but these they had not the barbarous gratification of cutting up. Their wounded men left within our reach were sent to the native hospitals, and every comfort administered to them. They were in the same wards with our wounded men, where friendship presided instead of murder. Had the war been between native and native, the cruelties would have been equal on both sides.

When this strange rencounter had subsided, the storming party was ordered for twelve o'clock. Reader, imagine my disappointment when my doctor most positively forbade my being employed on this occasion, as my wound in the forehead was still in such a state that, should I get heated or catch cold, he feared an inflammation of the brain would take place. I could have thrown what few brains I had in his face; but I was obliged to obey. The forlorn hope was led by Lieutenant Templer, of the 76th regiment, as brave a little fellow as ever wore a red coat. I looked on at a short distance from the scene of action, and a desperate hard struggle it was. No sooner did our brave boys gain the top of the breach, than the well-directed fire from the fort swept them off. Footing they had none; they literally hung on the bosom of the bastion. A third retreat was the result; leaving behind them upwards of five hundred dead and wounded: indeed, they might all be said to be dead, for death was inevitable. The enemy again manned the breach in swarms, shouting victory! It would have been better for me had I been there, for I am sure I fought and struggled as hard as any one engaged. I cannot describe my feelings and those of the other spectators of this dreadful scene; but what can eight or ten men a-breast do against a legion, posted aloft, and protected by walls, bastions, &c., and where every possible engine is in requisition for their destruction? Thus exposed, there was never any real chance of success. The whole circumference of the bastion, if lined with men, would not have contained more than fifteen or twenty men a-breast; and the whole means of the fort were levelled on this small space, to their certain defeat and destruction. All that was in the power of mortal man to do was done, but all our efforts were in vain.

The storming party was again ordered for the following day. I suffered an excruciating headache, but said nothing of the badness of my wound, which at that time bore a most frightful appearance, resolved to die rather than give up my past honour. I assured my doctors that I was well, and felt quite adequate to take my station, and entreated that they would not stand between me and glory. At last they consented, and I made the most of the short period between that and the storm, in supplicating the Divine protection, and in penning a letter to my only relation, on account of arranging my little affairs. I had made up my mind that I could not, in all human probability, escape a third time; but He alone who created life can destroy it. In the evening I left my tent, to seek in solitude that consolation for my troubled bosom which the drunken and tumultuous riot of a camp could but ill afford. The captain of our company, under whose care I had been brought up, was one of the best and most pious of men. In gratitude I mention the name of Captain Effingham Lindsay, now colonel on the half-pay of the 22nd regiment of Foot. To this beloved individual I am indebted for having implanted in my bosom, in early youth, those religious principles and feelings by which I have ever since endeavoured to direct my conduct, and from which, in the hour of affliction and of peril, I have ever derived inexpressible comfort. It was with the view of gaining consolation and support from private meditation and prayer, that I now retired from the riotous company of my companions in arms, the evening previous to my leading, for the third time, the forlorn hope at Bhurtpore. Scarcely had I gone beyond the discordant sound of revelry, and begun to muse upon the subjects that were ever uppermost in my mind, *viz.*, the possibility of my ever returning to my native village, or ever seeing my poor father, when an object presented itself to my sight, that for a moment startled, and, I must confess, a little alarmed me. The moon was just peeping from behind the high towers of the fort, and shedding her bright rays through the tree near which I stood, when by her light I perceived that the object which arrested my attention was a European soldier, prostrated on the ground—as I supposed, dead. I approached him, but could not hear him breathe. I laid my hand on his cheek; it was cold and chilly; which confirmed me in my first opinion, that he was dead. At last, I ventured to grasp his icy hand, which roused him, and he rose up and said, "Why did you disturb me? I have had a sweet sleep."

Then, looking at and suddenly recognizing me, he said, "Is that you, Shipp?"

I replied, "Yes; what brought you to this dreary spot?"

He replied, "The same, in all probability, that guided you here."

"What," said I, "do you suppose that to be?"

He replied, "To reflect on the scene before us to-morrow. Yes, sergeant," he continued, "I have this night stolen like a thief from the riotous parties I have too long joined, to spend an hour or two alone; and, if I must confess it, in prayer. Having offered up my prayers, I felt my poor heart relieved of a burden I cannot describe, and thus I fell asleep, and am now glad to meet a friend in this lonely spot."

We then, together, made the earth our communion-table, and offered up our poor but fervent devotions to the throne of mercy. It was the will of the Almighty to call my companion in prayer the next day from the world, and to spare me, but with a wound in the head, to show my dependence upon His mercy.

Two o'clock in the afternoon of the next day was ordered for the assault. I forgot my aches and wounds, and was at my old post. Lieutenant Templer, of his majesty's 76th regiment (he was a little man, but he possessed the heart of a lion) accompanied me on this occasion, with a small union jack, to plant on the enemy's bastion. He gave me his hand, and smilingly said, "Shipp, I am come to rob you of part of your glory; you are a regular monopolist of that commodity." He continued, "I will place Old England's banner on their haughty bastion, or die in the attempt!" He fell a victim to his zeal, having first planted his colour on the bastion.

On the way down from the camp, we met his excellency the commander-in-chief, and suite. His lordship addressed me and my forlorn hope: "Sergeant, it is with sincere regret I again see you wounded, and again at the head of your little band of heroes. I will not check your praiseworthy spirit; go into glory, my lads, and may Heaven prosper your zeal, and crown you with triumph!" His lordship addressed every corps that passed him; but when the remnant of the two companies of the 22nd regiment marched by, he was seen to turn from them, and the tear fell down his cheek; but, fearful it might be observed, he took off his hat and cheered them. This was not the tear of Judas, for his lordship often shed tears of sorrow for our great loss at this place. He was a true soldier's friend, and valued their lives as much as he did his own.

The storming party marched out in the usual steady order; yet, from our recent calamitous defeats, there was not that spirit amongst the men which I had witnessed on former occasions. We had already experienced three disastrous repulses from this fort, and there now seemed a cloud on every brow, which proceeded, I have no hesitation, in asserting, from a well-grounded apprehension that this, our fourth assault, would be concluded by another retreat. If any sight could be exhibited to the human eye that was calculated to work upon the feelings of men already disappointed and dispirited, it was the scene that was exposed to our view on approaching to this breach; for there lay our poor comrades who had fallen in previous attempts, many of them in a state of nudity, some without heads, some without arms or legs, and others whose bodies exhibited the most barbarous cruelties, for they were literally cut to pieces. The sight was truly awful and appalling, and the eye of pity closed instinctively on such a spectacle of woe. Those who attempted to extend the hand of relief were added to the number of the slain, as the spot was much exposed to a cross-fire from the fort. Could any sight be more distressing for affectionate comrades to look on? I say affectionate, for, among men living together in one barrack, and, perhaps under one tent, in familiar intercourse, there must be a greater regard for each other than is found to subsist among those who meet casually, once a day or once a week. In a soldier's barrack, the peculiarities, good or bad, of every individual are known; added to which, arduous services will always link men together in the bond of union and affection. Many of these mutilated objects still breathed, and could be seen to heave the agonized bosom; some raised their heads clotted with blood; others their legs and arms; and, in this manner, either made signs to us or faintly cried for help and pity. It was a sight to turn nature's current, and to melt a heart of stone. Such was its effect upon our lines, that, after a short conflict of the softer feelings, the eye of every man flashed the vivid spark of vengeance against the cruel race who had committed such wanton barbarities; and, if mortal effort could have surmounted the obstacles in our path, those who witnessed the horrid scene I have just described must infallibly have succeeded. But the effort was beyond mortal power. Braver hearts, or more loyal, never left the isle of Albion, than those who fell like withered leaves, and found a soldier's grave at Bhurtpore.

Our ascent was found, for the fourth time, to be quite impossible: every man who showed himself was sure of death. The soldiers in the fort were in chain armour. I speak this from positive conviction, for I myself fired at one man three times in the bastion, who was not six yards from me, and he did not even bob his head. We were told afterwards, that every man defending the breach was in full armour, which was a coat, breast-plate, shoulder-plates, and armlets, with a helmet and chain face-guard; so that our shots could avail but little. I had not been on the breach more than five minutes, when I was struck with a large shot on my back, thrown down from the top of the bastion, which made me lose my footing, and I was rolling down sideways, when I was brought up by a bayonet of one of our grenadiers passing through the shoe, into the fleshy part of the foot, and under the great toe. My fall carried everything down that was under me. The man who assisted me in getting up, was at that moment shot dead: his name was Courtenay, of the 22nd light company. I regained my place in time enough to see poor Lieutenant Templer, who had planted the colour on the top, cut to pieces, by one of the enemy rushing out, and cutting him almost in two, as he lay flat upon his face on the top of the breach. The man was immediately shot dead, and trotted to the bottom of the ditch. I had not been in my new place long, when a stink-pot, or other earthen pot, containing combustible matter, fell on my pouch, in which were about fifty rounds of ball cartridges. The whole exploded; my pouch I never saw more, and I was precipitated from the top to the bottom of the bastion. How I got there in safety, I know not; but, when I came to myself, I found I was lying under the breach, with my legs in the water. I was much hurt from the fall, my face was severely scorched, my clothes much burnt, and all the hair on the back of my head burnt off. I for a time could not tell where I was. I crawled to the opposite side of the bank, and seated myself by a soldier of the same company, who did not know me. I sat here, quite unable to move, for some little time, till a cannon-ball struck in the ditch, which knocked the mud all over me. This added greatly to the elegance of my appearance; and in this state I contrived, somehow or other, to crawl out of the ditch. At this moment the retreat was sounded, after every mortal effort had been made in vain.

The case was now deemed completely hopeless, and we were obliged to give up the contest, having lost, in killed and wounded, upwards of three thousand men—braver, or more zealous, never lived—against this fort. Of the twelve gallant fellows who composed the third forlorn hope led by me, not one returned to reap the proffered reward of the commander-in-chief: add to this, the loss of one of the best officers in our army, Captain Menzies, of the 22nd grenadier company, aid-de-camp to Lord Lake. He fell endeavouring to rally some native troops that were exposed to a galling fire, and began to give way. In this heroic attempt he lost his life, regretted by the whole army. Of our two companies, scarce a soul escaped uninjured. Near the breach, the dead, dying, and wounded would have melted the heart of the most callous wretch; and, had not the little party who stormed the eleven-gun battery proved successful, few, if any, would have escaped the dreadful carnage. You must permit me to draw the gloomy shroud of mourning over this scene of misery and terror. The sad details of this siege have years ago been before the public; and here my personal services at Bhurtpore ended, leaving impressions, both on mind and body, that can never be obliterated.

In the course of the siege, frequent overtures were made from the fort, but of what nature I do not pretend to know. They were at last, however, obliged to come to our terms, which compelled them to pay all the expenses of the siege, &c.; after which we raised the siege, and returned to camp. The loss of the enemy must have been immense: report said, five thousand men, women, and children; and, from the immense concourse of inhabitants in the town, with their families, that number does not appear to be at all improbable. Certain it is, that they must have been as heartily tired of it as we were.

Our sad failures, on the occasion of this memorable siege, may unquestionably, in my opinion, fairly be attributed to our total want of means. What were four breaching-guns against such a fort as that of Bhurtpore? Forty would not have been too many: as a proof of which, if we contrast the means of attack at our disposal, with those possessed by Lord Combermere, in his successful siege of the same fort, it will be found, that the number of guns employed on the latter occasion, compared with the former, was at least ten to one. With the original force of Bhurtpore—calculated at not less than a hundred thousand men—it was scarcely possible that, with a less number of guns, the place could be taken by assault. It should be recollected, also, that, with the means we had, the ditch which surrounds the fort made it quite inaccessible to us. Sapping and mining, the only way by which Bhurtpore could have fallen, was, at the period of the first siege of that place, scarcely known in India; and shelling was then only in its infancy. The former of these methods was resorted to by the present commander-in-chief, with great success; and the latter, from the improvements which, since 1805, have been made in this destructive system of warfare, with at least ten times the vigour and effect that it was possible for us to impart to it.

After our last failure, conciliatory orders were published to our disheartened troops; everything was done to console and comfort them; and, with these judicious measures, though the men could scarcely bear the stigma of being defeated, yet, after a few days' reflection, their features began to brighten up, and they began to weigh things in a proper light; when an unexpected and untoward event happened, that was likely to have been attended with the most frightful consequences. The peace having been ratified, the garrison had permission to visit our camp. Imagine our mortification and surprise, when many of them had the presumption to appear, under our very noses, with the coats, sashes, and arms they had torn from the dead bodies of our poor comrades. This news flew through the camp in a moment; the whole army was out; every eye flashed vengeance: but, by the timely interference of the commander-in-chief, and the officers in general, the men were calmed, and the mischief stopped. In the next general orders my name appeared as Ensign in his majesty's 65th regiment, with many flattering encomiums by the commander-in-chief. From the whole of this regiment, during the short time I remained with them, I received the most marked attentions; and whenever I served with, or met them afterwards, I experienced from them the most disinterested friendship.

On the day of my appointment, I was metamorphosed into a gentleman; hair cut and curled; new coat, &c., &c.; had an invitation to dine with the commander-in-chief; but, of course, kept myself in the background. The gentleman did not seem to sit easy on me; for, you must know, I was then a blushing modest youth: but the extremely kind inquiries of his lordship, and of his equally kind son, if I was there, tended greatly to dissipate my shyness. His lordship, on hearing I had arrived, approached me with extended hand, and shook mine cordially, saying, "I congratulate you as a brave young fellow, and I shall not lose sight of your merit." He requested I would sit next to him at dinner. I did so; and, after the cloth was removed, he made me fight the forlorn hopes over again; at the recital of which his lordship was much affected. The next day his lordship again sent for me, when he addressed me in these words, "Shipp, I have been thinking a good deal about your case. You, of course, have not much money. I know your generous Lindsay will do anything to serve you, but he must really leave a little for me to do. You may therefore draw on me, through the field paymaster, for what you want." His lordship afterwards sent me a tent, two camels, and a horse, as presents. The rest of my fitting-out my excellent friend, Captain Lindsay, generously gave me.

Lord Lake was truly my friend, as he was that of every soldier in the army. He was munificent in his charities, being ever the first in subscribing large sums to whatever cases of distress appeared. I will relate one instance of his benevolence and generosity. A very old lieutenant could not purchase a company then vacant; indeed, knowing he could not purchase, he had thought nothing of the vacancy. In the evening I was standing with this officer, when the orderly-book, publishing his promotion by purchase, was put into his hands. He said, "There must be some mistake, for he had not a *rupee* he could call his own." At that moment Colonel Lake, his lordship's son, came up, and wished him joy of his promotion. The other said, "Colonel, there must be some mistake in this; I cannot purchase." Colonel Lake said, "My father knows you cannot, and has therefore lent you the money, which he never intends to take back." These were the sort of acts in which his lordship delighted; and, in consequence, he was loved by his army, and admired by the people wherever he came.

In about three weeks after, having been appointed ensign in the 65th regiment, his lordship promoted me to the rank of lieutenant in his majesty's 76th regiment, thus faithfully keeping his promise of not losing an opportunity of serving me. In this regiment I became a great favourite with my colonel, the Honourable William Monson, then brigadier-general of the army.

One of the articles of treaty was, that Holkar should be driven from under the walls of the fort of Bhurtpore. This had been done; but he still hovered about camp, annoying our foraging-parties and small escorts coming into camp with supplies. A few days after having joined the 76th regiment, I was appointed an extra aid-de-camp to the brigadier, to proceed on a foraging-party, consisting of one regiment of native cavalry and four six-pounders, with five hundred of irregular or local horse. We had not proceeded many miles from camp, when we saw Holkar's troops in immense force, posted on an eminence. They showed symptoms of fight. We collected our elephants, camels, and bullocks, and left them in charge of the five hundred irregular horse; then, placing two of the six-pounders behind the regiment of native cavalry, we moved slowly on till within two or three hundred yards of the enemy, when we gave them about twenty rounds of grape, killing great numbers. We then charged them, and cut up a great number more. I had a narrow escape; my horse was killed by a spear-wound in the chest, which entered his heart, and I fell under him. The horseman was about to give me a few inches of the same spear, when the honourable brigadier cut him down, and thus I escaped, taking the liberty of riding my well-meaning adversary's horse to camp. I was a good deal hurt by the fall, but this, with one or two men wounded, and some few horses killed, were the only casualties of the day.

Holkar, finding that our hands were so unoccupied that we had more leisure than suited his purposes, made towards Jeypore. We crossed the river Chumlah, near Daulpore, in pursuit; but he retired to his old haunts, with his colleague Ameer-Khan, and we to quarters in Futtypore Seccrah.

The following year, everything wearing the pacific garb, and the gallant regiment to which I belonged being literally cut to pieces—so much so, that we had scarcely a sound man left in the regiment—it was considered to be time that the corps had some cessation from war. Twenty-five years had they been in India, and stood the brunt of all Lord Lake's conquests, and those on the coast. When I was in the regiment (1805) I believe there were only two men of the original corps—Lieutenant Montgomery, and Quarter-Master Hopkins.

The regiment now embarked for Calcutta. I preceded them in charge of invalids. Many of these poor fellows were without arms and legs; and some of them so dreadfully cut up, that scarcely a human feature could be traced. Many died from their wounds. Mine, by the blessing of Divine Providence, continued to do well; but I was visited with the most excruciating headaches and dizziness from the wound in my head; and the terrific spectacle of the last scene at Bhurtpore so affected my mind, that scarcely a night passed in which I did not dream of "hair-breadth 'scapes i' th' imminent deadly breach," and fancy I was fighting my battles over again. My head was so much injured, that the report of a gun would startle me dreadfully; but, with an excellent constitution, care, and avoiding drink, I soon recovered, though the wound across my forehead has considerably impaired my sight. Twelve pieces, or splints, came away from the upper part of the wound; and when you put your finger upon it, the skull was so thin that you could feel the pulsation, like the pendulum of a clock. My wounds are still a certain and sure weather-glass. That on my forehead will, to this day, swell and expand on any change of the weather, or variation in the atmosphere.

CHAPTER 9

The 24th Dragoons

You have now, reader, followed me through my military enterprises, up to the time of my being appointed lieutenant in the 76th regiment. The time has arrived when I have to request that you will beat the silvery wave with me; for I am bound to my native country with my regiment, after an absence of ten years. On arriving at Calcutta, our reception was gratifying in the extreme. Every house opened its hospitable doors, and the tables groaned under a profusion of good cheer. Every one was anxious to hear the tale of war; and, wherever I went, I was thought ill-natured if I refused to repeat storm after storm, and all my battles over and over again. But, the ship being about to weigh anchor, our stay here was but short. We embarked at Balloh Ghaut, on board small sloops, and in three days reached the vessel, the *Lord Duncan,* Captain Bradford, in safety. We had on board a great number of passengers, and about two hundred invalids, under the command of Captain Lindsay, of my old corps. Two days afterwards we bade adieu to the Indian shores, leaving many dear and respected friends behind us.

We were at this time at war with France, and the Indian Seas were well watched by cruisers from off the Isle of France. Our fleet consisted of thirteen Indiamen of the first-rate convoyed by the *Tremendous,* seventy-four, and *Hindostan,* seventy-four. We sailed in two lines, headed by the two seventy-fours. All seemed order and discipline, and we thought ourselves a match for any ships of France we might have fallen in with. Everything went on smoothly, practising and drilling our guns once a week, and keeping a constant look-out for the enemy. Off the coast of Madagascar a ship was discovered, early in the morning, standing right down upon us. Seeing her a single vessel, we conceived her to be one of our cruisers from off the Cape of Good Hope; but, when she was within one mile and a half from us, she could not answer our signals, and consequently ran towards the land, which was to windward of us. The *Tremendous*, being a fast sailer, went in chase of her. The Frenchman soon found that he was mistaken. He, no doubt, at first took us for a French fleet that was then out in these seas, and relied upon his fast and superior sailing to enable him to get away, should he prove mistaken; but our commodore overhauled him hand over hand. The Frenchman tacked, turned, and twisted, but he found it was of no use. He therefore resorted to his natural cunning, shortened sail, and at last backed maintopsail, and waited till the English vessel came within pistol-shot. The commodore, conceiving that the Frenchman was about to strike, did not wish to injure her, and therefore would not fire. The French captain availed himself of this interval, and gave the *Tremendous* a whole broadside, by which she was so disabled as to become an immoveable log on the water. The Frenchman up-helm, and off he started. The commodore, at last, got his ship's broadside to bear, and nearly tore her out of the water. However, she was a faster sailer than any ship in our fleet, and, finally, made her escape, to the mortification of the whole fleet, except one Captain Brusée, a French prisoner of war, a passenger on board our ship, who danced with ineffable delight;—natural enough, but not very pleasant to the sight of an Englishman.

The following day we experienced a most violent hurricane, which lasted for two days without cessation. Fortunately, our fleet suffered but little injury, with the exception of one vessel, the *Lady Castlereagh*, which we thought must inevitably have been lost. She was about a quarter of a mile from us, and we could at one time see her whole keel. There was a general shriek of terror from all on board of us, and our captain said that he feared she would never right. The next gigantic wave, however, brought her up, and she did right, in spite of our predictions, but seemed to roll, pitch, and labour dreadfully. Some parts of her masts were carried away; but what, I do not now recollect. Three of our ships separated from the fleet, and we imagined that they had fallen into the hands of the French, for we learned, at St. Helena, that they had been seen a few days before from that island. The name of the French ship which we had fallen in with was *Le Cannonier*, a sixty-four, from the Isle of France. We understood that she was so badly wounded, that she was obliged to put into Simon's Bay, not aware, at that time, that the Cape was again in possession of the English. She soon found this out, cut and ran, and got clear to the Isle of France. Our three strayed ships made their appearance at St. Helena the following day, having seen the French fleet the night after the affair between the *Tremendous* and *Le Cannonier*, and, under cover of the night, escaped unobserved, or they must have been taken, as the French fleet consisted of five sail or more.

Our reception at St. Helena, by Governor Brooke, was truly splendid and hospitable. We remained there, I think, eight or ten days, after which we again stood towards Old England.

We arrived in England some time in October, 1807. We landed at Long Reach, and proceeded to Dartford, in Kent, from whence I marched my invalids, or rather had them carried, to Chelsea Hospital—a journey which I was three days in accomplishing. On the fourth day I reached the place of destination; and, having made my report to the commandant of Chelsea, I returned to join the regiment at Dartford. Here we remained for about a week or ten days, receiving the greatest kindness from the gentlemen in that town and its vicinity. From thence the regiment was ordered to Nottingham, and I obtained leave of absence to proceed home.

My primary object in coming to England was the hope of seeing my father; and I anxiously availed myself of the opportunity which now offered of revisiting my native village, full of anticipation of the pleasure with which I should relate my adventures to all who had formerly known me. The coach which was to convey me to the village of my birth, had not proceeded many miles, when a coincidence happened, which, though "true as holy writ," might be thought, without this assurance, to bear the marks of fiction. On the coach, next to me, sat a pilot from Aldborough, in Suffolk, who, suddenly addressing himself to me, said, "I really cannot help thinking, Sir, from your extraordinary resemblance to a person I once knew, that you are his son." The words, "*once* knew," turned my blood cold, and it was some minutes before I could muster courage to ask the name of the person to whom he referred. What was my astonishment when he at once replied, "Shipp!"

"Is he then dead, Sir?" exclaimed I, convinced now that it was my father of whom he spoke. "I regret to say he is," replied the pilot; and he added, while his lip quivered, and the tear of sympathy stood in his eye, "You are his son John—I feel sure that I cannot be mistaken now." At this moment the coach stopped to change horses, and I jumped off, and, instead of supping with the rest of the passengers, took a solitary stroll, to hide my grief. I had left India at a great sacrifice to my prospects. There were all my friends, and there lay all my interest. I might have made a very advantageous exchange, and remained in that country; but I could not resist the temptation of coming to England, from anticipations of the delight I should enjoy in recounting my life to a parent who had almost from my infancy been estranged from me. I had now heard, in the sudden and unexpected manner I have related, of that parent's death! But, not to dwell long on this painful subject, I made up my mind, that, notwithstanding what I had just learnt, I would still proceed to Saxmundham. On arriving there, I found living my father's two brothers, and my mother's sister. With the latter I took up my quarters, and spent a most happy fortnight under her roof. To enumerate the alterations which had been made, both in places and persons, since I left my native village, or to detail the inquiries I had to answer, and the congratulations which poured in upon me from all quarters, would be as uninteresting to the reader as it would be tedious to myself.

I soon returned to Nottingham, and rejoined my regiment. From thence I was ordered to Wakefield, in Yorkshire, on the recruiting service. Here nothing but gaiety prevailed; and, as I was the only officer at the place for a considerable time, I received invitation upon invitation, to dinners, balls, and suppers; and, to confess the truth, I thought myself no small personage, which, as I was now in the grenadier company, was not, in its literal sense, very easily to be controverted.

While I was at this place, I was called upon to perform the office of second, in an affair of honour between a military officer of rather diminutive person, and a huge fellow of a civilian. The circumstances which gave rise to the quarrel were as follow:—

Among the fair attendants of a ball which was given one evening in the town, was a very pretty girl, on whose charms the tall gentleman had for some time looked with amorous inclination, and whom, it is to be presumed, he therefore wished to exclude from the attentions of all but himself. The young lady herself, however, was not so exclusive in her notions; and, accordingly, finding her conversation courted, and the favour of her hand solicited, by a dashing little officer in handsome uniform, and who, though a warrior of somewhat small dimensions, was really a dapper, good-looking little fellow, she made no scruple either of listening to his flattering tongue, or of accepting his hand for the dance. This preference of the man of steel so irritated his huge rival, that he determined to pass some insult upon him. He accordingly found a more compassionate lady as his partner; and, no sooner had the dance commenced, than he took the first opportunity which presented itself of treading, with all his weight, on the little officer's toes. In dancing down a second time, he played him the same trick. Our little hero did not think it much of a joke to have the full weight of a gentleman full six-feet-three in height, and stout in proportion, twice on his toes within a few minutes; but as his tormentor made the most ample apologies on both occasions, he felt fully disposed to endure the pain with as much fortitude as possible, and to attribute the occurrence to accident; when his little rustic beauty, who had more carefully watched and better understood the manoeuvres of the neglected swain, whispered in his ear, "A pointed insult, Sir." These words roused the blood of the son of Mars in a moment; he watched the movements of his toe-treading foe, and, just as he was coming down the middle a third time, to repeat the trick, he jumped upon a chair, and from thence sprung on his enemy's back, and, seizing his nose, he wrung it in so unmerciful a manner, as to compel its proprietor to cry out most piteously for help. The parties were at length separated by the master of the ceremonies, and a challenge was of course the result; the gentleman whose nose had been thus scurvily treated, in the presence of almost the whole town, being compelled either to fight or to quit society.

Mortal combat having been appointed to take place the next morning, it was arranged by the seconds that the principals were to be placed back to back, and that from thence each party was to step six paces, and then to fire together by signal.

Preliminaries being thus concerted, and the fatal morning having arrived, the parties met punctually at the appointed spot, and were duly ranged with their backs to each other. At this moment the contrast between the courage of the two gentlemen was to the full as apparent as the ludicrous disproportion in their size. When I was placing them on the line drawn by me for their march, my little man, who possessed true "pluck," and was as cool as a cucumber, observing the trepidation of his opponent, whispered to me, just loud enough to be overheard, "Where shall I hit him, Shipp? Shall I wing him?" On hearing this, the knees of the six-foot Yorkshireman, which were already on the trot, broke into a full gallop; and, when his second placed the pistol, duly primed and loaded, into his hand, he seized it by the muzzle. This mistake, as I always loved fair play, I rectified; and, at last, the word "March" was given. Away went long-legs, getting over at least three yards of ground at each stride; and, had we permitted him to proceed at this rate, the one might as well have fired from the top of St. Paul's, and the other from Table Mountain; so the seconds saved him the trouble of extending his walk any further, by measuring twelve paces; and the signal having been given to fire, the little one's ball cut through the collar of his affrighted opponent's coat, and the big one's nearly shot his own toes off. At this crisis of the affair, the gigantic rustic was scarcely so tall as his little rival, and his knees and body were so inclined to take a more firm position, that we expected every moment he would fall flat on the earth; when his second roused him by saying, "Come, Sir, we must have another shot." This brought him fully to his senses, and he exclaimed, throwing down his pistol, "I'll see you d——d first; he has put it through my coat already, and the next time I may get it where the tailor cannot mend it. No, no; I am perfectly satisfied; so I wish you a good morning." And off he trudged, at a pretty round pace, to the great amusement of the other three, as well as of some country bumpkins, who were grinning from behind an adjoining hedge, and who roared out, "Well done, little un; bravo, little robin-redbreast." By the result of this affair, the six-feet-three gentleman lost his honour as well as his dearie, and the subject was the theme of many a song in Wakefield for years after.

The routine of dissipation which was kept up at Wakefield, was not to be sustained by me without expense; and to meet these expenses I spent more than my income. This extravagance—with the loss of fifty pounds, of which I was robbed by my servant, and the assistance of a designing sergeant, who took advantage of my youth and inexperience—soon involved me in debts, to liquidate which I was obliged to apply for permission to sell my commission. This, in consideration of my services, was readily granted; and, having effected a sale, I paid every shilling of my debts, and with the residue of the money repaired to London, where, in about six months, I found myself without a shilling, without a home, and without a friend. Thus circumstanced, my fondness of the profession induced me to turn my thoughts to the army again. I could see no earthly difficulty why I should not rise in the same way I had before; and accordingly I enlisted at Westminster, in his majesty's 24th Dragoons,[1] and in two or three days after went with the recruiting-sergeant to the cavalry depot at Maidstone, then under the command of Major-General George Hay. I had not been there long before an officer, who had served with me in campaigns in India, arrived at the depot, and, immediately recognizing me, my history was made known to the commanding officer, and I was promoted to the

---

1. The 24th Dragoons was raised in 1794 as the 27th Light Dragoons. After serving in San Domingo and at the Cape, it went to India and served with distinction in the campaigns under Lord Lake, for which it received a "standard of honour" from the East India Company. It was re-numbered the 24th Light Dragoons in 1803. It returned home from India in 1818 and was disbanded. The uniform in Shipp's time was French grey, with bright yellow facings and silver lace and buttons.

rank of sergeant. I remained at the depot about three months, at the expiration of which we were ordered to India, and I embarked as acting quarter-master on board the *New Warren Hastings*, Captain Larkins, and sailed from Spithead on the 8th day of January, 1808.

We experienced a most terrific gale in the British Channel, and were at last obliged to run for Torbay, where we brought up near where the East Indiaman, the *Abergavenny*, was lost. Near us lay a ship of war, from which, at the imminent hazard of the lives of an officer and six men, a boat was sent off to our ship, the crew of which, after riding in safety over the mountainous waves, desired us, in a most authoritative tone, to throw out a rope. All hands were at the leeward side in a moment, when there was a general whispering amongst the tars. "Shiver my timbers," said one, "but that looks like a press."

"Start me," said another, "but so it does." Thus went round the general buzz, when the man of authority, in size not much larger than a quaker,[2] with a sword as long as himself, and a huge cocked-hat, as big as a gaff top-sail, which he skulled off with as much grace and majesty as a grand *bashaw*, flew up the side of the ship in an instant. He saluted the quarter-deck, as is usual, then mounted on tiptoe, and danced up to the captain, who was on deck, and, with the authority of an admiral of the red, demanded to see the ship's books. At this sound every sailor writhed his features and limbs into the most ludicrous distortions; some limped, others stooped, and all did their utmost to appear as decrepit and unfit for service as possible. As our ship was then in imminent danger of going ashore, the captain remonstrated, setting forth the perilous situation of his ship, the number of lives, and the amount of property on board; but notwithstanding that we were at that moment dragging our two anchors, the little officer persisted in obeying the orders of his commander, and walked off with six of our very best seamen. By the loss of these men, our ship was involved in double the danger she was in before, as they were our ablest hands. Whether or not this was a justifiable act, I am unacquainted; but its enforcement at such a conjuncture seems sadly at variance with the principles of humanity. Fortunately for us, however, the storm soon abated, and the following morning, ere the feathered tribe were on the wing, we again stood on our way towards our destined port. Our ship had suffered but little injury, and she now scudded sweetly along the blue waters, her white sails swollen with majestic pride, and the eye of every one on board lingering, until it was lost in the distance, on that dear isle from which we were so rapidly departing. After this, we had a long

---

2. A false gun, made of wood, about two feet long.

and tedious voyage, in which much misery was experienced by all the troops on board, in consequence of the cruel and despotic conduct of our commanding officer. This gentleman is now no more; and, if it were on this account only, I should refrain from mentioning his name. For this, and other reasons, I shall withhold from the reader all detail of conduct which I have myself long tried to forget; and content myself by stating, in justification of the epithets applied by me to such conduct, that the cat-o'-nine-tails was constantly at work; so much so, that Captain Larkins at length interfered, and protested "that he would not have his quarter-deck converted into a slaughterhouse, nor the eyes of the ladies on board disgusted with the sight of the naked back of a poor screaming soldier, every time they came upon deck."

The distant low-land peeping from afar, and the company of little messengers from the myrtle grove, at length apprised us that we were in sight of the long-looked-for haven. The wind was contrary, and night had begun to throw over the silvery deep her sombre mantle; so that we were obliged to stand out to sea, to avoid getting into the currents that prevail near this land. Early in the morning it was dark and hazy, but at about ten o'clock it cleared up: the sun shed his bright beams over the Indian Ocean; the little harbinger of peace was again on the wing; and we again beheld the land.

All the passengers were now promenading the quarter-deck: some viewing the beauty of the scenery; others whispering sad notes of farewell love; and all anxiously looking forward to the moment of disembarkation.

We were crowding all possible sail to get the ship safe into the river by night. The wind was fair, and the sky was spotless, save here and there some little white clouds, that seemed to dance about us. In an instant after, the ship was thrown on her beam-ends, her gunwales under water, and passengers tumbling and rolling over each other. The crew had to struggle hard to keep her head above water. Every eye was wildly fixed on the captain, and every cheek wore a death-like paleness. At last, away went her fore-top mast, top-gallant and royal-mast, foreyard, main-royal-mast, main-top-gallant, and main-top-mast; and her mizen-mast was much injured. In that short moment the cup of bliss was dashed from our lips, and we lay a complete wreck upon the water; but, the masts having gone, carrying everything before them, and the ship having righted, every hand was as instantaneously set to work, and busily employed in remedying the evils and clearing the wreck. It was imagined at first that the ship had gone ashore; but, on trying her pumps, it appeared that she had made no water. We soon discovered that our misfortune was occasioned by what are termed, in those seas, white squalls. These come on without any previous indication; and, though of short duration, are so destructive while they last, that no ship under heavy sail can stand against them. These squalls are most frequent when the sky is clearest. They are supposed to be contained in those little white flying clouds, which, previous to the storm, are seen hovering over the ship, as though watching to catch the mariners off their guard.

We were again obliged to stand out to sea; but we soon cleared away, and once more stood towards land. The day was rainy and hazy, when through the darksome mist we beheld a sail, and soon discovered, to our great joy, that it was the boat of a Calcutta pilot, who immediately came on board our vessel. On examining the masts, we discovered that the maintop-mast would not bear her sails; therefore splinters and stays were immediately put on. The day brightened up, but the wind blew strong; so, not being able to discover landmarks, we cast anchor for the night. The next morning we found that we were so close to land that we could see men walking on the sea-beach, and distinguish huts and towns in the distance. We weighed anchor early, and stood towards Saugar, the wind blowing a smart gale. At one time we approached so near the breakers that we expected to go ashore, and a few minutes after we shipped a tremendous sea, the major part of which went over the poop and through the great cabin windows, carrying trunks, boxes, beds, and everything before it. I was on deck at the time: the ship's stern seemed to be fastened, and she shook much; but at last on she went. I have no hesitation in saying that her stern struck the ground, but no injury was done beyond sousing a few trunks and beds. We at last reached Saugar in safety; but before we arrived there our feelings were excited to a high pitch of sympathy by an interesting scene. Captain Larkins was standing on the poop, close by where I stood, with his glass at his eye examining the ships which were lying at anchor, when he suddenly exclaimed, "I surely know that ship lying yonder: my eyes cannot deceive me—it's my old ship, the *Warren Hastings*." The pilot was requested to go within hail of her. All hands were upon deck; every eye fixed upon the strange ship; and sailors and soldiers manned the rigging. The captain got the large speaking-trumpet, and bellowed out, "What ship, a-hoy?" Answer, "The *Warren Hastings*—what ship are you?" Answer, "The *New Warren Hastings*." Here the shouting of the crews of both ships was quite deafening. Our captain could not say a syllable more, but was so much affected as to shed a tear to the memory of his old ship, which he had manfully defended, but lost to some French ship-of-war. She had been retaken by some of our cruisers.

A short time after this we came to anchor a little above Saugar; and the following day we were shipped on board sloops, and sailed up the river Hoogley, and in about a week came to anchor off Fort William, Calcutta, and were again placed on *terra firma*. We remained in the fort about a fortnight; and, while boats were in preparation for our conveyance up the river Ganges, to our respective regiments, all was gaiety and mirth.

The monsoon, or rainy season, having commenced, we sailed from Calcutta, under the command of Colonel Wade, on route to Cawnpore, where we arrived in safety in about three months, with the loss of seven or eight men drowned, and of a few others, who died from having eaten too freely of unripe fruit.

CHAPTER 10

Return to India

The day before we arrived at Cawnpore, Colonel Wade sent for me, and gave me a strong and handsome letter of recommendation. In the evening of the next day we marched to tents which had been previously pitched for our reception. Here we found two officers of our own regiment, ready to receive us, with one of whom I had often dined when an officer in the same camp. He received me kindly, and promised me his friendship. Nothing of moment occurred during the short time I was at this station.

Having refitted, we started on route to Meerut, about three hundred miles by land, under the command of two officers, whose sole study was to promote our happiness and welfare. I do not know that I ever spent a happier time. Our march was always over by nine o'clock, and we encamped under the salubrious scent and pleasant shade of the lofty mango. After journeying in this pleasant manner, we reached Meerut on the 9th day of November, 1809, having been eleven months and a day from England. Here I was welcomed by all my old comrades, and found myself full sergeant in Captain Beattie's troop.

On the evening of our arrival we were inspected by the commanding officer, now Major-General Need. I was well received by all the officers, and indeed by all the corps, save two or three corporals whom I had supplanted in their long-cherished hopes of promotion. This naturally placed me in no very enviable situation with these men, and several attempts were made to try my courage; but I was too well versed with the rank I held, to permit myself to be imposed on or annoyed. When they found this, their ire passed away and their grievances were forgotten. After the inspection, my commanding officer called me on one side, and said, "I am much grieved to see you in your present situation, after the many laurels you have gained in India, but I feel pleasure in having it in my power to promote you to the rank of sergeant; and, if you conduct yourself well, be assured I shall not lose sight of your further promotion." I was obliged once more to go through a regular and systematic course of drills, both on horseback and on foot; but, as I was already well acquainted with both, I was soon dismissed.

I had not been in the regiment above one year, when a colonel, commanding a corps of the Company's native cavalry, who had known me before, offered me a riding-mastership, a situation equal to an ensigncy. I was elated with the idea; it was the situation which, of all others, I should have fancied. I dressed myself in my best, and off I marched with the colonel's kind invitation in my hand, not having the shadow of a doubt of the full and joyous concurrence of my commanding officer, who, I thought, would gladly embrace the opportunity of giving me a proof of the friendship he had so often professed for me. I presented the letter, and begged his consent and aid in the fulfilment of my wishes. He read it, paused, knitted his dark eyebrows, and it was so evident that he was displeased, that I began to muster my offences, but I could think of nothing in which I had offended him. Imagine my surprise and mortification when he returned the little document into my hand, accompanied with this sweet and consoling declaration, "I shall not recommend you for any such thing." He was just about to leave the room, when I presumed to remonstrate on the cruelty of such a denial, in preventing me from getting such a respectable situation; and I pushed the matter home by asking him if he thought me unworthy of it, or if I had displeased him in anything. He said, "No; but," continued he, "don't you think I like good men in my regiment as well as Colonel K—? Besides," he said, "what am I to do for a sergeant-major if you leave the regiment, or perhaps for an adjutant, if anything should happen to either of them?" Two of these persons were younger than myself, and in full and blooming health. I felt my pride wounded and my feelings hurt, and I could not help expressing my sentiments to that effect, and we parted at enmity. This was a death-blow to my present hopes. I made the best excuse I could to the colonel who had made me the kind offer, and I was in a short time made drill-corporal in my own regiment, and afterwards drill-sergeant. This was a situation I was fond of, and a preparatory step to that of regimental sergeant-major. For a time this new toy pleased me, for I would, at any time, sooner command than be commanded; but the duties of a drill-sergeant are very laborious.

I went on tolerably well with the troubles and vexations of this arduous office, when, one fine morning, it was rumoured through the

European Cavalry of Shipp's Day

lines that the sergeant-major was defunct in hospital. I was congratulated from all quarters as his successor, as a matter of course, and the eye of the whole regiment was upon the drill-sergeant. I expected a summons every moment from the commanding officer. So sanguine was I myself, that I had directed that all my "traps" might be put in moveable order; when, lo! another sergeant was appointed sergeant-major, leaving poor me the butt and jeer of the whole corps. I could not imagine what could possibly be the cause of this strange appointment. I say strange, for two reasons: first, that the situation had been promised to me; and, secondly, that the sergeant who was appointed was, of all others, the most unfit for it. I felt hurt beyond description, but my spirit was too proud to permit me to ask why I had thus been passed over. I bore it as patiently as I could, still trying to kill care by fagging at the drills; and no doubt some of the poor fellows under me felt the weight of my disappointed hopes, for I had them out late and early. I mentioned, however, the circumstance to my captain, and told him I would resign both my drill-sergeantship and also my three other stripes; but the captain, having more prudence and temper than his sergeant, advised me to put up with it, saying, that he had no doubt the colonel had something better in store for me. This supposition appeased my troubled mind, and I endeavoured to smother my grief by making myself a better drill; and in a short time the storm had blown over, and the event was nearly obliterated from my memory. After this affair I always avoided the colonel, and whenever chance threw me in his way, I gave him the customary salute due to his rank, but accompanied with a few dark looks, as tokens of my gratitude.

Thus I went on, chewing the cud of disappointment, when one morning I happened to be straying down a narrow lane, brooding over my misfortunes, and trying to assign some reason why my commanding officer had passed me over in promotion, when, in turning a corner, I almost came in contact with the object of my meditations, who could soon have put my mind at peace—the colonel himself. I tendered him a most formal salute, almost as stiff as my feelings were towards him; this dumb greeting being garnished with one of my blackest looks. I was passing on, with one eye looking over my shoulder, and at last I turned my whole body round to have a good stare at him; when, to my surprise, as if he had anticipated my thoughts, I found that he also had countermarched. We were now face to face, and retreat would have been unsoldier-like; so I commenced the attack, by approaching the spot where he stood, as if I was returning home to my barracks. When passing him, I of course gave him another salute, somewhat smoother than the former. From this amendment in my behaviour, I was in hopes he would speak to me as I passed, for I was ripe with a speech as long as my sabre, which I had been some time cementing together. I had hardly gone past, when he said, "Halloa, Shipp—come here." I approached him, and, after giving him a more conciliatory salute than usual, was just about to open my battery upon him, when he commenced a hedge-fire, by saying, in a kind and friendly manner, "Well, Shipp, how do you get on?" Here was a pretty preface to my intended speech! I stood at attention, knowing the respect due to my commanding officer, and replied, "I get on but badly, Sir."

"How is that?" said the colonel. I said, "I had but little encouragement to get on well, since he was pleased to pass me over in promotion."

"Why, then," said he, "did you not come and ask me for it?" Here my spirit nettled; I told him, no doubt impetuously, that, if he did not think me worthy of it unsolicited, I should never ask it of him. By this I struck the chord of his displeasure, and he replied, "Then you will never get it." I tipped him another salute, rather bordering on impudence, and was in the act of facing to the right-about, and for this purpose had drawn my right foot back to my left heel, when he turned his displeasure into kindness, and said, "Stop, sergeant; suppose I have something better for you than what I have taken from you, and which you did not think worth soliciting." He said this with an inquiring eye, and I replied, that my prospects in life depended entirely upon his friendship towards me. If he withheld that, I had nothing further to hope. He answered, "My good-will and friendship you have; but you must divest yourself of that impetuosity of temper, and depend upon it I shall not lose sight of your welfare: go home, and keep yourself quiet." Thus we parted. I wanted a balm of this kind to soothe and calm me; for, what with my disappointment, and the trouble I had with obstinate young soldiers and drunken old ones, my patience and temper were really worn threadbare, and, from constant bellowing at the drills, my voice had become as gruffly sonorous as a bad church organ. But, in all my distresses, I never lost sight of my duties and respect to my superiors, knowing that any neglect on my part would lose me everything. I was on good terms with every officer and man in the regiment, and made it my study to be the first on parade, and the last off. I had risen through the several gradations of lance-corporal to full—lance-sergeant to full—drill-corporal—drill-sergeant—pay-sergeant—and troop-sergeant-major—without being once confined, or on any occasion reprimanded by a superior officer.

In the year 1813, another sergeant-major made a retrograde movement, and tumbled into his grave; but I still could not make up my mind to solicit the appointment of my commanding officer, although I saw several other sergeants running down to ask for it. Notwithstanding this, I kept at home, where I dressed, expecting every moment to receive a summons from the colonel, who, I thought, surely would not again pass me over. Here I waited, looking every now and then out of my barrack-room window, but neither messenger nor orders arrived. I began to think it had been given away a second time, and a dreadful struggle ensued between pride and interest; the former said, "Don't go;" the latter, "Go, or you get nothing." After a long contest, pride succeeded, and I remained where I was. At evening drill I was early at my post, and was going through my regular course of evolutions, when the adjutant rode up to me, and said, "Why don't you go and ask the commanding officer to give you the vacancy?" I replied, "Sir, I should deem myself unworthy of such a situation, did I beg or cringe for it. If my commanding officer deemed me deserving of such an appointment, he would give it me without hesitation; and, should he be so kind, he may rely upon my strictly performing the duties entrusted to me, and thus proving my gratitude; but ask it I never can." After this fine speech, I went on with my drill; when the adjutant, after pausing a few seconds, said, "Well, if you are too proud to ask for it, I am not;" and off he galloped. In a quarter of an hour he returned, and said, "You are appointed sergeant-major." I thanked him most cordially, and assured him he should never have cause to regret his kindness. He replied, "Shipp, to be candid with you, I admire your proper spirit in not begging the situation, nor does your commanding officer think the worse of you for it: you will immediately move into the sergeant-major's bungalow, and assume the duties of that office. I need not, I am sure, inform you what they are." On the following morning I moved into my new house, and published my own appointment. Here all the cares and anxieties of my past life were forgotten. The very idea of having the whole regiment under my special command at drill, was to me inexpressibly delightful, and I looked forward to the day as the consummation of my military glory.

As a groundwork for proceeding properly in my new office, I established an inseparable vacuum between my rank and that of the other non-commissioned officers, treating them with every respect consistent with theirs, and, in time, making them sensible that such a difference must be established between their station and that of the privates under their command. I enforced prompt obedience and attention from them, and they from those under them. This they at first construed into pride on my part; but, in time, that prejudice wore off, and they obeyed with pleasure. Those who proved refractory were removed from their situations, and those more obedient promoted in their stead. Thus things went on smoothly and pleasantly; and, in two or three months, I could trust them in the discharge of their duties with confidence, and they soon learned how far they could go with me. I had a strict and vigilant adjutant; he made a strict and vigilant sergeant-major; he made good non-commissioned officers; and they good private soldiers. Thus, discipline and good-will towards each other went hand in hand together. My situation was a respectable one, and, what was equally pleasant, a lucrative one. I had as many titles as any peer in the kingdom:

    J. Shipp, R. S. M.—Regimental Sergeant-Major
    J. Shipp, G. K.—Gaol-Keeper
    J. Shipp, U.T.—Undertaker
    J. Shipp, L. M.—Log-Maker

The perquisites of all these situations brought my pay to a handsome amount; I was respected by the officers, and loved by the men; and I had scarcely a wish ungratified. The year round I always found the same people, with but little variation, in the congee-house; and one man, a fine young fellow, was never off my gaol-book. The moment he was released he was assuredly in the guard-room again, and from thence to his old place of abode. I once asked him how he could, month after month, prefer that solitary and secluded life to that of liberty. He replied, "Habit is second nature," for there, he said, "he could, alone and undisturbed, brood over his sad and hitherto melancholy career." He concluded in a most pathetic manner: "Sergeant-major, I have never done any good since the time your predecessor got me flogged. I assure you, I endeavour with all my energy to forget it, but I cannot; it crushes me to the ground, and that day's disgrace has been my ruin. I am of a good family, but I never can or will return to disgrace those dear parents with a scarified back." Some three months after this he died, in a sad state of inebriety.

One day I was going my usual round with the orderly-officer, who twice a day visited the congee-house. This officer was a famous one for scenting anything; he could smell a cigar a mile off. In going round the yard, which is enclosed by a tremendous high wall, he discovered a large beef-bone, recently dropped. The sergeant was called to account for this ominous appearance. This sergeant was a shrewd fellow, and he immediately said, "Oh, Sir, the pelicans have dropped it." This was very plausible, for these birds will carry enormous bones; and frequently, when fighting for them, they drop them, so that this might very probably have been the case. The moment the dinner-trumpet sounds, whole flocks of these birds are in attendance at the barrack doors, waiting for bones, or anything that the soldiers may be pleased to throw them. The men were in the habit of playing them many mischievous tricks; but, notwithstanding this, at the well-known sound of the dinner-trumpet they were regularly at their station. Some of the more mischievous boys would tie two large bones together, and throw to them: these would be swallowed with the greatest avidity by two of those poor hungry mendicants, who, in general, would both soar above the barrack-tops with their prey, pulling and hauling against each other, and attended by a hundred crows and kites, pecking them on the head most unmercifully. Sometimes they would throw out a single bone, a pretty large one, with a string and small kite at the end of it, or a large piece of rag. One of the pelicans having swallowed the bone, he would fly aloft, with the string and kite hanging out of his mouth, and with hundreds of his own tribe after him, in hopes he might throw up the bone again, which these birds can do with the greatest facility. Thus ascending, they are lost sight of amidst the clouds; but the same gentleman would frequently be in attendance the following day at dinner-hour, with a portion of the string hanging to him.

 We had not gone much further on our round, when the officer scented a bundle of cigars, which he picked up and archly said, "Sergeant, what luxurious dogs these pelicans must be! I have already seen beef, mutton, and pork bones, and here I find a bundle of cigars. I should not be surprised if I stumbled upon a bottle of brandy next." This the artful sergeant did not know how to account for; but the thing was obvious enough: the whole had been thrown over for the prisoners, by some of their friends. The sergeant was severely admonished for his neglect of duty, and a long conversation then took place between me and the orderly-officer, on the subject of these wonderful birds. They grow so tame that they will feed out of your hand. At night, they roost on the tops of the barracks, and on trees in their vicinity. In the morning early, they pay their respects to the river-side in search of any dead bodies that may be washed ashore; and it is a most appalling sight to see those ravenous creatures, with hundreds of enormous vultures, tearing human bodies to pieces. If you live on the banks of the Ganges, it is no uncommon sight to see crows, vultures, and hawks, riding down the river on dead bodies, feeding on them as they sail along. This is easily accounted for. Hindoos, in general, are committed to the pile after death, and burned to ashes; but the poor people, who cannot perform this last office to their departed relatives, burn the hair off the body, which is then committed to the Holy Gunga, as they call the Ganges. The bodies, when exposed to the sun, swell to an enormous and frightful size.

One day, I was walking on the banks of the Ganges, when I saw a group of people sitting together, and mumbling something to themselves. Near them I saw a corpse, wrapped in a white sheet, with its feet covered with water. A few moments after, a young man, I should think about twenty years of age, shouldered the corpse, and, walking slowly to an elevated bank, he hurled it into the river, in the same manner you would a log of wood. He then plunged in after the body, and deprived it of the winding-sheet, leaving the corpse to float down the tide in a state of nudity. When the youth reached the shore, I asked him who the young person was that he had thrown into the river.

He replied, with a kind of grin, "My wife."

I said, "You don't seem to be very sorry about her."

He said, "No; it was God's pleasure." I asked him how old she was, and he said, "Thirteen years old." I then inquired if he had any family. He replied, "Not now; she had one, a little girl, but that the Gunga had got the day before." I then asked him how long his wife had been dead, when he informed me that she died the moment before I came up. The father and mother of the unfortunate girl were both there, but seemed as indifferent as the rock on which they had perched themselves to watch her progress down the rippling stream—the cold grave of millions.

CHAPTER 11

Ensign of the 'Old Fogs'

Having now a respectable home, and an easy income, I began to look around me for a wife, to share my fortune, and to drink with me of the salubrious cup of contentment. I had been for some time intimately acquainted with a most respectable family, the father of which was a conductor to the commissariat department. He had three daughters, whom he took great pains to bring up in a respectable manner, and they all did credit to his fatherly care, and lived together in great affection and domestic comfort. To the eldest of these I became most sincerely attached. I asked her hand in marriage, and it was granted; but the father stipulated, that, in consideration of his daughter's tender years, the marriage was not to take place for the space of two years. In the meantime, every preparation was to be made for our mutual happiness.

Thus things went on till the latter end of the year 1815, when my good friend the colonel was promoted to the rank of major-general, and consequently bade farewell to his old corps, the 24th Dragoons, in which he was respected and loved. Scarcely had he departed, when I drew up a short memorial to the Marquis of Hastings, then Governor-General of India, and my new commanding officer, Lieutenant-Colonel Philpot, immediately dispatched it to headquarters, Calcutta, accompanied with a handsome recommendatory letter from himself. When I presented this memorial to my commanding officer, he replied, "Shipp, I am glad you have done so. I was yesterday speaking to your friend, Major Covell, about you. I will forward it with pleasure, and I hope it may succeed." Some twenty days after this, I was sent for in a great hurry to the riding-school, where the colonel was looking at some young stud horses. I immediately attended the summons. He was standing with his back towards the riding-school door when I entered, so I waited at some distance, when the adjutant said,

"Here is the sergeant-major." The colonel immediately came up to me, seized my left arm with the hand of his right, and thus led me out of the school. No sooner were we out of sight than he pulled out a letter, and I shall never forget his delight when he grasped my hand, and said, "Shipp, I sincerely congratulate you on your appointment. The Marquis of Hastings has been pleased to meet both your and my wishes; you are appointed to an ensigncy in his majesty's 87th regiment,[1] and directed to join that corps immediately: but this you must promise me, to keep the affair secret till to-morrow, or I shall be teased out of my life for your appointment. I would ask you to dine with me to-day, but for this wish to keep it a secret. I shall therefore have that pleasure another time." I expressed my most sincere thanks; the colonel put the letter into my hand; he went to his horses again; and I went to evening parade.

In the evening, after my duty was done, I went down to see my intended, and to tell her and her family of my good fortune. On my walk hither I had a most strange feeling; it was not that of elation of spirits, but rather of a dreary and gloomy turn. In this mood I reached the abode of my little wife, before I was aware of my near approach, and had almost stumbled upon her good father before I perceived him. Indeed, I should have passed him but for his usual salutation, "Ah, John, is that you? how are you?" This address roused me from my reverie, and I replied, with affected dignity, "Come, Sir, be a little more respectful to your superior officer, or I shall send you to the congee-house." Here I could not help lowering the ensign's mighty dignity, by bursting into a loud laugh. The old gentleman did not seem to know what to make of it; but I suppose he thought me tipsy, for at last he said, "What's the matter, John? you seem a little out of sorts this evening." I then took his arm; we walked together towards the house; and on the way I told him the whole affair. He replied, "Then of course that will break off the match with my poor Ann; you will now look higher." At this the ensign's blood rose, and he got nettled, and warmly replied, "You have mistaken your man, Sir. I could never, after winning the affections of any woman, forsake

---

1. The 87th "Prince of Wales's Own Irish" Regiment of Foot, re-entitled in 1827 the 87th "Royal Irish Fusiliers" (the facings being changed from deep-green to blue at the same time), now the 1st Royal Irish Fusiliers. In 1815, when Shipp was appointed to it, the 87th had *two* battalions, the first of which, after some years at the Cape and Mauritius, landed in Bengal in August that year. The second battalion, which had greatly distinguished itself in the Peninsula, under command of Sir Hugh, afterwards Viscount Gough, was at Colchester, where it was disbanded in February, 1817, the effective officers and men mostly joining the battalion in India.

or desert her. No: it was with tenfold pleasure I came down to assure her of my unalterable affection." Here my friend gave me his honest hand, and I have no doubt his heart with it; and thus, hand in hand, we entered where all the family were seated round a table at work, their usual evening's employment.

On entering the room, the father, addressing himself to the domestic circle assembled, said in a jocular manner, "Mrs. H. and children, permit me to introduce to your acquaintance Ensign John Shipp, Esq., of the Horse Marines—I mean His majesty's Own Irish Regiment of Foot." I made a bow worthy of his majesty's commission and of the corps to which I was appointed; but this profound obeisance only set the young ones tittering, and one of them, the youngest, had the impudence to point the finger of derision at me, saying, "He an ensign! so is my cat," which cat she immediately paraded on the table on his two hinder extremities, calling him "Ensign Shipp." After this I seated myself close to my little intended, and whispered the whole truth into her ear; but, instead of evincing the joy which I expected, she turned pale and gloomy. I inquired the cause. She was humble as she was good, and she replied, "I am sorry for it; for I suppose you will not condescend to look upon a poor conductor's daughter." Here the ensign's ire was again roused to a pitch far beyond that of a sergeant-major, and I said, "What the devil (I could not help the warm expression) do you all take me for?—man or beast? No, Ann; have a better opinion of me." I then extended my hand towards her, and pledged the honour of an ensign that it was hers, and hers only. She seized my hand and bathed it with her tears. I then directed the conversation into a new channel, by turning my indignation on the little one who had metamorphosed the cat into an ensign; but, as I bethought myself that I really had seen less sagacious animals bearing that commission, I kissed her for her impudence, and forgave her.

The following day I had my hair cut *à la ensign*, and ordered a new suit of regimentals; and the third day I dined at the mess of my old corps, to which I had a general invitation during the time I remained at the station. I received the most marked kindness from the regiment on my promotion. Invitation followed upon invitation, so that it took up nearly the whole of the ensign's time to make and write excuses; the officers vied with each other in politeness and liberality; and I shall ever remember the generosity of the late 24th regiment with feelings of gratitude.

Having arranged my affairs, I left Cawnpore for Dinapore, on the 1st day of January, 1816, having first concerted everything for my marriage as soon as I should be settled with my regiment. I reached the station where my corps was quartered, in five days—a distance of four hundred miles.

On the morning of the 5th day I landed, for the purpose of reporting my arrival to my commanding officer. After wandering about the station a considerable time, without seeing a single European soldier, at last I met a woman, and I asked her if she would have the goodness to inform me where I could find the commanding officer of the 87th regiment. I found by her manners (I mean ill manners) that she had early paid her devoirs to the shrine of rum. I repeated, "Will you, my good woman, have the goodness to inform me where I can find the 87th regiment?"

"What! the old Fogs?"[2] said she.

"Fogs!" said I, "no: the 87th regiment, I mean."

"Is it making fun of me you are?"

I replied, "No, my good woman: I really want to find where the 87th regiment are."

"Sure they are just after laving this place, becase they are gone away these three big days."

"Gone!" I repeated, "where?"

"Fait, to fight against Paul."

"Paul!" said I, "who the devil is he?"

"Arrah! bad luck to you, is it after mocking Judy Flanagan you are, you tafe?" I again assured the woman that I was in earnest (for she had put herself in a boxing attitude), and informed her that I was an officer of that corps. Here she burst into a loud horse-laugh, slapping her legs with both her hands, "You an officer of the old Fogs! ha, ha, ha! Arrah, none of your blarney, honey."

"However you may laugh," said I, "I am an officer of the old Fogs, as you call them, and I am come to join them."

"Then," replied she, "you might have saved yourself the trouble, joy; for the divel a one is here, except the quarter-master, and I could not find him this morning; but does your honour really belong to the old Fogaboloughs?" I pledged the honour of an ensign, upon which she stretched forth her brawny paw, and grasped my hand, saying, "Give us your daddle, your honour; sure I am always glad to see any of the old corps here." She gave me positive proof of her attachment to the regiment, by nearly squeezing my hand off, and she was about

---

2. The 87th was popularly known as the "Ould Fogs" from its Erse shout in charging *Faugh a Ballagh* (Clear the Way). The sobriquet is often wrongly assigned to the Connaught Rangers.

to confirm the whole with a kiss, but I parried her in this kind intention. She then entered on a eulogium of the regiment. "The divel a better corps within a whole day's march. The regiment is a credit to your honour. Och, thase are the boys for fighting!" Here she pulled up her petticoats nearly to her knees, and commenced capering and humming a tune. I could not help laughing, for she footed it with the skill of a dancing-master. When she had pretty nearly winded herself, she again seized my hand, and asked me for something "to drink his honour's health, and success to the old Fogs." I told her that, if she could inform me if there was any person belonging to the regiment at the station, I might be inclined to give her something to drink.

"Thank your honour," said she; "sure, the adjutant, and one Captain Bell, are left behind."

"The adjutant here?" answered I, "what—sick or on duty?"

"Neither, your honour: he is confined as snug as a bug to his own room, and is a prisoner besides. Sure, there has been a mighty blusteration and hubbub between him and the same Captain Bell."

I inquired what had been the matter.

"Matter, your honour! matter enough: there has been bloody murder betwixt them; and sure there is no end to the murders in this regiment."

"What! have they been fighting?" said I, meaning a duel.

"Fighting! sure enough."

"Is the captain also a prisoner?"

"Snug enough, joy."

"Will you be kind enough to show me where the adjutant's quarters are?"

"To be sure, honey: he lives just over against the corner house, just over by the other side of the chapel, and forenent the main guard-room: sure anybody will inform you that knows."

"I fear I shall never find it, with all these leading points," said I; "give me some place near it."

"Well, your honour, do you see yonder woman standing all alone, with a man spaking to her? Or can you see the house round the corner?"

Finding now, from the information proffered by this lady, that the more explanatory she attempted to be, the more unintelligible she became, I cut the matter short by giving her a *rupee*, and I took my leave of this ardent admirer of the old Fogs, with her parting benediction, "God bless your honour; may your honour never die till the side of an old house fall on you and kill you!"

Having parted from this pretty specimen of my new regiment, I inquired for the adjutant's quarters, which were pointed out to me. At the door I met a soldier, of whom I inquired if the adjutant was at home, and was informed he had just gone out. I said I would wait till he returned; so I seated myself, and in about five minutes after he came in; and, when I informed him who I was, he gave me a hearty welcome, invited me to breakfast, and I remained with him the two days I stopped at the station. From this officer I learned that the regiment had left two days before, against the Nepaulese. This was a piece of news that delighted me much, although I had not a single thing prepared for such a campaign, nor was it probable I could procure what was necessary, after the whole country had been drained of cattle, &c., to supply the army. But, notwithstanding this, in two days I was ready, so far as carriage; but, as I could not, by any possibility, get a tent, I was obliged to manufacture one, something like what our gipsies use, out of a *setterenge*, or Indian cotton carpet.

Thus provided, I commenced my march to join the old Fogs, who had preceded me five marches. The first day I accomplished a distance equal to the regiment's first two days' marches. The next day I completed two more, and was handsomely treated by an indigo-planter, in the district of Tirhoot, where their liberality is noted. I sent on my things, the next morning, twenty miles, and desired that they might be conveyed twenty more, should I not reach them that night. I spent the day with my liberal host, the planter; slept there, and, after eating a hearty breakfast, started the next morning on horseback, my kind entertainer having laid horses for me on the road. I overtook my things about two miles from their destination, and put up at another indigo-planter's. Here I met a young officer, who was also on his way to rejoin the same division, and, as it proved after a little conversation, the same regiment. He was very young, and seemed delicate; and, I thought, but little calculated for such an arduous campaign as the one in prospect. Here we regaled ourselves till next morning, when we thanked our host for his liberality, and bade him farewell. This was the last indigo factory on our road, and travelling without protection was attended with some little danger, the lowlands being proverbial for murders and robberies. We were, therefore, now obliged to proceed with caution. In the day-time we remained in our tents, and at night slept in some hut or temple. Neither tents nor mud walls were any safeguard against the desperate thieves in these districts; besides, these lowlands abounded with tigers, bears, hyenas, wolves, jackals, &c.; and, as these had not been much accustomed to the sight of Europeans, we could not tell how far they might be induced to go for such unusual delicacies; so safety was the parole.

The first march I taught my young companion the art of becoming his own butcher, cook, &c.; for I killed, skinned, washed, cooked, and eat a fine young kid, of part of which I made a curry, and grilled the remainder; of this my young friend partook, with most excellent appetite. After tea we moved into a village for the night; for some suspicious fellows had already been seen loitering about. When thus travelling, I would recommend people to show their fire-arms, and in the dusk of the evening to fire them off. The dacoits, or low thieves, in India, although a most desperate set, have the greatest dread of fire-arms, and will seldom approach those whom they know to possess them, however ill-disposed they might be under other circumstances. Thus, I have often, on the rivers Hoogley and Ganges, when coming home at night in a lone boat, escaped being robbed, and perhaps murdered, by frequently discharging my fire-arms, while others, who have neglected this precaution, or perhaps not had fire-arms with them, have been plundered, and in many instances murdered, in spite of the police kept on those rivers.

The regiment was now only twenty miles ahead of us. We therefore retired early to rest, intending to reach the corps the following day. We had not reposed more than an hour, lying upon our things, when I was awoke by a noise something like the crowing of the domestic cock, and then like the barking of a dog. I had been too long in the country not to know that these crowings and barkings were sure indications of robbers being on the look-out. I therefore seized my pistol, resolving to have a shot at whatever first made its appearance. For a time all was still. There were two doorways to the hut in which we had sheltered ourselves; and, across each of these doorways lay myself and my young friend. I was wide awake, and he was just dozing, when, all of a sudden, he jumped up, and bellowed out, so that his voice re-echoed again, "Who is that?" I jumped up and said, "What's the matter?" He answered, "Some person's hand touched my face." I replied, "You must have been dreaming." He said he was confident that what he said was true. "Well, then, if it is, don't be afraid," said I. This nettled the young soldier, and he replied, "No, Sir, I am not so easily frightened as you may imagine." I thought at one time he was going to give me proof of his valour, by coming to an open rupture with me; but, at last, we both lay down to repose again, I thinking to myself, "I shall try your courage by-and-by, my lad." I pretended to be asleep, and soon heard the thieves on the move again. I therefore stole silently from my bed, and discharged both my pistols in the air, bellowing out, with the lungs of an ensign, *"Choor! choor! choor!"* which my companion perfectly understood to be, thieves! thieves! thieves! Hearing this, he made a desperate jump over my bed, and was out with me in a moment; but he afterwards confessed that he was most dreadfully alarmed. We retired to rest once more, but had not lain long before I felt a hand cross my face. I immediately seized the fellow, but he was so oiled that he slipped through my hands like an eel, and was out of sight in a moment. I ran out after him, but he was gone like a whisper on the breeze. At this juncture I heard my companion crying out, "Where are you, Sir? Where are you, Mr. Shipp? Don't leave me." When I returned, I found him in a dreadful state of alarm, and, I must confess, I did not myself half like it. These nocturnal robbers go perfectly naked, with their heads shaved, and oiled from head to foot. They seemed bent upon robbing us, for it was strange that they should have returned after I had fired. However, I reloaded my pistols, and I said, "Now, Sir, I think we may repose till the morning."

"Repose, Sir!" he replied; "I don't think I shall sleep again for a week."

"Nonsense!" said I; "we soldiers must not mind these little skirmishes. Such things as these happen every day, and we laugh at them. If we had nothing more to disturb our peace than these little annoyances, soldiering would be a delightful life indeed. The grand thing is to keep a good watch, so as not to be taken by surprise."

CHAPTER 12

On Campaign to Nepaul

The next morning we were in marching order betimes, and started with the determination of joining our regiment as early in the day as possible. We overtook them about nine o'clock, just as they had crossed a *nullah*, and had halted on the opposite bank. I immediately sought the acting adjutant, from whom, after I had announced my name and delivered my credentials, I received every politeness and attention. He introduced me at once to the commanding officer, Lieutenant-Colonel Miller, C. B., who received me in the most cordial manner, congratulated me on my appointment, and expressed himself much pleased at my accession to the regiment. All the officers of the corps flocked round me, and greeted me in the most handsome and friendly manner, every one of them inviting me to breakfast. That invitation, however, I had previously received from the kind commander of the Prince's Own Irish regiment. This liberal conduct was the more gratifying to my feelings, as I must confess I did not anticipate any such friendly reception. I was well aware of the existing prejudice, and the caution with which officers promoted from the ranks were usually received; but no such prejudice prevailed in this distinguished corps: on the contrary, had I been the son of a duke, my reception could not have been more flattering or friendly. It is true that I had the most flattering letters of introduction from my late commanding officer to my present; but as I had not delivered them, the kindness which I experienced was wholly spontaneous and unsolicited, and the result of liberal and benevolent feeling. My young companion was received by all in the same handsome manner.

As I found that the jacket, which I had had made for me in haste when I was ordered to join the regiment, was widely different from the uniform of the corps, I apologized for this to the colonel while at breakfast, and he relieved me from all anxiety on that score, by replying, "Ah, never mind; the one you have will do very well for fighting in, as it is supposed we shall have some pretty hard service."

The following day the regiment reached the ground on which the army engaged in the arduous campaign of Nepaul, in the years 1815 and 1816, had been directed to form. It was at a place called Ammowah, about thirty-five miles from the great forest of Nepaul. At the back of this forest were the strong forts and stockades of the enemy, on hills whose summits were crowned with milk-white clouds, fringed with glittering gold; and in the distance were to be seen the snowy mountains proudly towering over the heads of the more humble hills below.

Considerable delay now occurred in the formation of the army, and time began to hang heavy on our hands, although we had good hunting, shooting, and racing, and did our best to amuse ourselves when off active duty. But this was not the sort of sport for which we were assembled in arms in this wild and romantic territory of the Nepaulese. Our object was to reduce this artful and warlike tribe to subjection; for our disasters the year before had made them bold and overbearing, and had incited them to laugh to scorn all overtures of amicable arrangement. They trusted, and not without good cause, to the almost inaccessible nature of their country, and, from their tremendous fortified hills and stockades, looked down with contempt on the little foe below.

The necessary preliminaries to this arduous enterprise having been at length duly arranged, things began to take a more active turn, and in three days after we bent our way towards that forest that for ages past had been the terror of the East, and was indeed a bulwark to the Nepaul territory. Our march was necessarily slow and tedious; but in three days we reached a place called Summarabassah, on the very margin of that terrific forest. On the last day I was in the rear-guard, which did not reach camp until late in the evening, although a distance of not more than ten miles. The roads in which we marched might, with great propriety, be termed bogs. They abounded with deep *nullahs*, or ravines, with abrupt banks of a clayey nature. Our heavy guns we were compelled to get over by means of men and drag-ropes, for the bullocks had no footing, and many of these poor creatures were much hurt in the attempt to perform this labour. After the camp was in sight, we were three hours before we reached it. We had marched at about four o'clock in the morning, without breakfast, expecting to reach our ground by nine, the usual time, instead of which we did not get in until past four o'clock in the afternoon, and then half famished.

We at last reached camp, in front of which, in a kind of inlet to the forest, stood a large building, two stories high, forming a square. This was built of stone, and tiled, and had only one entrance, which was a small door. This security was, no doubt, to protect the inmates against depredation, and from the nocturnal visits of savage animals. It was supposed to have been the residence of the collector of the lowlands or valleys. At this place we established a strong depot, or principal post of communication, where we could deposit cumbersome or superfluous stores with safety. On the forest side we erected a strong breastwork or stockade, with a wide and deep ditch, and embrasures for some guns—I now forget the number—I think four.

The following day, Captain Gully, Lieutenants Masterson, Lee, Bowes, and Ensign Shipp, must needs take a morning ride, and a peep into this dark and dreary forest—the awe of man, and the haunt of beasts. We had not gone far, when we saw several bears near a waterbrook—no doubt for the purpose of a morning swim, for the weather was warm. A little further, we struck into a path, about a yard wide, which we all agreed to explore. On each side of this path the underwood was thick and dark; the trees were of an enormous and gigantic size; every hundred yards were places where it was evident that fires had been kindled; and large trees had been cut down, and were piled across the pathway, for the prevention, beyond question, of intruders. We rode on till prudence suggested the propriety of returning; but our curiosity was not yet satisfied, so we mutually agreed to proceed about two miles further. At last we came to a fire which was still burning. Here we called a consultation, and at last again agreed to proceed about two miles further. This distance brought us so close to the hills, that we could discover men moving on them. About a mile further was the end of the dark and frightful forest of Nepaul, which, the year before, had kept five thousand men at bay. At the end was some open ground, with large clumps of bamboo trees, and the open space pebbly. It was evident that this space was covered with water during the monsoons. We still rode on a little further, until at last we saw some men running across the road, whereupon we unanimously agreed that it was high time to return, having satisfied our curiosity to the full, and at the risk of our lives. We were fearful that they might have observed us, and have dispatched a detachment to cut off our retreat; and we now began to count our beads of repentance; but the trial was to be made; so on we pushed, and reached camp without molestation, thanking the auspicious stars that were our safeguards. The distance we had ridden was about thirteen miles, which, being doubled, made a pretty good morning's ride; add to which, that during the excursion we had leapt over about a hundred large trees. For this piece of palpable indiscretion, we were, as we richly deserved, most severely admonished; but the information which we had gained was truly acceptable, and we the following day commenced our march, taking the road which we had so rashly explored, preceded by pioneers, who soon cleared a way, and made a good carriage-road. We had scarcely any stoppage, nor did we see a soul of the enemy. If small stockades had been thrown across this narrow pathway, our loss of men must have been great; but the supposed inaccessible nature of their mountains made the enemy slumber in security. We soon got through the avenue, and continued our march through the pebbly bed before alluded to. About a mile ahead of this, a small plain opened to view, studded with small bushes, at the extreme end of which the bed of the dry ravine took a direction to the left. Here a most magnificent scene burst upon the sight. The hills at this point represented a flight of stairs; one reared its golden summit above the other in beautiful succession; the whole of them were wooded with the most beautiful variegated trees and shrubs; and, here and there, majestic rocks elevated their proud heads, and seemed to bid defiance to the besieging enemy. At the foot or base of these hills were posted two strong piquets of the enemy; one on a hill to the right, in a house similar to the one described at Summarabassah: but on our approach they flew into the hills in the vicinity, without giving us a shot in earnest of being our enemy. This silence on the part of a subtle and cunning foe informed us, in plain terms, that something was brewing for us. They seemed to coax and invite us to advance and view their picturesque country. It was necessary to establish here a post of communication, through which we could obtain supplies; for which purpose the house just spoken of was fortified, and a depot established. Here we waited until this post was well stored with every requisite for war. During this time, the quartermaster-general's department was busily employed in reconnoitring the surrounding country; but, from the intricacy of its nature, but little information could be obtained which we could on sure grounds act upon. At last, after our patience was worn almost threadbare with this delay, it was given out, as the firm opinion of the quarter-master-general (grounded on unquestionable information from his trustworthy spies), that to force an entrance at this point would be attended with the most disastrous consequences. To risk a failure at the commencement of a war against such a foe, would have been the basis of our ultimate defeat and destruction; and it appeared, from information not to be doubted, that in the direction which we had thought of taking, there were stockade upon stockade, and fort upon fort. The attempt, therefore, to prosecute our enterprise in this direction, under all these circumstances, could be considered in no other light than wantonly knocking our heads against the flinty rocks, or offering our shattered limbs as wadding for the enemy's guns, or our bodies to fill up some deep vacuity in their new and numerous stockades. We had more than fifty years' dear-bought experience, and an officer seventy years of age for our guide. The young and inexperienced officers, in the ardour of youth, felt mortified at this information; and, had their will and feelings been consulted, they would have madly rushed to their graves.

It was the opinion of the more calm-thinking and experienced men, that if, after the information we possessed, we had proceeded in the same track, and a failure had been the result, the whole dishonour of the catastrophe would have fallen on the head of the commander, and have been visited with the government's disapprobation and censure; but we had at our head a soldier possessing every requisite for such a critical campaign, and whose thoughts were now turned to some more practicable part of the country. Every one was actively engaged in the attempt to discover some new road, path, or ascent. Spies had now been absent two days, and some apprehensions were entertained as to their safety, knowing the barbarity of the Nepaulese; but on the evening of the third day they returned; but not a syllable could be gleaned from the quarter-master-general's department; every ear was on the listen to catch the slightest hint, but all was silence and secrecy throughout the camp. Rumours were flying about, and strange stories were circulated; but the prevailing opinion was, that we must give up the campaign, on account of an impossibility of access into the enemy's country. This was a death-blow to our hopes. The attempt to force the entrance above alluded to, would have been through the Chirecah Ghattie pass; but this was wisely given up as hopeless. There was a small ravine branching off from the bed of a dry river, in which our encampment lay, and its entrance looked like the dreary access to some deep cavern. From thence the spies last came. The moon rose in all her splendour, gilding the tops of the golden-leaved trees; and all was silent, save the falling of the distant cataract, when a faint whisper, borne on the refreshing breeze of night, said, "Prepare to move;" and in one hour after, we entered this little gaping cavern, leaving the principal part of our force for the protection of our standing tents and baggage. We were equipped as lightly as possible. Two six-pounders were conveyed on elephants, and our march seemed to lie through the bed of this ravine, which was rocky, and watered by a crystal current that rippled along its flinty bed. We did not proceed at the rate of more than one or two hundred yards an hour, ascending and descending every twenty paces; at one time deep sunk in some dark excavation, and shortly afterwards perched upon the summit of a rock, the falling of the numerous cataracts drowning the noise made by our approach. The night was cold and chilly, but as light as noonday; not a cloud was to be seen; the sky was one sheet of beautiful blue; but in some of the excavations, where the blessed moon never condescended to show her bright face, we were obliged to go back to boyhood, and have a game of blind-man's-buff, for in those places we were obliged to grope our way completely in the dark. In these excavations the water was deep and cold; but even in these dreary spots we experienced some pleasure, for occasionally, through little fissures in the rock, we could espy the distant moonlit landscape, which appeared as if viewed through a spy-glass, and was beautiful in the extreme.

Had the enemy been aware of our nocturnal excursion, they might have annihilated us, by rolling down rocks and stones upon our heads; but, fortunately for us, they slumbered on the couch of fancied security, and heard us not. What with falling and slipping, we became wet through; but as I had that night the honour of bearing my country's banner, this was a charge, the care of which afforded me neither time nor inclination to attend either to personal annoyance or personal comfort. I felt that, while it was untarnished, I should be proud and happy. My covering-sergeant once had the assurance to ask me to permit him to deprive me of the encumbrance. I really thought I should have jumped down the fellow's throat. "An encumbrance!" I repeated; "how dare you cast such an imputation on England's pride? No, sergeant: he who takes this colour, when before an enemy, will take with it my life."

"I beg pardon, Sir; I did not intend to offend you, or cast a reflection on that flag under which I have fought and bled." I replied, "No, sergeant, I know you did not intend to offend me, or cast a stigma upon the colour; but supposing that I should be so imprudent as to give up such a charge to you, and you should lose it, or be killed, or meet with any other accident, which in the course of war we are all liable to, what answer should I make my justly-offended country, when asked, Where is the banner which was entrusted to your charge? What excuse would it be to say, I gave it to a sergeant to carry? Should I not deserve to be carried to the gallows? No, sergeant, the post of ensign is one of most distinguished trust, and, so long as I hold that commission, nothing but death shall part me and my flag, while it is my duty to bear it; but your offer was that of kindness. Come, let us drink to its prosperity." Here I gave him my little pistol or brandy-bottle; and, in the most prophetic manner, he said, "Well, Sir, God bless and prosper our old banner; and, ere to-morrow's dawn, may you wave it over a conquered foe." I took a drop, and said, "Amen." My young friend, who had journeyed with me from Dinapore, and who was now my chum, had the honour of carrying the other flag, and he also gloried in the distinction; and although he had some twenty desperate falls, and sprained his thumb, he would not part with it.

Our march now became more and more tardy, and the ascents and descents more difficult and intricate. In some places rocks of gigantic size hung some hundred feet over head. These sudden and tremendous hills and dales indicated that we could not have far to go; for the last hill was scarcely accessible. The soles of both my boots had long refused to bear me company any further; but I had one faithful soul that bore me through every difficulty and hardship.

The morn now began to break through the cerulean chambers of the east, the faithful moon still lingering on the tops of the western hills, loth to bid us farewell. I was of course in the centre of my regiment. We halted a considerable time, till broad daylight, when we could see, from where I stood, the soldiers in advance of us, ascending by means of projecting rocks and boughs. We were halted in a kind of basin, surrounded by high hills. In the course of a couple of hours, the whole of the 87th regiment, with our gallant general and suite, ascended this difficult *ghaut*. From this eminence we could see a great distance; and on every hill we could discern signals, which were communicated from post to post. From this we concluded that the enemy had gained information of our approach; but I do not think they knew whereabouts we were, as will appear afterwards, but merely that some of our troops had marched from their old ground.

What will not good examples effect on the minds of soldiers? Our gallant general walked every yard of this critical march, encouraging his men. These well-timed examples will accomplish wonders. The question now was, how to get the guns up, and the powder and shot; but those who are accustomed to wars in India are not often at a loss for expedients. Having got all the men up, except the rear-guard, the pioneers went to work with their pickaxes, some making a road, and others felling trees. As we were but two regiments, the general's primary object was to place our little force to the best advantage. This accomplished, the guns were our next object. Having cut a good deal of the most prominent part of the hill away, and laid trees on the ascent as a footing for elephants, these animals were made to approach it, which the first did with some reluctance and fear. He looked up, shook his head, and, when forced by his driver, he roared piteously. There can be no question, in my opinion, that this sagacious animal was competent instinctively to judge of the practicability of the artificial flight of steps thus constructed; for the moment some little alteration had been made, he seemed willing to approach. He then commenced his examination and scrutiny, by pressing with his trunk the trees that had been thrown across; and after this he put his fore leg on, with great caution, raising the fore part of his body so as to throw its weight on the tree. This done, he seemed satisfied as to its stability. The next step for him to ascend by was a projecting rock, which we could not remove. Here the same sagacious examination took place, the elephant keeping his flat side close to the side of the bank, and leaning against it. The next step was against a tree; but this, on the first pressure of his trunk, he did not like. Here his driver made use of the most endearing epithets, such as "Wonderful, my life"

"Well done, my dear"

"My dove"

"My son"

"My wife;" but all these endearing appellations, of which elephants are so fond, would not induce him to try again. Force was at length resorted to, and the elephant roared terrifically, but would not move. Something was then removed; he seemed satisfied, as before; and he in time ascended that stupendous *ghaut*. On his reaching the top, his delight was visible in a most eminent degree; he caressed his keeper, and threw the dirt about in a most playful manner. Another elephant, a much younger animal, was now to follow. He had watched the ascent of the other with the most intense interest, making motions all the while, as though he was assisting him by shouldering him up the acclivity; such gestures as I have seen some men make when spectators of gymnastic exercises. When he saw his comrade up, he evinced his pleasure by giving a salute, something like the sound of a trumpet. When called upon to take his turn, however, he seemed much alarmed, and would not act at all without force. When he was two steps up, he slipped, but recovered himself by digging his toes in the earth. With the exception of this little accident, he ascended exceedingly well. When this elephant was near the top, the other, who had already performed his task, extended his trunk to the assistance of his brother in distress, round which the younger animal entwined his, and thus reached the summit of the *ghaut* in safety. Having both accomplished their task, their greeting was as cordial as if they had been long separated from each other, and had just escaped from some perilous achievement. They mutually embraced each other, and stood face to face for a considerable time, as if whispering congratulations. Their driver then made them salaam to the general, who ordered them five *rupees* each for sweetmeats. On this reward of their merit being ordered, they immediately returned thanks by another salaam.

At the top of this *ghaut* we left five companies of native infantry to protect our baggage, that must necessarily follow through this pass. Pioneers were also left to cut down the hill, so that our large guns might be dragged up by means of men. This arranged, we pushed on for about a couple of miles. Our route lay through the bed of a river, which was then dry, but which, from the enormous trees that had been washed down its current, must be rapid and destructive during the monsoons. I believe the whole distance we had accomplished did not exceed five miles, and we had been upwards of sixteen hours on the move. By the evening, the enemy had learnt of our being in their country with a large force, with elephants, guns, &c., which so much alarmed them, that they dared not so much as take a peep at us. They said that we were not men, but devils, and that we must have descended from the skies. Some set forth that we were seen soaring in the air in aerial cars, drawn by elephants. Thus, their idolatrous superstition frightened them out of their wits; and until some of them, more courageous than the rest, had ventured and felt that we were men, they could not be prevailed upon to return to their posts, nor would they ever believe that we had ascended the *ghaut*; and, indeed, to view it even after the hill had undergone such a metamorphosis, it was then almost beyond credit that the whole army, with twenty-four pounders, should have been got up.

Our next object was to keep firm possession of what we had attained with so much difficulty; for which purpose a small hill was selected for the general safety, on which we established outlying piquets. From hence we could reconnoitre the surrounding neighbourhood; but we had scared the foe far into the woods and hills. The beauteous sun, which had in mercy dried our wet clothes, was now on the decline, but assumed such an awful colour, that it looked like a blood-stained banner. It had, when this idea came across my mind, half buried itself behind the highest hill visible from our new and exalted situation. When the sun had wholly retired behind the hills, the golden rays which lingered on the scene rendered it truly magnificent and ravishing. The mountains in the distance were so high, that their tops seemed to touch the clear blue clouds, while those which exceeded the others in height seemed pushing their smaller neighbours headlong, to crush the foe below.

When the sombre robe of eve began to spread itself over the beauteous scene, fires were seen as far as the eye could reach. These were signals of alarm, and we could not expect anything less than a desperate effort to drive us down the *ghaut* again; for the prevention of which every possible preparation was promptly made. We were cold, hungry, and barefooted. There had been an order that every man should bring three days' provisions; but, by some mistake, this order had been neglected to be properly communicated, for it ought to have been verbally published on the morning of the day we marched. The expectation of something to do in the night made us forget the cold and hunger. An additional outlying and advanced piquet was ordered, and I was the next for duty. This piquet was thrown out about two hundred yards in front of the others—a subaltern's piquet. The first line of piquets threw out a chain of double sentinels, the extremities of which formed a link with those thrown out from the hill above, forming one-eighth of a circle round the general body. Mine was rather a piquet for reconnoitring, and, in case of alarm, to join the first piquet behind me. It was now about twenty hours since we had had anything to eat. I was therefore hungry, and, consequently, in good watching order, for an Englishman is always irritable and peevish when his belly is empty. Repose was quite out of the question, for bedding we had none, except the earth. I could not sleep myself, and I took care that my little piquet did not slumber on their posts. Of water there was plenty, for a most lovely crystal brook murmured close by; but we were quite cold enough without that. It grew dark and lonely, fires being forbidden to those on piquet, while those on the hill had enormous ones. Speaking beyond a whisper was also forbidden. Thus posted, we fully expected to be attacked; for the enemy was famous for night-work. I visited my sentinels every quarter of an hour. I could always find them by their teeth chattering. I had forbidden them from challenging me, as I gave them to understand I should always whistle when I was going round, and thus the enemy would stumble upon my little piquet, and we could, if overpowered, retreat to a stronger. Thus things went on till the moon rose in all her eastern splendour, which enlivened the scene considerably; for when she was thoroughly roused from her slumbers, we could see a great distance. All was hushed as the tomb, save the crackling faggot, and the distant roaring of beasts of prey. All of a sudden, two of my sentinels bellowed out so that the echo resounded again, "Who comes there? Who comes there?" Bang! bang! went both their muskets, and, in an instant, my whole piquet were on the spot; and the whole line were ferreted out of their beds of dried leaves—guns loaded—matches lit; all was ready for the conflict: when it was found that the alarm was occasioned by a bear or tiger lurking close upon our post, and which, in all probability, if not timely disturbed, would have walked off with one of our men. The circumstance was explained to an aid-de-camp who had arrived, and all was again quiet; and the two sentinels got finely roasted by their comrades, who had been obliged to turn out from their hiding-places. Naught now was heard, save some pathetic execrations on the disturbers of the night, by some poor fellow who had lost his warm berth. Thus passed the night. This was in the month of January, and a bitter night it was.

The following morning it was truly laughable to see the men crawling from a huge heap of dried leaves, like pigs out of their straw. Thus enveloped, they had managed to keep themselves warm during the night. Some companies' liquor and biscuit had arrived; and, a short time after daylight, my men and myself had something to eat, in the delights of which meal we forgot the cares of a soldier, smiled on the hardships that were passed, and thought little of those to come. I had some tea, which revived me much. I must confess I do love to be on duty on any kind of service with the Irish. There is a promptness to obey, a hilarity, a cheerful obedience, and willingness to act, which I have rarely met with in any other body of men; but whether, in this particular case, those qualifications had been instilled into them by the rigid discipline of their corps, I know not, or whether these are characteristics of the Irish nation; but I have also observed in that corps (I mean the 87th regiment, or Prince's Own Irish) a degree of liberality amongst the men I have never seen in any other corps—a willingness to share their crust and drop on service with their comrades, an indescribable cheerfulness in obliging and accommodating each other, and an anxiety to serve each other, and to hide each other's faults. In that corps there was a unity I have never seen in any other; and as for fighting, they were very devils. During the Peninsular war, some general officer observed to the Duke of Wellington, how unsteadily that corps marched. The noble duke replied, "Yes, general, they do indeed; but they fight like devils."

So they always will while they are Irish. In some situations they are, perhaps, too impetuous, but if I know anything of the service, this is a fault on the right side; and, what at the moment was thought rashness and madness, has gained Old England many a glorious victory.

Our magical or aerial flight up the *ghauts*, with guns and elephants, seemed to have bewildered the enemy, for we could not get a glimpse of one of them; and it is not clear to me that they had not flown to their capital, to see if some of us had alighted there, or that we were not soaring in the air in that vicinity.

The sun rose in majestic splendour, and the scene before us was a little world of woody hills and valleys. The brilliant rays of the luminary of day exhibited to the eye nature's masterpiece in scenery. Golden woods, that would have defied the pencil of an artist, and which surpassed the sublimest creation of the imagination; glittering hills, that vied in brilliancy with the rising sun; rippling rills, that whispered, "Come, ye thirsty souls, and drink of the crystal brook; and, ye passing seraphs, stay and dip your wings in the pure stream, ere ye ascend to the realms of love;" lofty towering pines, that nodded, "Come and see the things on high;" and cataracts, that rushed headlong down the rocky cliff, and imparted a wild beauty to the whole, beyond the power of words to describe. There sighed the weeping willows, which, by the cool brookside, dipped their new-born leaves in the rippling waters, to steal more tears that they might weep again. There sported the golden fish, sheltering themselves from the meridian sun, beneath the shade of the overhanging foliage. There grew the blushing rose, calmly reposing on its downy moss, and smiling that it had, when fair maidens were asleep, robbed their cheeks of all their beauty. There flourished the gaudy tulip; and the blue-eyed violet dwelt on the mossy banks. The little minstrels of the grove tuned their morning notes, and their seraphic melody lulled the whole to sweet repose. Oh, that ever human blood should defile these beauteous scenes! or that the horrors of war should disturb the sweet harmony established by nature in the fertile valleys of this sweet and picturesque country! But in this paradise of beauty dwelt a cruel and barbarous people, proverbial for their bloody deeds, whose hearts were more callous than the flinty rocks that reared their majestic heads above their woody mountains. They are more savage in their nature than the hungry tiger that prowls through their dreary glens; cruel as the vulture; cold-hearted as their snowy mountains; subtle and cunning as the fiend of night; powerful as the rocks on which they live; and active as the goat upon the mountain's brow.

We were obliged to proceed with caution, and with our eyes open, step by step. We had intended to have remained here the whole of this day, to enable our supplies to come up; but these having arrived early we commenced our march in continuation of the same bed of the river. We had not been in motion an hour, before the enemy's fires were lighted, as signals that we were again on the move. Our march was difficult, as we were obliged to cut our way through underwood, and pass through several rivers, which much impeded our progress. These streams are fed and nourished from the tremendous cataracts from the high hills before us. We found that the enemy had strictly watched our movements during the night; for, every quarter of a mile we advanced, we found fires still burning, and some earthen cooking-vessels in which they had boiled their rice. Having proceeded about a mile, we came to a sudden and abrupt turning in the river. Here we halted, and the light company was sent on to reconnoitre. We then moved on again, and when we had rounded the turning of the river, which swept round the bottom of a little hill, a small plain opened to our view. It was fertile with a kind of yellow grass, that perfumed the air with its odour, something like sandalwood. This grass, we were informed afterwards, was a deadly poison. Here we came to another halt, our spies having returned, and informed us that we were not far from a very strong post of the enemy. This news flew through the ranks like wildfire; the flints were adjusted—bayonets firmly fixed on—cartridges arranged—and every eye beamed delight. I did not much like my present situation, in the centre of the regiment; it was not what I had been used to; but being one of the youngest ensigns, I was obliged to comply. I thought it strange that the colours should be in the centre, and would, if I had dared to make such a proposition, have suggested that they might be moved to the front; but my commanding officer, good and kind as he was, would, I am sure, have rode me down for my impudence; so I contented myself by getting on the toes of my lower extremities, and peeping over the men's heads to see what was going on. The light company were busy all this time in exploring and examining the localities on our right and left, that we might not be hemmed in. This is a necessary precaution in a mountainous country; for the enemy may open the door to you and bid you enter, and, when well in, may shut you in, so as to leave you no possibility of escape. Young officer, never be inveigled in this manner, but take care, especial care, that you can always insure that last extremity—a good retreat. My eyes lingered on the light bobs as they ascended the surrounding hills, and I wished to be with them, to see what was to be seen. This was a most critical campaign, and required more prudence and caution than I ever possessed in the whole course of my life. In such a country you could not tell but your next step might be in the cannon's mouth. I was thus thinking, when I saw the adjutant running towards the centre of the regiment, vociferating, "Pass the word for Mr. Shipp; pass the word for Mr. Shipp."

"Holloa!" thought I, "what's all this about?". At last he came up to me, and said I was to join the light company immediately. This was making me a light bob, indeed. I made over the colour to my covering sergeant, by the adjutant's desire; but at that moment a thought struck me, that perhaps this was the last time I should ever bear it; for I could not foresee but that that day—nay, that fleeting hour—might be my last; so I pressed the colour to my bosom and kissed it: why should I be ashamed of it? I was a soldier, and the oft blood-stained banner was my pride.

I soon joined the light bobs, for I could run and jump with the best of them, and the column now proceeded slowly. The fine light company of the 25th regiment of Bengal Native Infantry were with us, and there was the greatest intimacy between this native company and ours, and more familiarity and good-fellowship than I had ever witnessed during my course of service in India. We now ascended a small hill, at the bottom of which we saw several men running away. Our soldiers were not cruel, nor did they ever wantonly throw away their fire. A soldier ought to guard every round entrusted to his care, for the protection of his country and himself, as the apple of his eye; many a brave man has lost his life in battle for the want of a round of ammunition, which, in all probability, he had been careless of at the beginning. It is not only a crime, but a folly, for men to be wanton in this particular. I took about ten men with me, and the acting adjutant followed, and we soon came up with these poor frightened and bewildered creatures. They threw themselves on the earth, but did not supplicate for mercy—a thing unknown among themselves. They seemed rather to meet the pointed bayonet, than to run or cringe from it; but, when they saw that we did not lay on them the finger of harm, they kissed our feet and then the earth, in token of gratitude. These poor creatures were not soldiers, but poor, solitary, and oppressed villagers, that had been sent for rice, of which they carry great loads, by a strap or belt over their heads, in baskets made of the willow-twig. We were directed by our general to let them go, that they might tell our enemies that we were not bloodthirsty murderers. When this was communicated to them by one of their countrymen, the eye of fear brightened up; we could see the tear of joy in their eyes; they bowed, a hundred times in the most abject prostrations to our feet; then stood towards their village, seemingly dispossessed of any fear. I dare say these poor starving creatures would willingly have sought protection under the shadow of our mercy, rather than return to be the slaves of a tyrannic government.

We now came to a wider river with a rocky bed, and, a little higher up, was the strong post before alluded to. We could see the ends of the houses standing some thirty yards from the river, whose banks, at this place, were high and abrupt. We therefore crossed a little lower down, when the 87th light company was pushed on at a good round trot. Here was a square building, something like what I have before described at Summarabassah, but on a much larger and stronger scale. This we surrounded and entered. About fifty men were in this place; but, on seeing us enter, they ran out at an opposite door, but were met by the European soldiers. Many of them escaped; the others, some of whom showed fight, were killed. The house was empty, except that some unshelled rice and saltpetre were strewn about it. On looking round, we discovered another building of a similar nature, about three hundred yards further in the wood, to which there was a narrow path. Into this we struck, and expected every moment to be saluted with the contents of a canister of grape, or with a volley of musketry; for the building commanded this road or pathway from two or three hundred loop-holes. In this building, or, rather, near the door of it, lay a man dead, dreadfully mutilated. We pushed in, and the few soldiers that occupied the house ran out into the wood, which was close to this building, and thus escaped, with the exception of about five or six, who were shot by some good marksmen. This house was also empty, save that some little grain was scattered about here and there. They did not, I should suppose, expect us to dinner, although their cooking utensils, well filled, were boiling on the fire. These we broke for fear of poison, a crime they were fully capable of. On looking at the poor mutilated man, he was discovered to be one of our spies, respecting whom our kind-hearted quarter-master-general had expressed the most anxious solicitude. My expressions, in describing these savages, may have been thought to have been too severe and exaggerated, when I accused them of being barbarous and cruel; but the reader shall now judge for himself whether or not this accusation was unfounded.

In all nations, even in Europe, the practice of punishing spies is recognized as just; but their execution is generally public, and not without the sanction and approbation of the governor or commander-in-chief; and no piquet, post, or guard, dare inflict the penalty of death. This poor creature was seized, and literally cut to pieces; and it was supposed, by the medical people, that he must have died a death of extreme agony, for the ground under him was dug up with his struggling under the torture which had been inflicted on him. His arms had been cut off, about half way up from the elbow to the shoulder; after which it appeared that two deep incisions had been cut in his body, just above the hips, into which the two arms had been thrust. His features were distorted in a most frightful manner. Our poor fellows wept bitterly over the sight, and swore, in the bitterness of their anger, that they would revenge this foul and bloody deed; and I had great difficulty, with their gallant captain, in restraining them from following those savages into the wood. The pioneers having arrived, the poor wretch was committed to his last home, amidst the sympathy of all around.

Ettoondah was the name of the place where this barbarous murder had been committed; and a more lovely or more picturesque spot there is not in the created world.

Here we had some tolerably good fishing, by tying our horse-blankets together, and then dragging the stream. We remained here some days, for the purpose of making this our grand depot; for which purpose, in the lower house, which was better situated than the other, and not so near the wood, we built a large and strong stockade, with six embrasures for guns. This house we converted into store-rooms, and here we left all our superfluous baggage. I had no superfluities; one thing on and one off was quite enough for any man on such a service, and I often regretted, with many of my brother officers, that we had not brought packs, like the men, which would have carried our all safely, and entirely relieved us from the apprehension which we now felt of losing those things not immediately in our presence.

The domestic fowls, kept by the natives, had strayed into the adjoining woods, and there bred, and had become very numerous. At night they roosted on the trees, without any apparent fear of molestation. Firing was most strictly prohibited within a mile of camp; and justly so, or we should, if permitted, have had the soldiers firing away their ammunition, and the camp alarmed. Many of the fowls, however, were caught and eaten.

Chapter 13

Fighting the Nepaulese

In three or four days we again moved on. The 87th being the only European corps with this part of the division, we always led the column, or, rather, formed the advance-guard. We commenced our march; and, rather wishing to see, instead of groping, our way, we went on through a dense thick wood for a couple of miles, through which there was a tolerably good road, so that our troops travelled with comparative facility. When at the end of two miles, we came to a small open space, where several fires were still alight and burning, and earthen pots left behind. About the middle of this little plain was a river about knee-deep. On the margin of the wood on the opposite side of this river, several people were seen peeping through the green foliage, watching our movements. We entered another thick wood, which brought us to the bank of another river; but the road did not cross it, but went along the left bank, under a small hill, from which it had apparently been cut by manual labour. This was rather a dangerous place to enter. A high and inaccessible hill was on one side, and a deep bank and river on the other; and on the opposite side of the river, was a kind of rising bank, behind which the enemy might be lying in ambush, and waiting till we had got well in before they commenced firing. In this case their fire must have been very destructive from both sides, without the possibility of escape or defence, and the confusion would have been dreadful. But Major-General Sir David Ochterlony was not to be entrapped in that manner; these points were scrupulously explored before we attempted to enter such a place of insecurity.

At the end of this winding road, there opened to the view an extensive valley, and, here and there, small straggling villages, consisting of some ten or more huts; but very few people could be seen, and those few were poor villagers. We continued our march for about half a mile further, when we saw on our left an extensive village, and, on the hills immediately in its rear, an immense number of people, seemingly soldiers; for we could see spears, colours, &c. We immediately bent our way towards this village, as we saw numerous people running to and fro. When near, we got into double-quick time, and then separated into files, with our pieces loaded. I went into several huts, where nothing but a set of poor decrepit old people could be seen. About twenty or thirty yards further, I saw a two-story brick house, probably the *zemindar*'s, for there was no other. Here I saw several good-looking and well-dressed men run in and shut the door. I broke it open, with the assistance of some of my men. When I entered the lower floor, I found there were several men there. One was sitting; but, having gone from the light, and a bright sun, into comparative darkness, I could scarcely see. I was therefore obliged to prick my way with my old 24th dragoon sabre; and I just recovered my vision in time to see a man aiming an arrow at me. I struck at the arrow, which was close to me; but, from the indistinct light, I could not make sure of my aim. He let fly, and the arrow could not have been more than a hair-breadth from the side of my head. It stuck in the door-post, when a soldier of the company, by name Quanbury, stopped his shooting, by shooting him, for firing at his officer. The others begged for mercy, which was willingly granted. Never did I see a man in the 87th regiment wantonly commit an act of cruelty. We took them prisoners, but they were ultimately discharged, and permitted to return to their villages or homes.

A little further on we came in sight of Muckwanpore Valley, and an immense long line of huts. These, we afterwards were given to understand, were the summer quarters of the enemy's soldiers. On our left ran a ridge of hills, covered with variegated shrubs and trees. On this range of hills we could see soldiers posted in immense force, but they attempted not to molest our line of march, although sometimes, I am sure, within shot of their *ginjalls*. They seemed rather to be on the defensive than the offensive, as we should have imagined. Various were the opinions as to their apparent indifference to our running all over the country. From these huts, or military cantonments, we could see the fort of Muckwanpore, and innumerable large stockades on the hill in the rear of the one immediately in front of the before-mentioned huts. The fort appeared some miles off, and looked like a speck in the sky; but, no doubt, the approaches to it, protected as it was by the stockades, which we could see with the spy-glass, were extremely perilous. We encamped in the lines which had been left by the enemy, and could not have been more than one mile and a half from the summit of this hill. However, they still continued passive, sitting upon their legs, watching our movements. Our position was secure and strong, being on two sides surrounded with a deep *nullah*, with a nice rippling stream.

The following morning was occupied in looking about our new encampment, and seeing what was in the adjoining woods. We found nothing but a few partridges and woodcocks, and these we could not shoot, being too near camp. About a mile behind the camp the whole scenery around was truly romantic, from the white and craggy rocks, apparently living in the clouds, behind which not a tree or a shrub was to be seen. These could only be seen night and morning, or when the sky was clear; at other times, these hills could not be discovered through the clouds. The fort itself seemed high, and almost beyond the power of mortal ascent. For the first time these ten nights I obtained some sleep, having no charge, and no care on my mind. Sleeping in my clothes was no inconvenience to me. I slept soundly till the broad daylight broke in through the crevices of the tent. I rose in the morning sprightly as a lark, and indulged myself with dry and clean linen, which was quite a treat. I felt so refreshed, that I was quite another being from the day before, and fit for anything. I took a stroll round my brother-officers' tents; paid my devoirs to my commanding-officer, which I never failed to do once a day, as a duty, and a respect due to his rank. I was invited to breakfast with him; after which, as we were standing looking at the hill, we were not a little surprised to find that the strong piquet of the enemy, which was posted there the night before, was not to be seen. Two of our men were brought before the commanding-officer for having gone beyond the outlying piquet. The fact was, that these imprudent fellows had been upon the hill, where the piquet had been, unarmed. After admonishing them for their imprudence and disobedience of orders, the commanding-officer asked one of them what he saw; he replied, "Nothing at all, your honour, but a great big piquet; and sure they were not there, but all gone." He added, that "all their fires were alight, because he saw them burning."

"And what did you see on the other side of this first hill?" asked the colonel, trying to smother a laugh.

"Nothing at all, your honour."

"Are there hills or valleys on the other side?"

"Neither, your honour; only a mighty big mountain, as big as the Hill of Howth."

"Did you see any men?"

"Divel a one, your honour, except one poor old woman in one of the huts, and she was after going when she saw me and Pat Logan coming near her."

"What took you there?"

"Fait! we both went to take a big walk, for we were quite tired doing nothing—that's all, your honour; so I hope no offence."

"Fall in, the light company!"

"Light company, fall in!" was bellowed through the whole line of encampment. The colonel flew to the right—the adjutant to the left; I ran one way, and the two men jumped another, for they both belonged to the light company. Scarcely had I reached the parade, when three parts of the company were under arms, with our noble general at the head, getting men together. It was five minutes only from the first order when we marched off, not a man absent. We soon found, by the direction we took, that the taking of the hill was to be our object. We moved on slowly, for it was a good half mile up the hill, and the ascent winding and steep. Our lads seemed as merry as crickets. In five minutes after, we heard firing on the top of the hill to our right. This proceeded from a small reconnoitring party that had a short period before gone up, under Lieutenant Lee, of the 87th regiment, and Lieutenant Turrell, of the 20th native infantry, a brave young volunteer, who fell an early victim to his zeal. The design with which this reconnoitring party had been dispatched up the hill, was to protect the quarter-master-general in the execution of the duties incident to his department. This party being observed from the fort of Muckwanpore, which overlooked the ground on which they were reconnoitring, a large body of the enemy, who had, without orders, vacated the post immediately in front of our encampment, were dispatched to re-occupy the position which they had deserted, and in their advance they fell in with our reconnoitring party, who, as they were not in all above twenty men, were of course obliged to make a precipitate retreat. In this disastrous skirmish, poor Lieutenant Turrell was cut to pieces, and several others of the party killed and wounded. As the party which had been thus surprised was making the best of their way down the hill, we made the best of our way up. We were supported by our old friends, the light company of the 25th native infantry. The ascent was most difficult, there being only one narrow pathway, by which we were obliged to ascend almost one by one. When about half way, or three parts up, we came to a small flat spot, about fifty yards long, and twenty wide. Here our noble captain sounded the assembly. We could now see the enemy, like ants, creeping and lurking about, and busily engaged in secreting themselves behind trees and stones. I presumed to recommend to the captain of the light company, that our forming in a body would bring on us a destructive fire, and that we had better fight them on their own system, which was extending, and every man availing himself of tree or stone, and a rest for his piece. This was sure to be attended with success; and, however brave a man may be, he never ought to be above advice. Our captain readily saw the danger that would attend our forming, and therefore immediately sounded the extend; then the advance; and the fighting soon became warm on both sides. The enemy maintained their ground and fought manfully. I hate a runaway foe; you have no credit for beating them. Those we were now dealing with were no flinchers; but, on the contrary, I never saw more steadiness or more bravery exhibited by any set of men in my life. Run they would not; and of death they seemed to have no fear, though their comrades were falling thick around them, for we were so near that every shot told. At last some of their men began to give way; and, as we were ascending rapidly, their commander, or one of their principal officers, attempted to rally them. Having succeeded in this attempt for the moment, the said officer had the impudence to attack and put his majesty's liege subject, John Shipp, ensign on full pay, and in the full vigour of his life and manhood, in bodily fear, on the king's high hill of Muckwanpore, on the afternoon of—I now forget the date, he so frightened me. He was a strong, powerful man, protected by two shields, one tied round his waist, and hanging over his thighs as low as his knees, and the other on the left arm, much larger than the one round his waist. From this gentleman there was no escape; and, fortunately for me, I had my old twenty-fourther with me, which I had two or three days before put in good shaving order. With this I was obliged to act on the defensive, till I could catch my formidable opponent off his guard. He cut, I guarded; he thrust, I parried; until he became aggravated, and set to work with that impetuosity and determination pretty generally understood by the phrase "hammer and tongs;" in the course of which he nearly cut my poor twenty-fourther in pieces. At last I found he was winded; but I could see nothing of the fellow, except his black face peeping above one shield, and his feet under the other; so I thought I would give him a cut five across his lower extremities; but he would not stand still a moment; he cut as many capers as a French dancing-master, till I was quite out of patience with his folly. I did not like to quit my man; so I tried his other extremities; but he would not stand still, all I could do. At length, I made a feint at his toes, to cut them; down went his shield from his face, to save his legs; up went the edge of my sword smack under his chin; in endeavouring to get away from which, he threw his head back, which nearly tumbled off, and down he fell; and I assure you, reader, I was not sorry for it, for he was a most unsociable neighbour. I don't know whether I had a right or not, but I took the liberty of taking his sword, gold crescent, turban-chain, and large shield. The latter I sported on my left arm during the action, and it was fortunate for me that I did, for I found that the shield was ball-proof, and I should have been severely wounded, had I been deprived of this trophy. Our gallant captain fought like one of the old Fogs, and his men, as I had been told, were indeed "divels to fight." The very noise they made would have frightened old Harry himself.

The enemy fought furiously before they gave up the hill; indeed, many of them rushed upon our bayonets in the most reckless and desperate manner. Being at last compelled to give way, they took up their station on the adjoining hills, and in the ravines and valleys below, and their fire for a time was destructive. As we had now gained the hill, we had proceeded to the extent of our orders. Here reinforcements poured up to our assistance, and two six-pounders, which had been sent up immediately after us, now began to play with grape on the poor and brave fellows who had sought refuge in the dells below. The havoc was dreadful, for they still scorned to fly. During our ascent, some shells had been thrown by our artillery below, from some howitzers in front of our encampment, to the right of the ridge of the hill, where the enemy, in immense force, had been observed running down to the assistance of their beaten comrades. This reinforcement of the enemy brought down, to play upon our ascent, a small hill-gun, a three-pounder of about a yard long, which one man could carry. The whole of the ammunition brought by the enemy for this and other purposes, our shells from below reached and blew up, and great numbers were killed and wounded by the explosion. When their ammunition was gone, they rolled the little gun down the hill, where we, after the action, found it. Our troops having been distributed and posted along the range of hills, some of our men were killed and wounded by each other, by their cross-firing at random, where they heard the sound of muskets, but could not see the object. We frequently sounded "cease firing," but to no purpose; and, indeed, it was truly tantalizing to see thousands of the enemy under our very noses, and not to be allowed to fire at them; but, the woods being thick and high, we were fearful of again drawing on ourselves the fire of our men on the opposite hills. Our brave colonel had arrived upon the hill with the reinforcements which belonged to his brigade, and, fearing the same evil he sounded repeatedly the "cease firing;" but here and there some shots were still fired by the native troops. When he came to his light company, I could see the beam of delight in the veteran's eye; but that was no time for compliments. He desired us to cut the first man down who presumed to disobey his oft-repeated order of "cease firing;" and he told us to lie down, and on no account to attempt to proceed. At this moment, one of the enemy, who had been annoying us from a thicket some thirty paces from where I stood, not stomaching the grape, made a movement from his hiding-place. One of our company seeing so good an opportunity, was not to be restrained; he fired, and killed his man. The colonel had nothing but a walking-stick in his hand. Whether he thought it was his sword or not, I cannot say; but he immediately ran at the man and struck him across the nose—in which, by-the-by, nature had been very bountiful to this individual—exclaiming at the same time, "You rascal! I have a great mind to have you shot this moment for this pointed disobedience of my orders." At this moment, seeing the enemy, who had secreted themselves in the underwood, ferreted out by our shells, and running off, some of our fellows must, if they died for it, have a shot. This exasperated our little colonel beyond bounds. He was a little lion when roused. He immediately selected one of the men of the light company of the 25th regiment, and ordered him to be shot, which would certainly have been done, had not the adjutant-general of the forces at that time joined the colonel with orders. By this the colonel's attention was drawn off, and he ran off towards the right. The man, seeing this, ran towards the left, and thus escaped the punishment he justly deserved. Prompt and implicit obedience is one of the grand principles of military discipline; and any officer would have been justifiable in shooting, or cutting down, any such disobedient soldier. Any breach of orders I would at all times punish with a great and heavy penalty. Encourage this, and there is an end to military obedience and discipline at once. The soldier who was struck on this occasion was sensible of the enormity of his crime, and therefore quietly pocketed the more lenient penalty, and the countermarch his nose had made towards his cheek, and thought himself fortunate that he had not been deprived of his life.

 Naught was now heard but the roaring of the two six-pounders and the whistling of shells. The dying and the wounded lay in masses in the dells and ravines below. In our own company we had, I think, eleven killed and twenty wounded, our total number being eighty only. I do repeat again, I never saw such soldiers. I began to think myself, in comparison with them, but yet a novice. When the evening began to spread her mantle over the dreary scene, the sombre appearance of the lowering sky seemed to mourn, and put on a garb of black, to shield from human eye the ghastly sight below. As long as it was light, we could plainly see the last struggles of the dying. Some poor fellows could be seen raising their knees up to their chins, and then flinging them down with all their might. Some attempted to rise, but failed in the attempt. One poor fellow I saw get on his legs, put his hand to his bleeding head, then fall, and roll down the hill, to rise no more. This was the scene that the evening now closed upon. Reader, believe me when I assure you that these results of war were no sights of exultation or triumph to the soldiers who witnessed them. Willingly would we one and all have extended the hand of aid to them, and dressed their gaping wounds. No brave man will ever exult over a bleeding and wounded enemy. The weapon of destruction is no sooner out of his hands, than he is our prisoner, but not our foe. The sympathetic expressions that fell from the lips of our brave soldiers, on witnessing these sights, would have done credit to any set of men.

The dark clouds omened a coming storm. I have been told that any particular noise in mountainous countries—more particularly the roaring of cannon—will bring the clouds down from above, and that rain will follow; and I once heard a gentleman account for it in this way. He said that all dark and thick-looking clouds might be said to be reservoirs of water; that any convulsion would bring them down; and that, when at a certain distance from the earth, the earth's attractive power would draw the rain from them, and, when lightened of this burden, the clouds would again rise. How far this may be the case, I know not. I can only say that, if convulsion could cause rain, there was convulsion enough, for the roaring of the cannon kept up one continued re-echo. The evening closed in pitchy darkness.

The pioneers had been sent up, and we commenced entrenching and stockading the hill round the huts, which were in number about twenty. Some refreshments had at this time come up, both for officers and men. After partaking of some food, it was resolved between my captain and me, that we should watch four hours round, and that he should commence the first four. He accordingly went to post his men, and I took possession, with several men, of a small hut full of good straw, on which I lay down to repose. Scarcely had I closed my eyes in balmy sleep, when I heard the unwelcome vociferation, "Pass the word for Lieutenant Shipp; pass the word for Mr. Shipp; send Mr. Shipp to me."

It was the colonel's voice that I heard; so, jumping from my straw, I exclaimed, "Here I am, colonel; here am I, Sir."

"That's right," said the colonel; "I want you to go on duty." He then took me by the hand, and said, "Shipp, you have verified the recommendations I received from your late commanding officer of the 24th Light Dragoons, and I shall not lose sight of your conduct. From the information our spies have brought, we have every reason to believe that the enemy will, under the darkness of the night, make an effort to regain their lost post, which is of much consequence to them, and more to us. We must therefore prepare to meet them with determined force and resistance, or we shall have all our work to do over again. You must take a steady sergeant and twelve men, and proceed down close to the reservoir of water. On this side of the reservoir take up your station. Let your sentinels form a link with the other sentinels on your right and left; and by no means permit your men to lie down or sleep, but see that they watch, and are on the alert. Go; I know I need not explain more to you. Your captain I have posted in a similar situation."

The rain now fell in torrents; the thunder rolled in its bitterest anger; and the lightning shot in massive sheets along the mountain-tops, and, by its vivid blaze, showed us a glimpse of the dead and the dying. I found that, close to my post, lay numbers whom I believed dead; but I afterwards distinctly heard, during the cessation of the thunder, the moaning of those below. I don't know any situation more painful than mine was at that moment: a tempest raging in all its terrific forms, surrounded by the dead and the dying, and expecting every moment to be attacked by a cruel and barbarous foe, from whom no mercy could be expected, should fate throw us into their hands. Nothing but a sense of duty, and the recollection that I was engaged in the service of my country, could have supported me under such circumstances. A high sense of the duties, and an ardent attachment to the profession of a soldier, will enable a man to do that, with comparative cheerfulness, from which, under other circumstances, his feelings would revolt. The enemy were noted for barbarity and craft, and the danger of surprise was great.

Upon the principle that all stratagems are justifiable in warfare as well as in love, a ready excuse may be found for the craft and cunning exercised by this or any other tribe in their own defence; and it is impossible to look even upon the cruelties practised by them, with any other than an eye of pity and commiseration. They are taught from their infancy the art of war; they fight under the banner of gloomy superstition; cruelty is their creed; and murder of their foes the zenith of their glory. Let us not, therefore, condemn too severely these untaught babes of idolatry.

Notwithstanding my dismal forebodings, and the dangerous position which we occupied, the night passed off quietly enough. Towards morning the rain ceased, and the sun rose in all its splendour and majesty; but the scene of death below marred and defiled the more distant prospect, which was magnificent beyond description. The piquets from below were withdrawn after daylight. On going round the hill afterwards, the dead bodies there astonished me. It was scarcely possible to walk without stepping on them. I could not have imagined that the one-twentieth part had fallen; but, as I have before said, self, in action, is the grand and primary object of man's regard. I paid a visit to the dead body of my antagonist of the preceding day. I found that his head hung only by the skin of his neck. He had also a cut in the abdomen, through which the bowels protruded. I found that, in addition to this, he had received a ball in the fleshy part of the thigh; but whether he got this before or after the fall, I do not pretend to say, but I should imagine before, from the direction of the ball. He was a fine-looking man, and was dressed in a full general's uniform, the same as that worn by our English generals twenty years ago, with the old frog lace, both on the skirts and sleeves, but without epaulettes. When engaged with him, I never dared take my eye off his. Had I not been thoroughly practised in the sword exercise, I must soon have fallen, for he was a very expert swordsman. In a letter addressed to me afterwards, by Captain Pickersgill, quarter-master-general of the army, I was congratulated on the fall of that distinguished *sobah*, or chieftain. His name, the quarter-master-general stated, was Khissna Rhannah Bahadur, and that he was the identical officer who had planned and executed the massacre at Summanpore and Persah, the season before. The letter went on to state that he was a great loss to the Nepaul government, and it was the opinion of the quarter-master-general, as well as of Sir David Ochterlony, that the death of this *sobah* contributed greatly to turn the current of affairs in the Nepaul campaign.

Our next object was to commit the poor fellows who were killed to the grave; for which purpose an enormous working-party was employed to bury the dead, and take the wounded to our hospitals. In two days, eleven hundred were committed to the grave, having almost one general tomb; and it would have much edified those babblers who rail so much against soldiers' cruelties and vices, to have seen the tear of compassion trickling down the cheeks of both natives and Europeans on this occasion. Having performed our sad duty, we were relieved at mid-day, and returned to the lines, amidst the greetings of our comrades at the foot of the hill. The orders of the day were flattering and complimentary to all engaged. These were little trophies gained that no man could rob or cheat us of. Having washed and dressed myself, I went to the hospital to visit both my friends and those that had been, a short day before, my mortal enemies. It had been a considerable time before our wounded men could be removed from the hill, and then the bringing them down so shook them, that, in many cases, inflammation had taken place. Some of these poor suffering fellows seemed to endure the most excruciating pangs. Every comfort that liberality could purchase was afforded to the sufferers, and it gladdened my heart when I went into the tents of the wounded of the enemy, to see some of our native soldiers on their knees, waiting on and administering comforts to them, while others were whispering sweet words of consolation into their attentive ears, which were the more necessary, as some of these poor creatures had an idea that their lives were only prolonged for a more cruel and lingering death. An amputation had been thought necessary on the leg of one of the native enemy. This he submitted to almost without a struggle. When his leg was off, and the stump dressed, it confirmed him in what he had been taught from his infancy, that almost all white men were cannibals; and he asked one of his friends who was lying by him (one of his countrymen), "when he thought they would take the other leg off; as, if he thought it would be long, he would destroy himself." This being understood by one of the hospital attendants, to ease his mind, it was thought proper to explain to him that the act was one of kindness, not of cruelty, and done to save his life. For this purpose one of his countrymen, a spy of ours, was sent for; nothing, however, but the sight of the same operation performed on one of our native men, could appease and satisfy him. After having witnessed this, he became calm, and felt satisfied that we were not such barbarians as he had been taught to suppose. Our humane general had directed that men of the same caste should attend the wounded prisoners of war, and volunteers in abundance came forward for this benevolent purpose. It was a truly pleasurable and delightful sight to witness those who, but a short day before, had fought hard in the bitterest rancour of their souls, now interchanging the most affectionate civilities.

I have, in the hurry of my narrative, forgotten a circumstance which reflects honour on the soldier whom it concerns. When on the top of the hill where the action raged most, one of the enemy showed himself most conspicuously, fighting like a hero. He had just shot one of our men close by where I stood, when I made towards him, with a man of the name of Quanbury. Finding that he was receding from us, and again loading, the soldier next me fired, and the man fell upon his knees. Quanbury immediately ran up to him—for he still grasped his firelock—and was in the act of running him through, when the man threw down his arms. Seeing this, the brave Irish soldier stayed his finishing blow, exclaiming, "By the powers, my fine fellow, but it was well you were after doing that self-same thing; for had you shot me as you did that other man, bad luck to me if I wouldn't have blown your brains out; so I would." Here the quarter-master-general came up and took charge of his prisoner, and we passed on to clear the hill of others who were keeping up a heavy fire.

Chapter 14

The End of the Ghoorka War

We were still obliged to carry on our approaches with all possible vigilance and activity; and our discipline was not relaxed in the slightest particular. We were compelled to watch the enemy with a jealous eye, not allowing our late little victory to feed our vanity, or to seduce us from our wonted caution. Every eye was now fixed on the hill which was in front of our head approach; and various and ludicrous were the reports and opinions, during the day and night, of the movements on the said hill. Fallen trees were magnified into guns and mortars; variegated bushes into soldiers; the light between the trees into flags; and the midnight *ignis fatuus*, on its nocturnal rambles, into torches and lights of the enemy. The rustling leaves, falling down the wintry glen, were construed into the coming foe; and, had one of our captains been the commander-in-chief, the hill would have been treeless and leafless, for he would have blown them all up instead of the enemy. The glass was never from this gentleman's eye. Could his thoughts and speculations by day and night have been committed to paper, his words would have shone forth in all the radiance of a military vocabulary. What shells would he not have expended upon the poor *ignis fatuus*! All we could do or say, he would not believe us. If he had been our general, we should have been in Khatmandoo, the capital of Nepaul, in half the time. His system was new and wonderful; for, when arguing on the best plan to be adopted, he had always the most happy knack of catching the enemy asleep. But in these notions he happened to have mistaken his men. The Nepaulese soldiers never sleep, or rather, such is their watchfulness, that you can never surprise them. This misconception of their character would have led him wrong as often as the *ignis fatuus*. It is quite preposterous to hear some men boasting of what they would do if they had the command. Soldiers are not to judge of the actions of their superiors, but implicitly to obey any orders that may be communicated to them. It is certain, at least, we have no right to promulgate our opinions to the prejudice of others. I longed for an opportunity of seeing this kill-devil of a captain well tried as a soldier; for, if he killed people as fast by the sword as he did by the tongue, two companies of such men would clear the universe, asleep or awake. However, I never had my wish gratified in this respect, though I do not despair that I may hear of some of his brilliant exploits when he is general; for his merits surely cannot be long before it reach the throne.

While we were parading the company in the evening, the captain observed a man looking extremely ill, and asked him what was the matter with him. "Nothing at all, your honour, only a little scratch one of them spalpeens gave me on the hill yesterday; but, sure, it's nothing worth while talking about." As the surgeon was standing near the parade, he was sent for, and the man went into a tent to show his scratch, as he called it, when it was found that the ball had carried away the point of his lower rib, and the wound having been neglected, the surgeon expressed some doubts as to whether the ball was still in or not; when the soldier replied, "I beg your pardon, that's a great big mistake, for here it is" (pulling it out of his pocket), "beat as flat as a crown-piece." He was then ordered to the hospital, but was almost obliged to be dragged there, for he bellowed out, "Arrah, captain, honey, are you going to send me to the hospital before I get satisfaction and revenge for this wound?" He was, of course, obliged to go, and he got better; but during the campaign against the Nepaulese, he never had the satisfaction he required.

The following day I went on outlying piquet, on a small hill about half a mile from the right of the camp. This was, strictly speaking, a piquet or post of observation, as, immediately behind it, was a small foot pathway from the hill, which our advanced post had not yet reached. It was, therefore, requisite to guard the mouth of this little pathway with great care.

I believe it was when on this service that I had occasion to notice an instance of sagacity in a dog, that may be deemed worthy of being recorded.

In passing the sentinels, I found it necessary to admonish one of them for not challenging in a louder voice. To my astonishment, the excuse which the man made was, that he was afraid of waking a faithful dog of his, which was asleep under a bush just by.

"What!" said I, "then I suppose you sometimes take nap about with this faithful animal."

"Why, yes," said the man, innocently, "sometimes, sir; and, to say the truth, I have but five minutes ago relieved him from his post."

"Very candid, truly," said I; "but are you not aware, my good fellow, that you could be shot for sleeping on your post?"

The sentinel admitted that he knew well the consequences to which he would be subjected by so doing; but notwithstanding this, he asserted that he could thoroughly confide in his faithful companion, who, on the slightest noise, would jump upon him, and awake him.

On further inquiry, I learnt that this sagacious and faithful creature would regularly, when his master was on watch, stand his hour and walk his round; that, in very dark nights, he would even put his ear to the ground, and listen; and that, during the period assigned to him as his turn to watch, he would never venture to lie down, but would steadily and slowly walk his round, which nothing could induce him to leave, such was his opinion of the nature and responsibility of his post. The man added, that he once gave him to an officer of the Company's service, who took him from the station where he was (Meerut) to Loodiana, a distance of four hundred miles, and that, the moment the officer let him loose, he returned to his old master, having performed that great distance in two days and a half; that he was on the main-guard the night he returned, and he was awoke by the dog licking his face. It appeared that he had been through the barrack, and visited every sleeping soldier on their separate cots, until he found his master. The man related several anecdotes of this animal: among the rest, he said he was one day out drinking toddy, some miles from camp, and from the intoxicating effect, and the extreme heat of the weather, he went to sleep. On awaking, he found his clothes torn in several places, and that he had been dragged more than three yards from the bush under which he had lain down; but what was his astonishment, on getting up, to find a large snake almost torn to pieces, no doubt by his faithful guard! He was a powerful dog—a kind of Persian hill greyhound—that would kill a wolf single-handed.

On the following day we opened our batteries on some stockades on the face of the hill intervening between us and the fort of Muckwanpore. The first stockade that we proposed to dislodge, was one about eight hundred or a thousand yards from our battery. We could not approach nearer than this, as a deep and enormous declivity lay between us. This being the case, we were under the necessity of commencing at this great distance. The stockade seemed alive with men. There was also a tent pitched in it, with several colours flying, in token of defiance. Some dozen shells, which were beautifully thrown into this stockade, put some of them to double-quick; the tent soon disappeared, as well as the colours, and most of the men, save now and then one or two taking a sly peep to see what we were about. The eighteen and twenty-four pound balls, however, I am convinced never had power to penetrate that little edifice of art. It was evidently built of green bamboos. These, when green, are very elastic, and, being interwoven, as this stockade seemed to be, there is no question that, at the distance from which we fired, they would resist the power of our balls. We frequently saw men running and picking up something, a hundred yards or more from the place. We could not suppose that they were picking up stones.

In the course of this day we received a communication to admit into camp a native from the fort, with his attendants, six in number.

"Halloa," said one, "what! they have had a sickener, have they?"

"They have had enough on't," said another.

A soldier standing near me bellowed out, "Arrah, Corporal Freeman, dear, sure the enemy have got the Corporal Forbes" (meaning the *cholera morbus*), "for the *rajah* is coming to take *ta* with Sir David Maloney."

This was what our men had christened him, I suppose to make his name shorter. Various were the reports in circulation, and every one had his own opinion. Here again the glass of the noble captain, of whom I have already made honourable mention, was constantly at his eye, looking for this messenger of peace. Sometimes he saw him on horseback; then in his palanquin, attended by one hundred followers.

"If he was the commander-in-chief, he would not permit one of them to come within a mile of the camp, armed."

One time he saw the *rajah* riding on a milk-white steed on the hill; but this procession, unfortunately, proved to be no other than little white clouds riding in the sky. Ten thousand were the methods and styles in which this messenger was to make his appearance, and not one was right, for he arrived carried in something like a sailor's hammock, with one follower. He was a dirty, ill-looking, thick-set fellow, with small eyes, wide face, and a low forehead. In spite of these disadvantages of person, however, he assumed all the consequence of a nabob; but when we commenced examining his hammock and person, to see that he had no hidden weapon, his ambassadorship was highly offended, and protested that, to use his own words, "He would not permit his holy person (for he was a priest) to be polluted or defiled by the contaminating touch of a Christian." He added, "that he was a high-priest, and that, rather than submit to such debasement, he would return to his *rajah*, and inform him of the prodigious indign scrutiny of his holy person."

He was soon informed, that if he did not submit to the required forms and rules of the East, he of course might return to his master, and tell him what he pleased. He was getting into his hammock for this purpose, when his holiness thought better of it, and said, "Well, you may examine."

While I searched his ponderous *cumerbund* (a long cloth that was round his waist) he endeavoured to avoid my touch, by cringing from me, as he would from the bite of a serpent; but I gave his holiness such a twist round, that he thought he would never have stopped. Upon this his eye darted vivid flashes of fire; I saw him clench his fists with rage; he foamed from the sides of his mouth; and at one time I really thought that the holy personage was about to forget his holiness, and coming to the scratch. Having no secreted weapon upon him, he was permitted to pass, and it was a very necessary precaution to examine such a fellow strictly, for he was a Goorkah, or bastard Tartar, a race pre-eminently bloodthirsty and cruel, and of the same sect with those who committed such wanton cruelties on the poor unfortunate spy of Ettoondah. In obedience to our instructions, we passed him into camp, and in about an hour he returned, his sallow face contracted and distorted with all the rage and malice that can make the human features terrific. He passed on in sullen silence, in his heart vowing vengeance, as he had no doubt been unsuccessful in his embassy. His sudden exit, and obvious displeasure, indicated a renewal of hostilities; at least so said the all-wise captain, who was the very fountain of information—a complete reservoir of the pure stream of knowledge, at least as far as his own opinion went.

Notwithstanding this sage prediction, however, two more days passed away, when another ambassador came into camp—if not so holy as the former, certainly more like a statesman. This second messenger remained a considerable time in deep and secret conversation with our noble general, who could see as far as most folks, although the service had deprived him of one eye. At last he left, his eye beaming delight. He smiled and bowed as he passed, and we, one and all, immediately flew to the sure channel of information. His opinion was peace; and, for once during the captain's campaigns, he was right, for, the day following, the firing from our batteries ceased, and the uncle to the then reigning *rajah*, who was regent, was expected in camp. Every eye was on the look-out for this great personage, and various were the opinions of the anxious multitude, and they were as ridiculous as they were varied. The wise captain was not idle, either with his glass or his tongue. To do honour to the reception of such a personage, the two flank companies of the 87th regiment, and the two flank companies of the 25th native infantry, formed a street to the general's tent, where every preparation was made to receive our visitor as regent, and uncle to the reigning *rajah*, who was a boy. Having waited some hours after the time, Sir David began to get nettled, and was in the act of withdrawing the troops and setting our batteries to work, when the shrill sound of the war-trumpet, and the roll of the war-drum, were heard, which were signals that the regent was on the move. Shortly afterwards we saw him descending the hill in a superb palanquin, attended by about twenty armed men on foot. At the end of the street he was met by the adjutant-general, quarter-master-general, and several other staff-officers; and, after a little hugging, they led him on, taking his hands in theirs in token of friendship. Thus they proceeded to the general's splendid tent, the street presenting arms, which he perfectly understood, and to which he bowed in a most majestic manner. I do not think that in the course of my service I ever beheld a more noble and venerable-looking man. He was most superbly dressed, with numberless daggers stuck in his *cumerbund*, and a sword by his side that seemed studded with diamonds and precious stones. His neck, turban, and hands were one mass of jewels. Our brave general met him at the door of his tent, when the greeting was most laughable; something like that of Doodle and Noodle, in "Tom Thumb." The manners of our visitor were those of a perfect courtier; but he was free, affable, and jocular. In two hours after the customary sprinkling of scents, the treaty of peace was ratified, and he returned towards home with pleasure in his eye. Here the wise captain ran about, delighted and delighting, saying, "Did I not tell you so? I knew it—I could not be deceived—the thing was plain. People must have been blind not to have foreseen this event."

Thus ended the fighting against the Nepaulese, this having been the second campaign in what is called the Goorkah war. It was a fortunate thing for all hands that hostilities were thus terminated, for seventy men of the 87th regiment had that morning gone to hospital with the dysentery, a complaint that was raging with great violence, from the damp situation of the valley, and the thick fogs that lodged there till nearly mid-day. Guns were ordered down, and we began to prepare for quarters. None were sorry for it, for already were our toes playing at hide-and-seek through our boots, and our wardrobes were much the worse for wear. We were given to understand, from the quarter-master-general, that the post which we took had been vacated by the enemy's troops, without orders, and that they were sent back reinforced to retake and keep it, in which attempt, if they did not succeed, their heads were to be the forfeit. This accounts for the desperate manner in which they fought and struggled to keep the post.

Having vacated the hill, and our enemies having now become our friends—for many of them had already come down into camp for the purpose of purchasing articles in our bazaars—some three or four of us made a party to visit the fort and stockades; for which purpose we started after breakfast, and reached their advanced outpost. Here we were stopped, and informed that we could not be permitted to proceed any further, without the permission of the *keeledar*, or governor of the fort; but that, if we would wait, a man should be sent to ask if we might advance. To this we consented, and, in about half an hour after, the man who had been sent on this errand came back, with two other men, and said the *keeledar* had been pleased to grant us permission to go, but that we must go unarmed, leaving our swords in the last stockade. The ascent of the hill towards the fort was extremely difficult; and at every turning of the road was a strong stockade with guns; so that our necessary loss in taking these hills and posts must have been enormous, for there was scarcely any footing.

We at last reached the grand fort of Muckwanpore, if it deserved the name. It was built of stone and brick, and was very high; but a dozen shots from our twenty-four-pounders would have levelled it with the ground. Indeed, one bastion had given warning of its intending to stand no longer. The tempests that rage in these hills had shaken its foundation. The gate was strong, but its hinges were small. On our entering, a small guard at the gate presented arms, a drummer beat the grenadiers' march, and a little fifer played the tune. Both the drum and the fife were of English manufacture. A little further was the tent we had seen in the stockade—at least some part of it. It was riddled like a sieve with our shells, and the top of it was hanging in ribbons. Here we were introduced to the governor, who was seated on a greasy cushion, the pillows of which, though they had once been white, were now the colour of his face. He received us cordially, and shook hands with us most heartily; and he was really a very jolly old fellow, some twenty or twenty-three stone, his fat sides hanging in large flaps over his hips, which we sometimes made shake again with laughter. He paid us many compliments about our fighting and system of warfare, and wanted to know how many thousands we had had killed. When we assured him that we had not lost more than forty he laughed heartily, and said, we meant forty hundred, for they had lost more than that. We spent a pleasant hour with this fat governor, who, after we had looked round the fort, had the politeness to parade his regiment for our inspection. I never saw a finer body of men in my life. They were as well armed, and as well equipped in every respect, as our native troops. After this we returned to camp, and the following morning marched towards cantonments.

As all treaties contracted in India, between native and European powers, are ever to be held with a jealous and watchful eye (for naught but time can make them valid), it was necessary for us to take up a position to watch the proceedings of our new friends. Under the cloak of friendship, some of the most barbarous massacres have been perpetrated; and treaties have been frequently signed and sealed, and, ere the signature was dry, the enemy have commenced infringing on their contracts and sacred ties. It has even been known that, during the time occupied by the parley necessary for completing such negotiations, the enemy have been busily engaged in making preparations for striking a more effectual blow. It was but prudent, therefore, that we should keep our eye upon them. In accordance with one of the covenants of the treaty, a British resident, and the usual escort, were to remain at the capital. This escort marched, on the same day we did, to Khatmandoo. Our march was through the pass of Cheriagotte, where the mad-brained young officers wanted to force an entrance. My description of this pass, as I proceed, will prove how fatal, and contrary to the dictates of reason, would have been any such attempt.

I was on the rear-guard the morning we left the valley of Muckwanpore. The enemy—or, perhaps, I should say our friends—flocked in great numbers, to bid us farewell, or see us depart. The whole of the baggage was nearly gone, when a number of these soldiers gathered round the guard, asking all manner of questions. A most respectable-looking young man, wearing the dress of an officer, came up to me and said, "Were you not in the action on the hill of Muckwanpore?"

I told him that I had had that honour.

He replied, "So was I; and I fired three shots at you from behind a tree—are you not wounded?"

I replied, "No."

"Well," said he, "I never missed my man before in my life."

I asked him at what period of the action it was that he aimed at me.

"When you were fighting with Sobah Khissna Rhannah," replied he.

"You were not far from your man, then," said I, "for one of your shots struck the peak of my cap."

Ghoorka Soldier

At this he laughed. He afterwards complimented me on my swordsmanship, and said that few could touch the *sobah* in that exercise. He then asked to look at one of my men's muskets, and he put himself through the manual and platoon exercises, giving himself the word of command in English. I never saw motions more clean or more compactly executed. I asked him where he learned English, and the English modes of drill. He replied, "From Browne," who was a deserter from the Company's European regiment. He added, that a man of the name of Bell, a deserter from the Company's Foot Artillery, had also taught him his exercise, and Browne had instructed him in English. The former, he said, had been made colonel of artillery, and the latter schoolmaster; but they had both been discharged from the service at the commencement of the war.

At last we moved off, the young stranger shaking me heartily by the hand, and saying, "I love a brave soldier; and the white men are all brave." This young man, it appeared, was the adjutant of the corps of which Khissna Rhannah, who fell under my fortunate sabre, was colonel.

Our first march was tolerably easy, as it lay under a winding hill; and we reached nearly the top of the pass, and encamped. On the following morning we dispatched our things very early, to prevent them falling into the hands of the people, should they attempt to prove treacherous—which was not at all improbable—after we had descended the *ghauts*. When under the base of the hill, the road, which had been before wide and tolerably good, narrowed off, and we soon found ourselves sinking down between two enormous hills. The road was scarcely wide enough, in some places, to admit an elephant, with his load, to pass. On each side of this terrific hill were huge rocks and stones piled up for our destruction. Some, of enormous size, the least touch would have precipitated upon our heads, and they seemed to have been rolled to the brink for that purpose. There were stockades upon stockades, all looking on and commanding this little and narrow excavated pathway. Had we once entered, as I have before mentioned was suggested by some rash-brained young officers, not a soul could have escaped destruction. I should think that, in the middle of this *ghaut*, the perpendicular rock on each side must have been five hundred feet high; and therefore, had there been no other weapons of destruction than the ponderous masses of rock and stone which they could have hurled upon us, our annihilation must have been inevitable, for escape was impossible.

When we reached the other side, the eye was met by stockades, fortified hills in all directions, and strong breastworks thrown across the roadway, which was here somewhat wider; though our road all along was, in fact, nothing more than the bed of a river, surrounded and commanded by numberless little fortified sugar-loaf hills. These the foe had been obliged to ascend by means of ladders. To complete the destruction these hills must have dealt upon us, they had poisoned a stream of water, either previous to our march from the ravine some ten days before, or since the treaty of peace was signed; but this was timely detected. The poisonous grass I have before alluded to, had been sunk in a kind of basin, which was constantly replenished by water that fell from the rocks behind it. This might be about twenty yards round, and two deep. On the morning of our return, an elephant, belonging to Lieutenant-Colonel Rose, of the Company's army, as also a horse belonging to that officer, had preceded the army, and even the baggage. The elephant got his fore feet in the water, of which he drank a little, but seemed not to relish it. The horse could not be induced to drink much, nor would the elephant again touch it. When urged by his keeper, such was his perverseness, that the driver descended, and, on looking at the water, he saw a yellowish colour rising to the surface, which was caused by the pressure of the elephant's feet on the grass. The keeper immediately introduced his hand, and pulled out the poisonous herb. This occurrence was without delay communicated to our gallant commander; and, never shall I forget his indignation and displeasure at this intelligence. The fact being ascertained by the medical department, and both the elephant and horse dying shortly afterwards, Sir David peremptorily called upon the Nepaul government for satisfaction for this diabolical attempt to poison his army; but they denied all knowledge of such a base transaction, protesting that the heads of the offenders should be the penalty, if they could discover the authors of such a scheme, which they affected to suppose must be the act of some individual who had sustained injury by the war. They promised that a most strict inquiry should be set on foot, and that the result should be made known to our government. Here, I believe, the business ended; at least, we heard no more of it. A guard was, after this discovery, placed on the poisoned water, to prevent any of the cattle that followed from drinking it; and the basin was afterwards filled up by our pioneers, as an effectual remedy to prevent any other travellers that might be journeying that way from becoming its victims.

    Nothing worth narrating happened during our march to our new place of encampment, or where a temporary cantonment was to be erected; save that we went to visit the still exposed bones of those poor creatures who were murdered at Summanpore and Persah. Skulls, and whole bodies, were here to be seen in all directions, and scarcely a tree that had not fifty shots in it. We dropped a tear to the memory of the poor fellows who had here fallen, and committed their fleshless bones to the earth.

Having arrived at our new place of encampment, we found that some temporary barracks had been erected there, for two regiments, the year before. The site of our new cantonment was marked out. It was on the banks of a beautiful lake, well stocked with fish and wild fowl. Here every one commenced building his hut, not knowing the moment we might be called upon to re-commence the campaign; for breach of treaties with such people was an everyday occurrence. From the long and uninterrupted friendship which has now subsisted between the two nations, we may, I think, with fairness conclude, that first impressions are the most durable; and, if in my power, I would take especial care not to run the risk of a failure at the beginning of a campaign. An effectual blow then makes the enemy shy and tame; and the complete victory gained over the Nepaulese, at Muckwanpore, beat them into principles they never knew before. They are, however, still tenacious of admitting strangers into their country, and it is with difficulty that a passport can be obtained to visit any part of their beautiful territory.

In the month of March we had built and completed our bungalows, or huts, containing two or three rooms each; but we had scarcely got housed when we received orders to proceed to Cawnpore by water—a tedious and long trip at that time of the year. I therefore, being almost tired of war's alarms, began to turn my mind towards the object of my affections, with whom I had kept up a constant correspondence during the whole campaign. I asked for permission to proceed by land to Cawnpore. This was readily granted, and I started alone on this long trip—a distance of four hundred and thirty miles.

CHAPTER 15

The Hattrass Campaign

I reached Cawnpore in twelve days, after a very harassing journey, the fatigues of which laid me on a bed of sickness; but the affectionate nursing of the fair object of my love, and the kind attentions of her excellent family, soon restored me to health, and I was married on the 4th of April, 1816.

I was received by my old regiment in the most cordial manner; and their continued marks of kindness to me and my young wife, kept pace with the liberality of their mess. No stranger was permitted to pass through the station without a liberal invitation from the 24th Light Dragoons. Soon after this, my own regiment arrived, when every hand was extended to bid me welcome; and the next eighteen months were spent by me in domestic felicity. At the expiration of that time, we were called upon again to put our limbs in marching order, on an expedition against the strong forts of Hattrass, Cummoun, and some other refractory dependencies of the Hattrass *rajah*.

The former of these forts is situate about thirty miles from Agra, and twelve from Muttra. It is a mud fort, standing in the middle of the most fertile country in Bengal, and is a place of immense strength, in consequence of its enormous ditch, eighty feet wide, by seventy and seventy-five feet deep, with but two small bridges, extremely narrow, and which the occupants of the fort could destroy in an instant.

On our arrival before this place, a negotiation was entered into with the political agent and a messenger from the fort; but still our operations went on in the most active manner. We could not expect success but by a regular and progressive siege, as, independently of the fort, there was also a walled town, which it would be necessary to take and occupy, before we could get near enough to the former to mine and breach it. For the taking of the town our first batteries were erecting during the parley, as convincing proofs that we were in earnest. This siege was under the command of Major-General Sir Dyson Marshall, K. C. B.

Mid-day was finally to determine peace or war. The embassy had been in camp all the morning, begging for time to consider of the proffered terms, or, more probably, to endeavour to meet the foe. This stratagem had often been resorted to on similar occasions, to gain the same end; and I have known instances when those creatures would swear by all their heathen gods and goddesses, that their great wish was to be reconciled, when, in reality, they were only plotting a more formidable resistance. I have often heard them swear by their most sacred Ganges, what was well known, both to us and them, to be the most palpable falsehood. I have seen these sycophants kiss the earth, and call everything dear to them to witness their asseverations, when they have been uttering the most abominable falsehoods to gain some end. I have also seen them beat their breasts and tear their hair, in indication of their love and friendship, when all the while the cankerworm was busy in their hearts. If you permit them, they will put off the evil day from week to week, and from month to month, having always something new to start. This day the *vakeel* had brought to camp the most positive assurance that his master, the *rajah*, would be in camp to sign and ratify a treaty on the proffered terms. On receiving this intelligence, our good general directed that our batteries should not open till the hour of twelve that day.

Ten o'clock arrived, but no *rajah*; eleven o'clock and half-past eleven passed away, but still no appearance of the great man from the fort. About a quarter before the awful hour, the *vakeel* was seen emerging from the political agent's tent, and mounting his rut; but his contracted brow betrayed the agitation of his mind. He set off at speed. I rode beside him as far as our grand battery, and he told me on the way that all was settled, and that the *rajah* was coming into camp. Scarcely had he uttered this lie, when the awful bell struck twelve, and our batteries opened at the same instant. In a moment the whole town was enveloped in one dense cloud of smoke. The instant the *vakeel* heard the guns, he leapt out of his carriage, and ran as fast as he could towards the fort, screaming in notes something like the angry tiger. This being the case, I took the liberty of taking the rut and horse to camp as prize property. Whether he reached the fort in safety I know not, for we never saw nor heard anything more of his fat ambassadorship; so I suppose he suffered with many hundreds of others during the siege. The moment our batteries opened, their guns also opened a heavy cannonade, evidencing the truth of what the *vakeel* had been hold-

The Fort of Hattrass

ing forth. Our siege went on progressively and systematically, keeping in view the grand point in all sieges, preservation of men's lives, and going to work with our eyes open. Our breaching-distance from the wall of the town was only about four hundred yards; and therefore, if we were inclined to take a peep at things, we were obliged to do it on the sly, for we were within half musket-shot; so near, indeed, that we were obliged to have screens for our embrasures, to protect the men when loading and laying the guns. The parts breached were the two extreme corners. When we commenced, the town was full of men; but we sent them a few shrapnells and a few rockets, which played beautifully along the tops of the houses, and up the narrow streets; and, in one hour, scarcely a man was to be seen on the ramparts; but we could hear them busily at work digging something, which we afterwards found to be holes, to hide from the shells, over which they covered themselves with old doors and pieces of plank. Some of our shells, however, found them, even in those dreary hiding-places. Many of their houses were on fire. The Congreve rocket is a most destructive instrument of death; its enormous shaking tail carries everything before it; and, when it explodes, it kills some yards round, and fires houses right and left. Our little whistling shrapnells quite discomposed the gravity of their hoary-headed priests, and drove them into the fort to seek refuge, and call in the aid of their heathen gods; but not one could be prevailed upon to interpose, even so far as to stop a single rocket or shell. Some long shots were then thrown from some of the large guns in the town, near and into camp; but these caused no other inconvenience than to put some ladies, who had come from Agra to be spectators of the scene, to the double-quick, who never thought themselves safe till in their own dear homes, some thirty miles off. One lady only remained; but she kept at a much more respectful distance than before.

A reward was given for all description of balls brought into camp, varying in amount according to size. Such is the avarice of the natives who hover about camps, that they will risk anything for money. Near the right of the line, balls used frequently to be thrown, and some of them rolled as far as the piquet. I was riding in that direction one morning when balls were flying pretty thick. A native saw one lob, and ran to stop it. In this attempt, one of his legs was so badly broken, that I believe it was afterwards amputated. If he had carried the ball to camp, he would have got about fourpence for it!

In two days the breaches began to wear a stormable appearance; and, on the third day, the storming parties were ordered to be in readiness about two o'clock in the afternoon. The day was calm, and the sky serene and cloudless. By three o'clock every soldier was at his post, ready and willing to perform the service of his country, and add new laurels to its crown. The left column was to be led by the 87th, or Prince's Own regiment, who were as merry as crickets; and the right column by the 14th regiment, a beautiful corps. About half-past three we moved off towards the town, in silence. Under cover of the village we halted, and an unaccountable delay ensued. Here we sat down and talked over the work before us. While thus engaged, the eye of an inquisitive officer was fixed on another officer of the same regiment, who had taken his epaulette from his shoulder, and his plate and feather off his cap, so that he looked for all the world like some discharged pensioner. This strange metamorphosis drew upon him the ridicule of his brother officers, and the scoffing of the soldiers. Whatever might be his motive for such an alteration in his dress, to say the least of it, it was extremely imprudent and improper; for, by such conduct, he incurred the animadversion of the soldiers of his own regiment, who would, in all probability, put the most illiberal construction on it. The officers did not fail to have their jokes and draw their conclusions from such a strange circumstance; and, when the question was put to him, why he did such a thing, his answer confirmed the ill-natured surmises that had gone abroad, his avowed object being that the enemy should not know him from a private soldier of the regiment. How far such an expedient may have deserved censure, I leave the public to judge. I merely introduce the instance to warn other young officers against doing anything that may justify the animadversions of the soldiers, or bring them under the lash and ridicule of their brother officers. Whatever might have been the feelings of this young officer—and I should be sorry to impute his conduct to anything but thoughtlessness—I can venture to assert that he never re-established his former character; in consequence of which, he some time after left the regiment. Therefore, young soldier, never be ashamed to let your foe know that you hold his majesty's commission. I would sooner cram it down their throats than have my honour or courage doubted. Be tenacious of your character, more especially in the point of courage. If you trifle with this, the sooner you cut and run the better.

The head engineer, conceiving the breaches not practicable, from his not knowing the depth and width of the ditch, had the storming postponed till the following day, with the view that an opportunity might be afforded him, under cover of the night, to obtain the necessary information. At night this officer stole down to the ditch unobserved, and, on his return, he seemed delighted beyond bounds that the storm did not take place, as the ditch was so wide and deep that an entrance was impossible. It appeared that what had been knocked off the bastion, had not actually filled up any part of the trench, but only hung to the sides of it.

On the following morning, we found that the enemy, having seen us march down the evening before, had fled when the night closed in, supposing we were going to storm in the night. On this being ascertained, a strong party was instantly dispatched to occupy the town. We found some difficulty in obtaining an entrance, as they had barricaded the two gates with stone and large bales of cotton. At last, we were obliged to scale the walls with ladders. With the exception of a few poor old people, not a living soul was to be seen in the town; but the number of the dead was considerable. Two elephants had been slain, and camels, horses, bullocks, goats, &c., lay killed in all directions. After sauntering about the town, and taking a peep on the other side, we found that the fort was quite close. The moment the enemy saw us, they commenced a heavy cannonade; and the tremendous peals of musketry which followed informed us that they had not run far. The prize agents now turned us all out, supposing, with a good deal of reason, that we were not to be trusted with gold *mohurs* and *rupees*, of which a few were found in some of the banking-houses.

On the following day, after reconnoitring the fort and the ground in its vicinity, spots were fixed upon for new breaching and shelling batteries; and, in twenty-four hours afterwards, we commenced our work of death on the fort and its obdurate inmates. Long ere the hour of the sun's decline, it grew as dark as midnight. About ten o'clock, the terrific shelling commenced, every whistling shell bearing on its lighted wings messengers of death and desolation. I never saw these implements of destruction so accurately thrown—some of them scarcely five inches above the walls of the fort. In five minutes the screams of the women in the fort were dreadful. In a place so confined, where numberless houses were crowded together, every shell must have found its way to some poor wretch's dwelling, and, perhaps, torn from mothers' bosoms their clinging babes. No person can estimate the dreadful carnage committed by shells, but those whose fate it has been to witness the effects of these messengers of death. On this occasion our shells were very numerous, and of enormous size, many of them thirteen and a half inches in calibre. The system of shelling had been so improved in the twelve years which had elapsed since the siege of Bhurtpore, that, instead of about one shell in five minutes from a single battery, it was by no means extraordinary to see twenty in one minute, from the numerous batteries which were brought to bear upon this place. It was, at times, truly awful to see ten of these soaring in the air together, seemingly riding on the midnight breeze, and disturbing the slumbering clouds on their pillows of rest—all transporting to a destined spot the implements of havoc and desolation contained within their iron sides. The moon hid herself, in seeming pensiveness, behind a dense black cloud, as though reluctant to look on such a scene; and the feathered tribe, that were wont, in those warm nights of summer, to melodize the breeze, retired far into the distant woods, there to tune their notes of sorrow. Mortal language cannot array such a scene in its garb of blackest woe. Some carcasses were also thrown. These, when in the air, are not unlike a fiery man soaring above. They are sent to burn houses, or blow up magazines. Far and wide they stretch forth their claws of death; and well might the poor natives call them devils of the night, or fiends of the clouds. To complete this dreadful scene, the roaring Congreves ran along the bastion's top, breaking legs and arms with their shaking tails. Nothing could be more grand to the eye, or more affecting to the sympathizing heart, than this horrid spectacle. Still, the superstitious foe were stimulated by some hoary priest with hopes of victory, thus imbruing their hands in the blood of their children, their parents, and their friends. Our shells found their way to their very cells, tearing babes from their mothers' bosoms, and dealing death and destruction around. Oh! what must be the anguish of a fond mother, to see nothing but the head of her fondling hanging to her bosom! I will relate one melancholy case of this kind, out of numbers that came within my observation, and actually happened at this place.

A female was lying on a bed of green silk; under her head was a pillow of the same material; her right arm had, no doubt, cradled her babe; and her left was extended as though for the purpose of keeping her child close to her. A large shell had perforated the tiled roof, and, having made its way through three floors, had gone through the foot of the bed, and penetrated some depth into the fourth floor. A piece of this shell had gone through the woman's forehead, carrying away a great part of the head; so that her death, according to the opinion of a medical man who saw her, must have been instantaneous. The lower part of the child's body, from the hips downward, was entirely gone; but, strange to say, its mother's nipple still hung in the left corner of its mouth, and its little right hand still held by its mother's clothes, which probably it had grasped at the first noise of the shell. We understood that this woman was the wife of a most respectable officer in the fort, who had also met his death some hours before her, and was, therefore, in pity spared the afflicting sight. Such, reader, are the scenes of war! Such are the sights which soldiers, in the course of service, are called upon to witness! The poor woman and her babe were committed to the grave—probably the first of her generation that ever returned to the earth as her last home; for she was a Hindoo woman.

The garrison of this fort had been solicited, in the warmest manner, to send their families to their homes, with a promise that they should be guarded to any part of the country, and their property guaranteed to them. To these proposals, dictated by the feelings of humanity, which our good general possessed in a most eminent degree, we received nothing but contemptuous answers. Be the blood of their slaughtered relatives, therefore, on their shoulders, not on ours! Wherever the troops of the Company have been employed, humanity has always marked their steps; yet I have only known one instance in my long service, in which the natives consented to avail themselves of the kind offer made to them, that their families should be protected. I shall have the pleasure of mentioning this in its proper place.

It was currently reported, and there seemed to be some foundation for such a report, that there were immense treasures in the fort. This was a more shining prospect than we had contemplated. Nothing could be more congenial to our minds than the chance of touching the coin. These anticipations gladdened our very hearts, and kept us watchful and vigilant. To say the truth, I do not know any class of people more deserving of money, or who can spend it in a more gentlemanlike manner, than soldiers. From our late gaieties at Cawnpore, and having danced my marriage rounds through the whole station, my purse, at this critical juncture, was in deep decline. It had undergone a most severe draining, and its contents had dwindled away to a single silver piece. My account with the paymaster had also made an oblique evolution, and settled on the wrong side, leaving me no credit by the position it had taken. Since this untoward account had taken that whim into its head, the paymaster was never at home. A confounded bore this—always to find people out, whom you particularly want to see, and have a little sterling confab with. Thus stood the case, or rather, thus stood my purse, yawning for lack of coin; and this was the case with many others. Was it a wonder, then, that we so readily gave credit to the reports which were in circulation touching the probability of our reaping a golden harvest by this siege?

With these prospects in view, the siege went on with all possible energy. Having viewed the gaping ditch, and assured ourselves of the impossibility of both descent and ascent, we had pushed our mining operations within thirty yards of the top of the glacis, and began to descend into the bowels of the earth. I was this day on a working-party, with one hundred men, and had just arrived in the tool-yard, about three hundred yards from the left of the trenches, when I was thrown flat on my face by some violent shock of the earth. Before the general shock, the earth seemed in dreadful convulsions. The walls surrounding the tool-yard were propelled forward from the fort, and fell to the ground. Stones, bricks, pieces of wood, and, nearer the fort, bodies and limbs, were to be seen soaring in the air in all directions. For the moment, consternation and dismay were depicted on every face. When I arose, I felt much alarmed; the earth seemed still to move under me; and at first I thought something had happened to me alone; but, on looking around, I found my men, some in the attitude of prayer, and others lying down, hiding their faces with fear. Having recovered my senses, I looked towards the fort, and saw it enveloped in one dense cloud of smoke or dust, and, now and then, streaks of fire issuing from its battlements. In the midst of this momentary alarm, there was an indistinct buzzing that the grand magazine of the enemy had been blown up. This report having reached my ears, I ran, or rather rolled, along the trenches, and was informed that their grand magazine had really been blown up by one of our shells. Again looking towards the tomb of destruction, what a sight met the eye! The smoke which arose from the ruins seemed to be a solid and substantial structure, gradually and majestically ascending to the skies, bearing on its top variegated volumes of vapour, that seemed to ride upon its summit. From this ascending mountain were ever and anon vomited forth sheets of vivid fire; and glittering sand fell in showers around the spot. Through this dense, but really unsubstantial mass, was to be seen the setting sun, spreading his luminous beams through the gigantic phenomenon; and the beauty of the sight was beyond human fancy to imagine. This tremendous volume of smoke seemed almost to rise perpendicularly, verging off a little with the wind, which scarcely breathed. When it had ascended so that the sun was visible under it, the mass above changed colour, and you might trace on it the most brilliant rays of the rainbow. This continued ascending in various forms, until, at last, it was lost in distance: after which, every eye was directed towards the destruction below; and the sight was frightful indeed. Heads, bodies, legs, arms, hands, spears, guns, muskets, planks, and colours, lay indiscriminately among the pile of ruin. Four thousand *maunds*, or three hundred and twenty thousand pounds of gunpowder, an accumulation of years, were contained in this magazine. This was buried in stone magazines, some hundreds of feet under the earth; and it was supposed that the major part of the garrison had sought refuge in those excavated vaults, from the destruction of our shells, and were there entombed in this pile of ruin and desolation. The cries of men, women, and children, and the groans of wounded horses, could be distinctly heard, and drew from every eye the tear of pity. Our guns had ceased firing, no one knew why. There were no shoutings of exultation; but, on the contrary, loud were the expressions of commiseration and sorrow. Amidst the convulsion, it was a most extraordinary fact, that the new and scarcely finished temple of the inmates of the fort still reared its superstitious head, and, on the very margin of their once boasted and inexhaustible mine of powder and ball, stood uninjured amidst the general wreck, divested only of its scaffolding. This coincidence, which they, no doubt, attributed to supernatural agency, still fed their deluded hopes, and they would not bend the stubborn knee and ask for mercy, but still persisted in their resistance, led on by some hoary-headed priest, who would not tear himself away from his ill-gotten stores. The night closed in as cold as the hearts of these obdurate creatures; the sky was serene and clear; and the moon rose in her most effulgent brightness.

The moon had now risen high above the tops of Rumnah (a place where they keep preserved game), when our guns re-opened, and more messengers of destruction were sent to complete the work of death. Every hand employed against the fort would willingly have carried these poor creatures the cup of peace and the balm of comfort, rather than send them more woe; but, notwithstanding these sympathetic feelings, there is a duty we owe ourselves and our country. We were in honour bound to push the siege; but this was our duty, not our inclination: nor is it true that soldiers, inured to scenes of war, do not possess the nicer feelings of the heart. The shelling again roared through their narrow streets, and tore up their little dwellings by the roots, each hurling additional victims into the gaping pile. About the hour of midnight, there seemed a bustle and clashing of arms amongst the people in the fort, and I began to think that they intended to give us leg; so I kept a good look-out. I crept close to the edge of the ditch, and listened. I could hear voices, but not distinctly what they said. I was observed from the fort, and nearly paid dear for my peeping. Several shots were fired, one of which struck close to my head. I moved my quarters to a more safe place; and, from the neighing of horses, it was pretty evident to me that they were on the bit: but, as I was no reservoir of news, I took good care to keep my opinion to myself, until the thing became more certain. Five minutes after, I saw some of them outside of the fort, on horseback, waiting to assemble in force, before they attempted to break through our mounted cavalry, which formed a chain of sentinels round this side. It was imagined impossible that they could make their escape. I communicated what I had seen to the commanding officer of the protecting party, who had a hundred native men under his command, which would, in all probability, have been sufficient to have stopped them; for, no doubt, they did not intend to go empty-handed away, but laden with gold *mohurs*. When I first communicated this intelligence to the officer on duty, he politely said it was only fancy—they were no flinchers. I told him that I could see them coming out; but he replied, sarcastically, "Then why don't you go and stop them? I will tell you what, Shipp—you are never easy unless your head is in the cannon's mouth."

At the first part of this reproof I got terribly nettled, and warmly replied, "Had I your means, Captain Brewer (alluding to the men under his command), I would stop them; but, as my men have only their pickaxes and shovels, it would be an act of pure madness to attempt such a thing; though it is by no means clear to me that I could not even stay their flight with these poor means." At this he instantly flew into a rage, and said, "Pray, Sir, what do you mean to insinuate by what you have this moment given utterance to?"

"My dear Brewer," said I, "you know I am as poor as the inside of a sentry-box, and it is really a pity to see these fellows under our very noses, walking off with the coin." He smilingly replied, "That's true; and I will prevent it if possible." So on we marched at double-quick; and, all I could do and say, I could not prevent my men, armed, as they were, with pickaxes and shovels, from following me. I threatened to cut the first man down who dared attempt to leave his post; but no sooner was I gone than my men were close at my heels; and one fellow came running up to me, and said, pointing to a small village, close by the entrance of the bridge, "By the powers, your honour, but there is a whole generation of cavalry, all mounted on horses. See, your honour, some of them that are halted are coming this way."

I replied, "What the devil has brought you here?"

"Does your honour think I would lave you in this blusteration?" said Paddy.

On getting pretty close to these "cavalry on horseback," my attention was drawn off from the soldier, who, on turning round, I found was close at my elbow, with a pickaxe on his shoulder. Here the enemy, observing us, rode off to the left at full speed. One I endeavoured to stop, and he rode at me. I gathered myself up in an attitude of defence, resolved, if possible, to dismount him; but, unfortunately, his horse's foot struck the inside of my thigh, and down I went, and he had the politeness to fire his matchlock at me, but it did not touch me. He rode on, and I jumped up, and again recovered my station at the head of the party. We now arrived at the end of the bridge, where there was a kind of half-moon battery or breastwork—at least there had been, but now nothing but the parapet and embrasures remained. Behind these my men, many of whom had followed me, took refuge, till we had again driven the enemy into the fort. We pushed on, and on the bridge the struggle was dreadful. The enemy wanted to come out, and we wanted to go in. They would not permit us to go in; and we, equally unaccommodating, would not let them out. This was the dispute; and, after a good deal of fighting, we not only stopped their intended journey, but put an end to many of their lives. They, for a time, disputed every inch of ground with us; but Jack Sepoy was not to be done; and we, after a hard struggle, gained possession not only of the bridge, but of the inner gate. Here they had the advantage for a time, for they had fastened the inner gate, which, however, yielded to force. At this moment I received a tremendous blow from a large piece of wood that was thrown from the ramparts, and hit me on the head; I fell to the ground, stunned for a moment, but soon got up again. When I was knocked down by the log of wood, a sergeant hallooed out, "By the powers, but he is kilt at last outright!"

"Not quite, sergeant," said I; "but it was a devil of a blow."

"Och! never mind that, your honour," said the sergeant, "it's all in the army."

"No, sergeant," I replied, "it is all on my head." A few seconds after this, the same sergeant received a similar salute, which made him hug the ground, when a soldier who was near him sang out, "Are you kilt, sergeant, dear?"

"Upon my conscience," groaned the sergeant, "I don't know; but I feel mighty queer, so I do."

I had not been on my legs again above a second, and had scarcely time to scratch my head, when there was a dreadful explosion of powder. The shock caused by this explosion nearly threw me down again. On looking behind, I found it necessary to give some orders, and I pointed to the object of my instructions. Some ill-natured fellow from the ramparts thought I was pointing the finger of derision at him, so he let fly his matchlock at me, and shot me through the very finger I was pointing with—the forefinger of the left hand. The shot passed through the finger, and, carrying away nearly the whole of the bone of the two first joints, grazed the palm of my hand, and passed through the lapel of my coat. At last the inner gate yielded to force, and we rushed into the body of the fort. On our first entrance, we could see women and children flying across the narrow streets; some mothers bearing their offspring in their bleeding arms; some dropping them in their flight; and others meeting death from the balls of our men, who were firing at random. Many poor childless mothers threw themselves on the points of our men's bayonets, and some begged for mercy. Putrid bodies, both of men and beasts, lay about in all directions—some of them three or four deep; and the smell was absolutely suffocating. The fighting soon ceased; and, though many attempted to escape by another bridge, they were taken prisoners.

The fort being now completely in our possession, as soon as the prisoners had been secured, I examined my wound. An hour having elapsed since I received it, my whole arm had begun to ache most dreadfully. Finding, therefore, that I could do no further good to the service, I was resolved I would do no harm to myself, so I bent my way towards camp, to get my wound dressed. To be candid, I may as well confess that I did not walk home, but rode one of the finest Persian horses I ever beheld. I found him loose, running about the fort. I caught him, and rode him with a piece of rope in his mouth. The good-natured prize-agents did not request me to give him up; nor, perhaps, were they aware that I had such an animal in my possession. Be that as it may, however, I sold him at Lucknow, to the king of Oude, for two thousand *rupees*—about two hundred pounds sterling. Having reported the capture of the fort to the major-general, who was, of course, much pleased with the information, and immediately made his arrangements accordingly, I got my wound dressed. My good-natured doctor was pleased to announce to me, that if I escaped with the loss of my finger, I might consider myself fortunate; but he feared that the dreadful manner in which the finger had been torn, would render amputation of the hand necessary. The wound was evidently from an iron and rugged ball. Iron ball-wounds immediately turn a rusty, or more of a yellow colour, and are bad healing wounds. In the morning my wound was again dressed by another medical friend; and it was so much better in the forenoon of the following day, that I got into my palanquin and rode down to the fort. I must beg to be excused from entering into a minute narration of the scene inside. Let it suffice, that it far exceeded anything that man could write, were he to sit down to draw a picture of the most abject misery and woe. The most depraved wretch could not have looked on the work of death which presented itself to our eyes, without being melted into sorrow. I soon turned from such a sight, and stood towards home.

Near a small village, a beautiful young woman, about sixteen years of age, had been seen, and ultimately seized. Her husband, to whom she had only been wedded about three months, was one of those who were entombed when the magazine blew up. From that period nothing could soothe her or appease her grief; no power could restrain her; and at last she escaped into the adjoining wood, or *runnah*. When I saw her, she was running wildly; but, at times, she would pause, hold up her finger, and tell you to listen; when she would exclaim, with the most heart-rending shriek, "That was him! It was he that did speak! Yet, now he is gone." Then the poor bewildered maniac would tear her sloe-black hair, which was hanging in ringlets down her back and bosom, and, at length, sink exhausted to the ground. She was taken to camp, and committed to the care of some of her relations, who had been taken prisoners.

CHAPTER 16

Recovering From Wounds

Amongst the prisoners captured in the fort of Hattrass, search was made by us for the *keeledar*, and his friend the negotiator, who had been so many times in camp; but neither of these gentlemen could be found; and we naturally concluded they must have escaped on the evening of the storm; for, strange to say, a great body of cavalry had cut their way through some of our cavalry piquets. The Europeans saddled the native corps of Hindostanee horse with this; and they in return threw the blame on the European cavalry. Some part of this flying enemy, however, passed the piquet of the 8th Light Dragoons, and several of the brave fellows of that regiment were wounded in endeavouring to stop them; but I have no doubt that the main body passed between the right of the 8th Dragoons and the left of the corps of Captain Badley's horse, between which flanks there was a wide space and a high-road. This road was watched by a regiment of native infantry. From the beautiful horses left in the fort, and the immense number of suits of chain armour we found strewed about the stables of the cavalry, the whole of the enemy's horse must have been in mail; so that our cavalry could have made but little impression, even if they had fallen in with them. By this escape one of our grand objects was defeated, by the loss of the person of the rebel governor, who was wanted to answer his rebellion to an offended government. How it was possible that a single individual could have escaped such a bombardment, was to us a mystery; for large houses were literally torn up by the roots. They had thrown a great number of their dead into a well, and many lay in the ditch, a melancholy and revolting sight, for the sun had swollen them to an enormous size.

It seems that, the moment any of their children were killed in houses remote from the well, they were thrown into the street. I counted five limbless babes in one street.

The day I left camp the maniac widow died; and it is with infinite pleasure I now bid farewell, for a time, to such distressing scenes.

Deputies from the other forts and dependencies of this *rajah* had witnessed the siege *incog.*, and were no doubt in camp when the explosion took place. Not being inclined to risk the same aerial ascent, or to be entombed, as many hundreds of the poor creatures in Hattrass had been, they readily surrendered to the wishes of the government. What had become of Diaram—for that was the *rajah's* name—we could not discover; but he was a dangerous man loose in a country like India, and might do much mischief if he joined the Pindarees, who were then in full force prowling about the country, not immediately in our provinces, but lingering on the borders. After some search, this *rajah* was found with Nawab Ameer-Khan, an independent chief; and, no sooner had the Company discovered the place of his residence, than, instead of punishing the rebel as he deserved, they munificently offered him a pension for himself and family, if he would reside in our provinces. With these terms the veteran *rajah* readily complied, and he is now residing in affluence, peace, and happiness, under the Company's banner of protection and shield of faith. I have heard from those who have since seen him, that his loss in lives at Hattrass was upwards of fifteen hundred in the fort, besides those in the town. Two of his nephews were amongst the dead; and he himself encouraged his men in person during the whole of the siege, and was scarcely ever from the ramparts.

My wound at this time assumed a dangerous appearance. It had been much irritated by the extraction of several pieces of shattered bone; and, as the weather at this period grew intensely hot, my doctor advised me not to travel with the regiment, as he apprehended that the extreme heat, and the constant shaking of the palanquin, might bring on inflammation. I therefore the next afternoon left my corps for Cawnpore, some hundred miles, by *dawk*,[1] and arrived there about the same time on the afternoon of the following day. From having been more than four-and-twenty hours without proper dressing, the whole of my arm, and indeed all my left side, became much inflamed, and were extremely painful; but the fond attentions of an affectionate wife, and the kindness of her good family, soon made me forget my pains and aches.

---

1. Travelling by *dawk* is a very speedy mode of conveyance, well known in India. The traveller is carried in a palanquin by eight bearers, who are relieved every ten miles; and by this arrangement a hundred miles are so certainly performed in twenty-four hours, that from Cawnpore to Calcutta, a distance of eight hundred miles, is reckoned an eight days' journey.

I had such a home as few were blessed with; and, in the bosom of my family, I forgot the toils of terrific war. By good nursing and good medical advice, my wound began to mend apace; but there were still pieces of bone protruding through the wound, which, however, were in time extracted by the hand of skill.

The moment I got my hand dressed on the night I was wounded, I took the precaution of sitting down to communicate the true particulars of the affair to my family by letter, knowing well what erroneous reports are often sent to the wives of soldiers, and communicated in the most blunt and abrupt manner.

In a few days the regiment arrived in cantonments; and in a month or six weeks I was again on parade with my company, little the worse, except that I had an ugly and troublesome finger, which was always in the way. I have since turned it to some use as a true register of the weather; but, beyond this, I do not think I could even now make it so far useful as efficiently to pull a man's nose with it.

I forgot to mention that, when I went down to visit the fort on the morning after its fall, the prize-agents were busy on the look-out for prize property, and to keep our lads from picking and stealing; but, had there been a thousand of them, all with the eyes of lynxes, this would have been impossible. I heard that a private of the Company's Foot Artillery passed the very noses of the prize-agents, with five hundred gold *mohurs* (sterling £1,000) in his hat or cap. Several of the men, when the troops got beyond the power of the prize-committee, boasted of their plunder; and, indeed, it is not much to be wondered at that men should make so free as to help themselves, when the dreadful metamorphosis that prize-money always goes through before it reaches the pockets of the captors, and the length of time before it is paid, are considered. All prize property is liable to many diseases and changes, incidental perhaps to the climate of India. When first taken, it shines in the full vigour of habit—is of good solid substance—of solidity of body—current, pure and clear; but in bulk rather protuberant and gross, and therefore, perhaps, somewhat inclined to be dropsical. Change of situation is in general resorted to; but the disease has taken fatal root, and nothing can eradicate the distemper but reduction of the system. Having been severely drained, and much inflammatory matter having been expressed, symptoms of decline but too often follow, and the poor sufferer is left but a shadow, if it escape total extinction. In this manner the solid substance extracted from the fort of Hattrass dwindled away, leaving, however, a residue of some £20,000, of which I pocketed eighty-six *rupees*; but as I had sold my share for

Travelling on the Ganges

two hundred, I may be said to have come off tolerably well. We afterwards learned, from undoubted authority, that immense treasures had been conveyed from Hattrass. The *rajah*, aware that he had fallen under the displeasure of the government, had the precaution to send his principal treasures away, as also the greater part of his family. This treasure passed through the city of Agra, the *rajah* having solicited the civil authorities to permit the female part of his family to pass through that district to some distant festival. As the *rajah* was an ally, this request could not be refused; and, accordingly, from twenty to twenty-four ruts, containing the treasures of that potentate, as well as his family, passed through Agra, to a place of safety.

The station now began to be gay, and nothing but parties, dinners, balls, suppers, &c., were the order of the day. This routine of gaiety and festivity was kept up for a considerable time, until the more active minds began to tire of it. In addition to this, our purses began to exhibit symptoms of an attack of their old complaints. Mine, in particular, had had such a regular and confirmed shaking-fit, that the disease threatened to be vital, unless some immediate remedy was applied.

The most noble the Marquis of Hastings was on his way up the river to this station. The object of his voyage up the country was quite secret. Strange were the surmises, and many of them as ridiculous as they were strange. Some said Scindia was to be attacked—others, Bhurtpore. His lordship was very particular and minute in the inspection of the troops of the upper provinces. The 87th regiment were in excellent order for service, and I longed to see them as a body again in the field. The noble marquis was as hospitable as majestic: dinners and drawing-rooms were now all the go at Cawnpore, and quite astonished the natives. His lordship's manners were truly winning and devoid of pride. At his parties he generally selected the greatest strangers to sit next him at dinner, and was to all extremely affable and condescending. Thus passed the time till the August following, when his lordship's grand scheme for the annihilation of the Pindarees was published, and set us all on the stir. Every one was as busy as trunk-makers, preparing. On every face was the smile of joy, except on those of affectionate wives, whose anxieties foreboded numberless ills that were never realized, and sorrows that never came. Farewell dinners passed in all directions; and, to wind up the farewell to each other, a station amateur play concluded the festivities. I played Lord Duberley in the "Heir-at-Law," and Lord Minikin in "Bon Ton." His lordship seemed highly amused with these performances, and was pleased to pass some eulogiums on my Lord Duberley. When the play had concluded, a gentleman came into the dressing-room, and addressed me thus: "Shipp, if you act your part as baggage-master, as you have that of Lord Duberley, you will do well."

"Baggage-master!" I replied, "I don't understand you."

"Why," said he, "you are appointed baggage-master to the left division of the grand army."

"My dear Sir," said I, "you must be mistaken; for I have not heard a syllable of the matter." He replied, "You may depend upon it as a fact; and, to be candid with you, I went to Lord Hastings and asked him for the appointment, when he himself told me you were already appointed, at the especial request and wish of Major-General Marshall, in consideration of your conduct at Hattrass, and of your being the only officer wounded during that siege."

Had I known this good news before, I would have thrown all the life and soul of a baggage-master into the character of Lord Duberley. As it was, no intelligence could be more welcome to me. On the following morning I wrote to the brigade-major to know if the information was true. He replied by note that it was, and apologized for having, through multiplicity of business, forgotten to mention to me that I must join the left division of the grand army forthwith. They had left Cawnpore two days before. Being now sure of this good news, I communicated it to my wife, and fixed the following day for my departure. I then waited on the noble marquis, to thank him for my preferment. His lordship received me with great kindness.

"Mr. Shipp," said he, "you have no occasion to thank me, but your own merit, and the kindness of Major-General Marshall, who requested the appointment of me as a favour conferred on him." His lordship concluded, "I will not ask you to dine to-day, as you would in all probability prefer spending the short time you have to spare with your family."

I expressed my grateful sense of his lordship's kindness, and returned home and spent the day with her whom I loved best on earth. In the evening I took leave of my brother officers, and on the following morning, ere the cock crew, I had taken an early breakfast, and by the time the sun left his slumbering couch I was some miles on my road, to join the left division of the grand army.

There is a kind of pensiveness by which the human mind is assailed on separating, though for a short time only, from pleasant acquaintances; but, when we part from objects bound to us by the dearest ties of love or consanguinity, an indescribable weight oppresses the heart. I felt this in parting from the most affectionate of women, to enter on a new series of wars, perhaps never to behold her again. These thoughts will intrude, in spite of all one's efforts to repress them, where the heart feels assured of reciprocal love. If I do not deceive myself, or my recollection fail me not, I was weak enough to weep on this occasion; for who could see the wife of his bosom writhing with anguish and clinging round his neck, whispering sweet words of love and constancy, and refrain from tears? She had two little sisters, too, who hung about my knees, crying, "Dear brother, do not go; see how sister cries. Pray do not go; sister will be ill." I tore myself from the endearing embraces which restrained me, and rushed out of the house.

CHAPTER 17

The Pindarees

The whole combined powers of the three Presidencies of India were now in motion, to effect the dispersion or annihilation of the Pindarees, a set of despotic marauders and savage barbarians, who were prowling about the country in immense hordes. Their numbers might be estimated at two hundred thousand, all horsemen, the remains of the old Mahratta sect of warriors, who had been driven from their homes by the civil wars of the several native powers of Hindostan. These marauders levied their exactions from the poor peasantry of the more remote districts of Hindostan, whom they robbed and plundered year after year; and murder is a common incident of the day. The horses on which they ride, and also their equipments, whether stolen or not, are the rider's own property, and respected by the rest as such. The craftiest and most daring among them are the greatest men, and call themselves, according to their several degrees of superiority, names of high office, such as those of our native officers of cavalry. Their weapons generally consist of a long spear, a sabre, a shield, and a matchlock; but many of them have pistols also, and some few I have seen with huge blunderbusses. Their families generally accompany them, and they are mounted on the best and fleetest horses. Should any of their women die or run away, they can easily be replaced at the next village. If any resistance is made, either on the part of the female herself, or of her father, mother, or husband, coercive means are unhesitatingly resorted to, and the poor creature is carried off in the same manner as any other commodity of which they may stand in need. As soon as they have drained one town or village, they take up their quarters in another, living entirely upon rapine and plunder.

In this manner these marauders had long prowled about uncontrolled, laying whole districts waste, and bringing with them, wherever they went, desolation and ruin. These desperadoes, who set the laws of the land at defiance, and the laws of humanity at naught, the Marquis of Hastings was now determined to destroy; for which purpose, every soldier that could be spared was now in the field, the noble marquis commanding in person the centre division of the army, and superintending and directing the whole plan of the war.

In four days I reached the division, then lying under the fort of Callenger, and reported myself to Major-General Marshall, commanding the division, with whom I breakfasted. His extremely kind manner of receiving me was truly flattering. I cannot say that I was very bashful, but I always endeavoured to be respectful to my superiors. I took the earliest opportunity of expressing my acknowledgments for his kind recommendation of me to his excellency the commander-in-chief. The general replied, "Shipp, you deserve what you have been appointed to. I have not forgotten your gallantry at Hattrass, although I was so extremely ill before that place; but I must confess that plaguey gout almost made me overlook your merit. I heartily wish you joy. There will be a knife and fork always laid at my table for you. Make my board your home." Thus saying, he shook me cordially by the hand.

I had now been told in person, both by the Marquis of Hastings and by the general in command of the division of the army in which I was now to act, that I had hitherto performed my duty like a brave and loyal soldier. These attestations to my military character and conduct caused my heart to glow with pride and satisfaction; and, indeed, nothing can be more gratifying to the feelings of a soldier than the consciousness that the approbation with which his superiors are pleased to regard him has been really deserved by him, on account of his ardent attachment to his profession, and his faithful performance of its perilous duties. It was with heartfelt pleasure that I heard I had earned the good opinion of men of high rank and command; and I felt highly gratified in the contemplation that, when retired from scenes of war, I could add to the enjoyments of the domestic circle the comfort of being able to look on my former life with satisfaction, and of fighting my battles over again and again with delight. Glory had been my motto; laurels were my crown!

I then paid my respects to Brigadier-General Watson, C. B., colonel of his majesty's 14th regiment, second in command of this division, whose cordiality and hospitality, for nearly a year that I was a constant guest at his table, I can never forget. After wishing me joy of my appointment, he said, "Shipp, as you are the only king's officer in this camp besides myself and staff, I hope you will take a seat at my table during the campaign." This hospitality I could not accept, the commanding officer having previously given me the same invitation; but the brigadier-general would take no excuse, but said he would settle that with General Marshall. I lived with him till the month of May following, in a most friendly manner, faring at his board in a very sumptuous style. In his private character, General Watson was generous, kind, and affable, and ever ready to do a good act; and in his public capacity a brave, active, and zealous officer, who seldom contented himself with directing things to be done, but actually saw them executed. From the extreme indisposition of the major-general, he undertook the more active parts of the several storms and sieges in which the left division was engaged, as the continuation of my narrative will show.

On the following day I visited the strong hill fort of Callenger. It is situated on an immense hill, on the ascent of which the greater part of the town stands. At the extremity of this ascent, the rocks are almost perpendicular. In some places they are fifty and sixty feet high. On these are built prodigious bastions and stone walls, with embrasures and loop-holes, so that any approach by assault or escalade was impossible. On its summit is a beautiful tank of clear water, nourished by a crystal spring. There are also fields, gardens, and woods, and two or three temples or mosques. The view from this elevation embraced an expanse of some miles of country. In its front, or more prominent part, lay the lowlands of the station of Banda, on the most beautiful and clear stream in Hindostan, the river Cane. This beautiful stream empties itself into the Jumna, about sixteen or twenty miles from this station. Between us and Banda stood some enormous hills; and temples were built on their very pinnacles, which are reached by winding steps, cut out of the rock by manual labour. These buildings, viewed from the base of the hills, look like little white spots in the sky.

When the sun arose on the following morning, I was invited to go up and witness the splendour of the scene; and I had no cause to regret such an invitation. The morning clouds seemed to slumber on the tops of those barren hills; but the rising sun's glittering beams roused them from their lethargy, and drove them from their thrones of night. Even at mid-day, I have seen the buildings on these hills entombed in the murky clouds, and their inmates, when visible, seemed beings of another world. They were Brahmin mendicants, who descended in the morning, and solicited alms all day in the name of Alla, re-ascending at eve to their aerial abodes, there to mumble forth their witchcrafts, and to contaminate the salubrious breeze of night with their invocations to blocks and stones. The breeze in these valleys is pure, renovating, and salubrious. Pea-fowls are seen in great abundance on these hills. They are both fed and worshipped by the mendicant priests, who are much annoyed if you disturb or shoot them, which, notwithstanding that, Europeans take the liberty of doing, wherever they can find them. These birds are, while young, as delicious as a young turkey. In former days, even during my time in India, shooting peacocks was strictly prohibited by the government, as interfering with the religious rites of the natives; but those orders or prohibitions have been long since rescinded, and they are now considered fair game. They are found in almost all the districts of Hindostan. Their plumage is splendid and beautiful, and, when parading before the sons of idolatry, who worship them, they seem as proud of their tails as the priests themselves do of their pretended and presumptuous knowledge of futurity.

By their ridiculous predictions of futurity these wretches live, and impose on the deluded villagers, whom they buoy up with the most felicitous prospects to come, feeding their fancies with the hope of future aggrandizement and wealth. Such is the confidence of the uninformed villagers in these promises of future bliss, that they will part with their all to insure a favourable prediction; but, when the auspicious and long-watched-for period arrives at which their hopes are to be realized, then they see how they have been deceived and robbed. But the miscreant priest has always a loophole to creep out at, either by asserting that his dupes have not dedicated a sufficient portion of their property to the priesthood; that it is necessary for them to do penance so many days; or give so much money, so much corn, and so many pieces of cloth to the priesthood, to enable them to invoke their gods for the promised mercies. This is frequently complied with, and the delusion goes on from one imposition and infatuation to another.

This is the description of the people inhabiting those beautiful mountains, on which the eye could dwell, and always find something new to feast on. This very fort of Callenger had, but a short time before, been stained with the purple stream flowing from Christian bosoms. It was in the storming of this fort, that his majesty's 53rd regiment of Foot suffered so severely before they succeeded in planting Old England's banner on its proud top. On the summit of the edifice is a monument, which was erected to the memory of the brave fellows who fell in the assault of this place.

We remained here three or four days, visiting this fort; and the oftener we went up, the more we were astonished how it was possible our troops could have got in on the occasion alluded to. To us who merely journeyed for amusement up its stupendous sides, the ascent was most difficult, and by the time we had gained its summit we were exhausted. That a fort like that of Callenger, often attempted by legions of native armies, should have been taken as it was, was matter of amazement to all who beheld it. It had once, we understood, been taken by stratagem in the following manner. A native *rajah*, who was going to war, solicited the governor's permission to lodge his treasures and family there as a place of security during the war. The governor, no doubt actuated by the hope of the ultimate possession of the treasures, readily granted the required asylum, for which purpose a hundred *doolies*, or covered *palanquins*, were to be sent up on the following morning. The infatuated and blinded governor, his soul burning with the prospect of gain, slumbered on his couch of supposed safety. Each of these *palanquins* was to be permitted to carry one female belonging to the *rajah*'s family; but, instead, each in reality contained a soldier dressed in the habiliments of the female sex, and veiled to hide his huge moustaches. To each of those *doolies* were eight bearers; in the *palanquins* were their arms, hidden from view. Those hundred *doolies* went up without the slightest suspicion, and they were ranged around the governor's house. The sequel may be readily guessed: no sooner were the supposed bearers relieved of their loads than they flew to arms, and thus got possession of the fort of Callenger.

The army being now formed and complete, with every requisite for a long campaign, I put the implements of my office in lashing order. My post of baggage-master being a situation which is, I believe, peculiar to India, it may not be improper to state its duties, &c. He is a staff-officer, and, when not employed in his particular department, is attached to the suite of the commander of the division, as much as the commissary-general, quartermaster-general, or any other staff-officer of the division. On the line of march, he is held entirely responsible that neither men nor baggage precede the column of march, and that they are on their proper flank, which is regulated by the general orders of the day. If the reader recollect what I before stated, that he may safely calculate ten followers in a Bengal army to every fighting man, and when he is informed that, according to calculations made in our camp, including the several native contingents we had with us, our followers were not less in number than eighty thousand, men, women, and children, some thirty thousand of whom followed the army for what they could pick up, by fair means or otherwise, my situation cannot be supposed to have been a sinecure. It was truly one of great labour and activity. I had twenty men belonging to a corps of local horse. These men were provided with long whips, and placed at my disposal. To attempt to talk the numberless camp-followers into obedience was quite out of the question; and, therefore, these whips were for the purpose of lashing them into something like discipline. To the great number of human beings I have spoken of must be added fifty elephants, six hundred camels, five thousand bullocks, five thousand horses, one thousand ponies, two hundred goats, two hundred sheep, fifty ruts, one hundred *palanquins*, one hundred dogs, and one hundred *hackeries*, or carts: presenting the following total:

Fighting men	8,000
Camp-followers	80,000
Elephants	50
Camels	600
Bullocks, horses, and tattoos	11,000
Goats, sheep, and dogs	500
Palanquins, *hackeries*, and ruts	250
Total	100,400

One hundred thousand four hundred were thus under my command, for the movements of the whole of whom, men, animals, and vehicles (except fighting men), I was responsible; and I am sure the reader will not class me amongst cruel men if I was obliged to use the whip, where obduracy and contempt of orders were frequent.

On the following morning we commenced our march; and I began the functions of my new situation by impressing upon the minds of some of the followers, that my arm was strong as well as the lash of my whip. I found I was soon obliged to take other measures besides merely bellowing to them; and in three days I had whipped the whole body into perfect obedience, which saved me a tremendous deal of labour afterwards, and some hundred yards of whip-cord. Sometimes some mischievous fellows would, to annoy me, get the whole baggage on the wrong flank; but I had influence enough to find them out, when they paid dearly for their trick. After a short time they found it would not do; so, my situation, instead of a task, was at last a pleasure to me; and the sight of my whip was sufficient to deter the most desperate from exceeding his limits. My commanding officer frequently said that, if he lived and commanded twenty armies, I should be his baggage-master.

In two days we arrived under the town and fort of Hedjeeghur, a strong hill fort, that had been recently taken by the Honourable Company's army. The refractory *rajah*, driven from his strong and proud walled fort, lived in the town below, where no doubt he panted for vengeance on his foes. He was a designing and crafty fellow, capable of the blackest crimes; but he was so pressed under the thumb of the government whom he had offended, that he dared not show himself in his true colours. What must have been his heart's writhings, when he saw that proud fort, which had been the residence and glory of his forefathers, forfeited by the most diabolical breach of treaty! It must have filled his cup of bitterness to the brim. In his disposition this conquered *rajah* was cunning, cruel, and despotic; but, from fear, he was the most cringing sycophant that ever lived.

The next march brought us to the foot of the *ghaut* we were to ascend. On its projecting bosom could be seen a kind of winding path or road, which, in some parts, seemed suspended from the clouds; and, how any mortal power could get up our twenty-four pounders, and all their gigantic appendages, seemed beyond human foresight to imagine. The pioneers went to work with the view of enlarging the road; in which occupation we will leave them, while I endeavour to describe the scene below. I imagined that no spot on this wide earth could equal in beauty the scene I beheld in Nepaul; but the one in which our encampment now lay appeared to me almost to surpass it in magnificence. The hill, from its base to its summit, was, I should think, a good English mile. Similar hills surrounded the encampment, and rippling and creeping streams wound through the camp in every direction. Here the trees, closely embraced by the fragrant woodbine, were of an enormous size; and, when in full leaf, their lofty tops vied with the encircling mountains. Every kind of wild flower was here in great profusion, and the grass under our feet was like the finest green carpet. The eye could wander far through beautiful trees, and through their verdure could be seen little huts of peace, standing by the brookside, which bespoke domestic bliss. But here, as at Nepaul, stalked idolatry in all its deformity, bidding defiance and evincing the most obdurate ingratitude to the sole Author of such blessings. Oh! that in God's good time the pure word of truth may flourish among this unenlightened race! May their seed bloom in the blossom of faith, and may sweet anthems of praise resound through their fertile valleys, and not only ascend to their mountain-top, but to the throne of heaven!

I was delighted to find, by the orders of the day, that the army would ascend the *ghaut* on the following morning; but that the baggage-master, with one thousand men as a working party, would remain behind. Immediately after the division had ascended, they were to follow, permitting all private baggage to be got up in the best manner it could. The working party which had been left below, was for the purpose of getting up public stores. I was up early, and saw them off; and it was a most terrific sight to see the cavalry hanging, apparently on the craggy cliff. Strange to say, elephants ascended carrying up their usual enormous loads; but the time occupied by these animals was considerable, from their trying to step one after another, and never venturing without first being well assured of the solidity of the ground. This reference to the extraordinary sagacity of elephants reminds me of two or three other anecdotes of these huge animals, which may be interesting to the reader.

In the year 1804, when we were in pursuit of Holkar, there was, in our encampment, a very large elephant, used for the purpose of carrying tents for some of the European corps. It was the season in which they become most unmanageable, and his legs were consequently loaded with huge chains, and he was constantly watched by his keepers. By day he was pretty passive, save when he saw one of his own species, when he roared and became violent; and, during those moments of ungovernable frenzy, it was dangerous for his keepers to approach him, or to irritate his feelings by any epithets that might prove repugnant to him. On the contrary, every endearing expression was used to soothe and appease him, which, with promises of sweetmeats, sometimes succeeded with the most turbulent to gain them to obedience, when coercive measures would have roused them to the most desperate acts of violence. By night, their extreme cunning told them that their keepers were not so watchful or vigilant. The elephant here alluded to, one dark night broke from his chains and ran wild through the encampment, driving men, women, children, camels, horses, cows, and indeed everything that could move, before him, and roaring and trumpeting with his trunk, which is, with elephants, a sure sign of displeasure, and that their usual docility has deserted them. Of course, no reasonable beings disputed the road he chose to take. Those that did soon found themselves floored. To record the mischief done by this infuriated animal in his nocturnal ramble, would fill a greater space than I can afford for such matter. Suffice it that, in his flight, followed by swordsmen and spearsmen shouting and screaming, he pulled down tents, upset everything that impeded his progress, wounded and injured many, and ultimately killed his keeper by a blow from his trunk. He was speared in some twenty places, which only infuriated him the more, and he struck away with his trunk at everything before him. His roaring was terrific, and he frequently struck the ground in indication of his rage. The instant he had struck his keeper, and found he did not rise, he suddenly stopped, seemed concerned, looked at him with the eye of pity, and stood riveted to the spot. He paused for some seconds, then ran towards the place from whence he had broken loose, and went quietly to his piquet, in front of which lay an infant, about two years old, the daughter of the keeper whom he had killed. The elephant seized the child round the waist as gently as its mother would, lifted it from the ground, and caressed and fondled it for some time, every beholder trembling for its safety, and expecting every moment it would share the fate of its unfortunate father; but the sagacious animal, having turned the child round three times, quietly laid it down again, and drew some clothing over it that had fallen off. After this it stood over the child, with its eyes fixed on it; and, if I did not see the penitential tear steal from its eye, I have never seen it in my life. He then submitted to be re-chained by some other keepers, stood motionless and dejected, and seemed sensible that he had done a wrong he could not repair. His dejection became more and more visible, as he stood and gazed on the fatherless babe, who, from constant familiarities with this elephant, seemed unintimidated, and played with its trunk. From this moment the animal became passive and quiet, and always seemed most delighted when the little orphan was within its sight. Often have I gone with others of the camp to see him fondling his little adopted; but there was a visible alteration in his health after his keeper's death, and he fell away, and died at Cawnpore, six months afterwards; people well acquainted with the history of the elephant, and who knew the story, did not scruple to say, from fretting for his before favourite keeper.

During the Nepaul war (1815) a female elephant, that had a young one some seven years old, died, leaving its young to lament its loss. I went to see it every day; and I pledge my word to the reader that the sorrow and sighing of this little animal was truly piteous and distressing. For some time it refused all kind of food. An old male elephant, that always stood near its mother, after some days seemed to take pity on it, fondled over and caressed it, and at last adopted it. It always travelled on the line of march close by its side, would feed out of its mouth, and gambolled with it as it was wont to do with its mother. Thus noticed, it grew fast, and, ere the campaign was over, its poor mother was forgotten, and all its affections seemed settled on its new friend. Its name was Pearee—love, or lovely, in English.

Colonel James Price, now major-general in the Company's army, knew, perhaps, more of the history of elephants than any man in India, having been one of the Company's breeders, at Chittygong, for many years. I have heard him recount the most affecting stories about these animals. He generally kept two or three himself. I was *tiffing* one day with him, when the subject turned on the sagacity of elephants, and he said he thought he had a young one as cunning as any one he had ever seen; and he offered to lay a bet, that if any one played this animal a trick, he would return it, if it was a month afterwards. The company seemed to doubt this, and the consequence was a small wager, taken by me. I cut the elephant some bread, of which these animals are extremely fond, but between the pieces I introduced a considerable quantity of cayenne pepper. Thus highly seasoned, I gave this bread to the elephant; but he soon discovered the trick, and I was obliged to run for it. I afterwards gave him some bread without any pepper, which he ate and seemed grateful for, and we parted. About a month or six weeks afterwards, I went to dine with the same colonel, and, prior to dinner being served, we took our usual walk to look at his stud. I had forgotten all about the elephant and the bet I had made respecting him, and accordingly played with and fondled him, without any suspicion. With this he seemed much pleased at the time; but, on my going away, he drenched me from head to foot with dirty water, in return for my cayenne pepper trick.

About mid-day, the whole of the private baggage was up, and some small guns had been drawn up by the working party. By six o'clock, no one but myself and the working party were remaining below. When I made my report to the commandant of the division that everything was up, he could scarcely credit my assertion; but when I assured him of its reality, he thanked me in the most cordial manner, and said he had given the following day for the completion of that job. The large guns took four hundred men, with double and treble drag-ropes, to pull up; and some of them were, in some of the most abrupt turnings in the ascent, actually hanging by the ropes, in a very dangerous state. One gun broke from its drag-ropes, but it was, fortunately, not far from a turning, which brought it up without any accident. Indeed, scarcely an accident happened worth the relation, save one, which I pledge my word was an absolute fact. A small *hackery*, or cart, belonging to some of the followers of the camp, fell down a precipice upwards of eighty yards deep, the sides of which were studded with trees of an enormous size. The two bullocks who drew this cart were dashed to pieces, and the driver so dreadfully injured that he had scarcely a feature left that could be recognized as human. Some ten feet from the cart lay a child about two years of age, perfectly uninjured, with the exception of one slight bruise on its little knee. It was supposed that the cart did not upset till at the bottom of the declivity, and that not until then did the child fall out; but it was certainly one of those extraordinary circumstances which sometimes happen, for which it would be difficult satisfactorily to account.

Chapter 18

The Mad Rajah

Having made my report that the whole of the stores, baggage, &c, had been safely got up the *ghaut*, I was still at the general's, when a messenger came from Rajah Buckeet Bellee, the *rajah* of Hadjepore, whom I have before alluded to; and the general requested I would escort him into camp. I therefore rode towards the top of the *ghaut*, where I found the *rajah* in waiting. The purpose of his visit was to make his peace with the general, who was much displeased at his not having complied with his requisition to furnish five hundred workmen to assist us to get up the baggage. The *rajah* had with him five elephants, and twenty horsemen, with spears, guns, &c. He was inclined to be affable and jocular with me; but I could see through his dark eyebrows the more inward workings of his heart. He broke silence by asking me if the general was displeased with him. Knowing the character of the fellow, I could hardly make up my mind to be civil to him, so I replied, "You had better put that question to him who can best answer it. If the general is not offended, he has good reason to be so." He then asked me what was the object of our campaign, and I told him that he had better reserve all these questions for the ear of the general himself, who, no doubt, would be able to satisfy his *nawabship*. Finding that I was not quite so elated with the honour of sitting on the same elephant with him, as he had expected I should be, and that he could get no information out of me, the *rajah* next admired my dress, and took a mighty fancy to my watch, but I would not let it out of my hand. He winked to a man on another elephant, and muttered something in the Mahratta language, which I did not thoroughly comprehend, but which sounded something like, "it won't do," or "he won't do." He then took a fancy to my whip, which I permitted him to look at. Some person happening to speak to me just as we arrived in the precincts of the camp, my whip was passed from one to another, and all protested they knew nothing about it; so that I had but little hope of ever seeing it again. On the *rajah*'s, return from the general, from whom he had met but a cool reception, he remounted his elephant, with indignation in his eye, and vowing vengeance, if ever in his power, against all Europeans. I had to see him out of the camp, when, having proceeded to the extent of my orders, I demanded my whip, protesting that he should be detained in camp until it was restored. Every search was made, but no whip was to be found. I was not to be hoaxed in this manner, so I persisted in having either my emblem of office returned, or its full value paid to me. The *nawab* asked what it cost. I said five gold *mohurs*; and, after some demur, and a good deal of parleying, I pocketed that sum, and we parted, to my perfect satisfaction.

We marched the following day. Our journey lay through a wild country, in which scarcely a human being was to be seen, though the soil seemed good and fertile. The fact was, that we were now entering those districts which had been recently the haunts of the Pindarees. The next day our march lay through a famous diamond country, belonging to the Punnah *rajah*. Having passed a small deserted stone fort, I was much astonished that, after the enormous ascent of nearly a mile, the whole country continued flat for a considerable distance. From the country having been deserted in consequence of the ravages of the Pindarees, all appeared desolate and dreary, except in the district in which the diamond speculation was carried on. Here were seen, in little groups, adventurers digging for these precious stones. In this venture, as in all others, some won and others lost; but the number of the latter greatly predominated. The adventurers purchase a certain extent of ground, say ten or twelve feet square, for which they pay from a hundred to a thousand *rupees*, which depends entirely on the situation. Terms having been agreed upon, they then dig, sift, and wash, and if they find any diamonds under a certain value, they are their own; if above (I think ten thousand *rupees* is the amount stipulated), they are the property of the *rajah*. Few of very high value are found; but, notwithstanding this, the speculators are well watched during the whole of their sifting and washing. A good deal of gold, silver, copper, and iron is also found in this part of the country, and there can be no doubt that the *rajah* is a rich man; though, notwithstanding his treasures, he must be devoid of happiness, as the following incident of his life will prove.

Some three years before the time that the division of the army to which I belonged passed through this district, the *rajah* had married a most beautiful woman, the daughter of a neighbouring *rajah*, making his third wife. This woman, of all his wives and concubines, he most loved, if such a tyrant can be supposed to be susceptible of such a feeling. In his court he had promoted a young man (his barber) from an indigent sphere to be his chief confidant. This confidant became his greatest favourite, and, indeed, ruler. Nothing could be done but through his interest. Thus things went on for some time, when the *rajah* was invited some hundreds of miles to an annual festival, which invitation he accepted. The times were turbulent, for the Pindarees were then roving about in large bodies; but, notwithstanding all this, the *rajah* imagined he could safely leave his confidant in charge of his family and his people. Having made this arrangement, he started on his journey, reposing the most implicit trust in the firmness and integrity of the new minister—for so he was denominated. Scarcely had one week elapsed, when the fiend, who was thus trusted, cast his sensual eye on the object of his master's best love; but he found her virtuous as she was beautiful. He protested his most ardent love, and that he could not exist without her honeyed smiles; that she was everything that could promote his happiness or destroy his life. He entreated, he conjured; but all were as words cast upon the wintry blast: she was firm, and threatened to expose his infamy to the *rajah*. Thus menaced, his crime seemed to stagger him, and he importuned no more; all the exasperated fury of an offended master rushed upon his mind. The *rajah*, as he well knew, was of a most violent and ungovernable temper—one of those unhappy mortals who act first and think afterwards; and such a report against his favourite would have wrought his jealous heart to a pitch of utter frenzy. The villain, seeing his danger, immediately turned his own dastardly crime upon her who had resisted his corrupt proposals, and, seeking an interview with the *rajah* on his return, he represented to him, clothed with the most infamous and plausible falsehoods, that his favourite wife had been unfaithful in his absence. Had the infuriated and jealous-hearted *rajah* but given this report one instant of consideration, he must have detected the wretch in his infamous falsehood; but the artful favourite knew and relied on his master's fury. The moment he whispered the poisonous words into his ears, the *rajah* grasped his sabre, flew like a madman into the *zenanah*, and without speaking one word, he cut his favourite mistress into pieces; then, gazing on the murdered beauty who lay lifeless at his feet, he sought refuge in the bosom of him who had destroyed his peace of mind, and the object of his most ardent attachment. Her lacerated body was committed to the pile, and burnt, after the usual lamentations. He was an independent *rajah*, and, consequently, beyond the reach of British justice. In his own country there was no law to punish such offences. In a short time, therefore, the circumstance passed away, and was forgotten; and not even did the relatives of the poor woman inquire the cause of the foul act, for murder was a common incident of the day.

At length, one of the other wives of the *rajah* lay on her death-bed. In this state, she expressed a wish that her whole court might be assembled, for she had something of the greatest importance to disclose, before she closed her earthly career. This was communicated to the confidant, who immediately imagined that the murdered victim had communicated to her the whole affair. He however took the necessary measures to summon the court into the chamber of death; but, when they had assembled, the favourite alone was missing, and, on search being made, it was found he had fled on horseback. The council having assembled, a full and clear disclosure of his infamous designs was made. The *rajah*, in bitterest anguish, tore his hair, beat his breast, and ran raving like a madman round the palace. Nothing could soothe or pacify him. Every horseman was dispatched in pursuit of the delinquent, but he was never found; and all the infuriated murderer could do, was to build a temple to the memory of his favourite mistress. This he did, and a most splendid edifice it is.

The unfortunate *rajah*, when I last saw him, which was in the year 1819, was a perfect madman. After looking on his blood-stained hands, he would wash them a hundred times a day; but neither water nor time can wash away the guilt of murder. In the temple before alluded to is her effigy, and two valuable diamonds occupy the place of her once smiling eyes.

We remained at Punnah some four or five days, waiting for instructions from headquarters. The left division was originally intended as an army of observation, to watch the several *ghauts* on the frontiers of our provinces, and to prevent the Pindarees from getting into our districts; but they having taken another direction towards Candish, we received orders to move on in the combined and general pursuit, and we stood towards Serronge Bopaul and Burrowah Saugar, through a most wild and desolate country, where tyrannic sway had driven far from their homes the poor villagers. At one time, having lost sight of the Pindarees, we began to be seriously alarmed about our families at the different stations. At one of the principal stations (Cawnpore) there was scarcely a soldier to be seen, and reports having reached them that the Pindarees had descended the *ghauts*, the alarm of the women and their families became dreadful. Their doors were barricaded with stones, bricks, tables, chairs, drawers, beds, and so forth, and not one dared to venture abroad. All was fear and consternation. Servants were dispatched for information, who brought back the most unfounded reports, which greatly increased their alarm. My wife's letters were filled with fears and forebodings. Many ladies had hired boats for the purpose of going down the river to a more secure place, when an event happened that, for a time, confirmed all their alarms, and almost frightened them out of their wits. A lady of the station, riding out early in her chair, or *tonjon*, saw, on the race-course, an immense dust, raised by a number of bullocks which were coming to the cantonment for grain, escorted by a party of local horse. She inquired who these were, when the person of whom she asked this question said "*Brinjarree*," meaning a small cattle that carry commissariat stores; but the lady understood him Pindaree, and the name was quite sufficient. She jumped out of her palanquin and ran towards home, screaming, "Pindarees, Pindarees!" and all she could answer to the questions put to her was, that the Pindarees were come, and were already in the cantonment. Servants were dispatched, who, seeing everybody running, vociferating "Pindarees," the alarm, as may well be supposed, spread like wildfire. Some took to their boats; some got under their beds; others into their cellars and go-downs; and the consternation was unbounded. My wife, fortunately, had a small guard of *sepoys* at her house, there being some commissariat stores there. On the news reaching her, her doors were locked and bolted, and a confidential servant was dispatched to ascertain the nature and the extent of the truth of the report. He returned, saying, that they were then plundering the great bazaar. The screaming of ladies and children which ensued, and the alarm of servants, beggars description; and it was not before evening that confidence and peace were restored, by the kindness and judicious interference of Captain Sissmore, the acting paymaster of the station.

We pushed on towards Bersiah, where we found Major Logie, of the Bengal Infantry, who had thought it advisable to stockade himself, for he had with him a considerable quantity of treasure for Colonel Adam's division. As the Pindarees were hovering about in large numbers, and a large body of Scindia's horse seemed to eye the treasure with delight, the major having only a few men, we found him on a small hill, well and securely fortified. The day before our arrival, this enormous body of Scindia's horse encamped close to the stockade, and in their manners were extremely insolent to Major Logie;

so much so, that he told them in plain terms, if they did not move their quarters, he would fire on them; and I do not know any man in the Company's army more likely to put his threat in execution. It is true they were the troops of an ally, but they were not to be trusted; and nothing but fear prevented them from seizing the treasure under Major Logie's care. At this place we received hourly information that the Pindarees were in the neighbourhood; but as they were in tens and twenties, it would have been folly for us to have gone in pursuit of them. Indeed, we might as well have attempted to catch the falling stars. Such a pursuit could not have redounded to the credit of the service, and it might probably have frightened and dispersed them, which was not our object. We rather encouraged their combining in large parties, that we might surprise and cut them up. With this view we remained here some time, watching their movements. Here, again, the munificence of the government of the East India Company was evinced. Proclamations were published through every village, calling on these marauders to become good subjects, offering to purchase their horses and arms at a fair valuation, and to give them land and a free pardon for all their former transgressions. Not one of these kind and liberal proposals had they a right to expect; but their obdurate hearts would not accept the proffered mercy, nor their indolent habits permit them to think of cultivating the earth. It is supposed that during the more inactive seasons of their lives, they will sleep from twelve to fifteen hours out of the twenty-four; and the few hours that they are awake are spent in rapine and sensual pleasures. There is no race of people on God's earth more depraved and debauched than a Mussulman Pindaree.

Chapter 19

Dhamoony

During our long stay at Bersiah, we frequently went out on parties of pleasure; and, as I had at this place nothing to do in my official situation, I generally accompanied these little excursions. About Bersiah the country was more fertile and beautiful than any part we had passed through, and we had excellent shooting, from the royal tiger to the royal snipe, without going a mile from camp. Thus we passed our time, living pleasantly enough. At length we found that the Pindarees had ascended another range of *ghauts*, and concentrated their forces at a place called Beechy Taull. Towards this place we bent our course, the extent of our daily marches being entirely regulated by the information brought in by our spies. Our wild enemy were, for a time, stationary; our marches were more regular; and they actually permitted us to approach them, without moving their quarters; taking care, however, to keep a wide and deep river between them and us, and an almost inaccessible *ghaut*, from whence they could see such a distance round, that our approach could be observed ten or fifteen miles off. When we were within forty miles of this place, we made a forced march in the morning, some twenty-two miles, through a thick woody country. Having completed this distance, we halted for our cattle and followers; but we started again when the moon rose, intending to surprise them by the following morning's dawn. Our road, however, lay through a dense thick wood, with a deep ditch or ravine every hundred paces, which we had so much difficulty in getting our guns over, that, when the morning dawned, we had not proceeded more than one-half of the distance, though we were in sight of the *ghaut*, which was about eight miles ahead. In an hour and a half after this, we reached and crossed the river Scend, about two miles from the top of the *ghaut*.

Our spies, who had just left the camp of the enemy, informed us that they were not encamped on the top of the *ghaut*, there being no water there, but that they were lying near a large lake of water, about two miles from the *ghaut*, apparently unconscious of our approach. The general immediately dispatched the 4th regiment of Native Cavalry, under Brigadier-General Newberry, who commanded the whole of the cavalry, with this division, also Cunningham's corps of Local Horse, under the command of Lieutenant W.W. Turner, with two six-pounders, called gallopers, as they would proceed as fast as the regiment could charge. I asked the general's permission to go, and I obtained his consent to act on the staff with Brigadier-General Newberry. The *ghaut* was high and difficult, being nothing more than a mass of loose stones, by which many of the poor horses broke their knees in getting up. As soon as we were up, we formed an extended line, and moved on slowly, as our horses had then been ten hours saddled, and without food. At the camp described we found a large body drawn up, and we gave them several long shots, and brought some of their spirited steeds and men a pitch lower. We then went off at a good smart gallop; but our long-jaded and hungry horses had but little chance. We soon emerged from the thick wood which surrounded their enormous encampment, and came up with some of them, and cut them up. About a mile to our left, and in our front, we could see tremendous volumes of dust; and, about a mile further on, we began to fall in with the enemy in considerable numbers. Some of them fought well and bravely: indeed, the greatest coward, when his life is at stake, will fight desperately, and this was the case with these marauders; but their struggle was ineffectual. We could see women riding across the country at speed, with one child on their backs, and one before them. Their horses flew along the plain with extraordinary rapidity.

Having gone about four or five miles, some few of the Pindarees formed, and seemed inclined to come to the scratch; but, before we could reach them, their hearts failed them, and they rode off, passing upon the gentlemen with the white faces some unpleasant epithets, which decency forbids me to mention. The declining sun had already dipped his golden beams in the distant lake, and bid us speed while yet he tarried. We had some hours of day remaining, and by the close of the evening we cut up numbers of them. At this time Lieutenant Turner's corps of Local Horse had separated themselves from the 4th Cavalry; and, before it was dark, the brigadier wished them to rejoin him, for the whole of the enemy's baggage was in sight. I was dispatched for the purpose of delivering the general's communications and wishes. When about half way on my road on this duty, I found that a number of straggling Pindarees were prowling about, some of them wounded; and, in riding over the ground again, it was evident to me that we had not been idle. Lieutenant Turner and his corps of Local Horse had also done the state good service. I was riding at speed to deliver my orders, when, from behind a large tree, a Pindaree had the impudence to discharge his matchlock in my very teeth; but the ball missed me. I had before this bent my faithful friend, the 24th Dragoon sabre, nearly double, by striking at the thick cotton-stuffed coats of the Pindarees; but, in the course of the battle, I had seized a large spear of one of the enemy, of which weapon I well knew the use, having been taught by one of the first spearsmen in the country—the *zemindar* of the elephants during the sieges of Bhurtpore and other places. In the moment of forgetfulness and irritation I threw away my sabre, and was resolved to chastise the Pin for firing at me, in his own way; so I ran at him with the spear laid across the first joint of my left arm, with the butt under my right arm. For a time he parried it, but at last I ran it into his neck, and I rode round him something like a brickmaker's horse going round, and twisted him completely off his horse. He soon fell, and, as I could see some of his comrades coming towards me, I rode off. I then began to regret having parted with my old friend, the twenty-fourther, which had so often stood my friend in the hour of peril; but this is man's ingratitude for services rendered.

I was some time before I could find Lieutenant Turner, the whole of whose troops were engaged when I came up. When I had communicated the brigadier-general's orders, they were reluctantly but promptly obeyed, and we soon joined the 4th Cavalry, agreeably to the general's desire.

Having come up with the enemy's baggage, the night beginning to close in, and our poor steeds being completely done up, we called a halt, to refresh ourselves, and more especially our poor goaded horses, who were so completely exhausted that we could not have proceeded another mile. The baggage of the enemy consisted of horses, ponies, cows, bullocks, goats, sheep, women, old men, and children, with their little all; and that all was nothing more than their wearing-apparel, cooking-things, &c. These people were only followers. None of their families were here, except about a hundred of their wives, mounted on ponies. Round these poor frightened creatures our gallant brigadier, more for their protection from the villagers than for his own gain or security, placed a considerable guard. I was immediately dispatched, with four horsemen, back to the main division of the army, who had encamped on the top of the *ghaut*, to communicate the purport of our little skirmishes. It was no very pleasant thing to ride over a field of battle, groping my way through the dark with only four men; but, as there was no remedy, it was as well to do it cheerfully. I found the division had taken up the enemy's position above the *ghauts*, where I arrived in safety, but completely exhausted, as was also my thoroughbred mare. From the time I mounted on the preceding night, it was twenty-four hours, in which time I could not have gone less than eighty miles. From the violent perspiration I was in, and the dust and powder with which I was covered, when General Marshall saw me, he burst into a loud fit of laughter. No poor dustman or sweep in London could have cut a more ridiculous figure; which may account for the impudence of the man who fired at me from behind the tree, who certainly must have taken me for some menial servant who had stolen his master's clothes.

Having communicated my orders, my next object was the care of my faithful horse. She looked the picture of woe, with her head almost down to the ground, and she had lost one of her shoes. I had a groom who prided himself on being a bit of a horse-doctor. My mare was a great favourite with him, and he begged, as a most particular favour, that I would leave the care of her entirely to him. Knowing his skill, I consented, when, to my astonishment, he told my bearer to bring him some warm water and half a bottle of brandy, with a little bran. He mixed the whole together, milk warm, and gave it to the animal, who drank every drop and neighed for more. This dose threw the mare into a violent perspiration, and the groom then set to, with three other men, and rubbed her well down with straw. She had not drank the warm mash long before she lay down on some clean straw, which had been prepared for her. The groom then commenced thumping her with his clenched fists all over, and shampooing her, which she submitted to with apparent pleasure. He then had her shoes removed and her feet pared and washed in warm water, and wisped dry. After this he made her get up, and rubbed her well over with his hands, and in one hour she looked as well as ever. He then gave her another mash, and clothed her for the night, and she slept well. On the following morning she was quite fresh. Having other horses, I gave her a rest; but she was so frisky that I was obliged to mount her before half the march was over.

The main body of the army was not able to reach the cavalry the next day, the distance was so great; nor did they till a late hour on the following day, when the property taken, such as cattle, &c., were sold in the bazaar. On the succeeding day we moved on, but learned that the hunted parties of the Pindarees had fallen into the hands of General

Donkin's division, with another portion of their baggage. Thus they were handed from division to division. Such was the judicious plan of the most noble the Marquis of Hastings, that, whichever way these marauders turned, they were sure to fall into the hands of their enemies. Thus harassed, they dispersed, in tens and twenties, all over the country, when the country people took courage and made head against them, and attacked them wherever they could find them; so that, at last, they sought refuge in any little fort that would give them admittance.

Things being in this state, we were directed to proceed against the fort of Dhamoony, a fort belonging to the Nagpore *rajah*, who had violated his treaty with the company. The *keeledar* of this fort would not submit to the proposals of the Company, but had received instructions from his refractory master to fight the English while he had a man left. Before we reached the fort, we understood that many of the Pindarees had accepted the offers of the government; numbers had been cut up, and others had flown to their homes, many of them in our provinces. Nothing but small parties could be heard of, and these sought refuge in the woods by day, and travelled towards their homes under cover of the night. Passing over numberless little skirmishes, marches, and countermarches, that would be tedious to detail, I shall leave the other divisions of the army to pursue the Pindarees, and proceed to relate the operations of that division with which my personal services stand connected; previous to which, however, a brief sketch of the character and mode of life of a Pindaree may not be unacceptable.

This predatory wanderer of the East, from the moment of his birth is nursed in the lap of depravity, and is nurtured and fondled in a bosom inured to cruelties and barbarities that would disgrace the wild savage of the interior of benighted Africa. His sire, perhaps, a short moment ere his birth, has imbrued his hands in the blood of innocence, or buried his spear in the bosom of some infant virgin who would not passively submit to his sensual embraces; and, peradventure, bears in his hand some gold or silver ornament torn from her before unpolluted bosom, with which he decks the body of his new-born babe. Should the little urchin be permitted to live, he is schooled in the camp of heartless assassins, mounted on horseback, and well instructed in the system of plunder. Scarcely can the boy lisp his parent's name, ere he is bedizened with his father's spoils. It often happens, however, that these children are not permitted to trouble their parents long, especially should they prove sickly or cross, in which case the father makes little scruple of dispatching them outright. Indeed, by less cruel parents these poor babes are thought but encumbrances to a flying and marauding force, whose motto is rapine, where the arm of resistance dare be put forth. When the boy attains five or six years of age, he bears the blood-stained weapons of his calling, and is schooled in all the intricacy and minutia of their predatory line of life. At the age of from ten to fourteen, he will be found a proficient in all the cruelties which are considered requisite qualities for his profession; and, perhaps, ere he has completed his sixteenth year, rapine and murder mark his youthful career, and he wanders through vast tracts of country unmolested and uncontrolled. The greatest blessing ever bestowed on this great nation, was the annihilation of those immense hordes of Pindarees, in the years 1817 and 1818, under the auspices of the Marquis of Hastings. They generally form themselves into small bodies, some six or seven hundred in number, putting themselves under the direction of the most daring and despotic of their sect, but one who is generally well acquainted with the localities of the country where plunder is to be had. The court paid to this fiend is disgusting beyond description. He is a little king, reigning on the throne of cruelty and bloodshed. These people take up their quarters in towns and in their vicinity, committing every kind of imposition on the poor unprotected inhabitants, against whom, should they prove refractory, in refusing them even the carrying off of their daughters or wives, the most coercive measures are unhesitatingly resorted to. On these occasions murder is not an uncommon event. From the unrepressed excesses of these marauders previous to the Pindaree war, their annual visitations were looked for and expected as a matter of course, but were esteemed by the poor plundered sufferers as a kind of pestilential visitation, which they had no power to avert, though, no doubt, they one and all had the inclination. They never remained long at a place; but, during their short sojourn, they would commit acts that disgrace the name of man, and would deservedly attach to them the designation of brutes and monsters. They are generally well mounted, and equipped in all the tawdry habiliments of the East. They are most debauched and profligate characters, and some of them have four and five women each as followers of their fortunes. These women are excellent horse-women, and can handle the matchlock or sabre with the best of them. They drink, riot, and smoke, the whole night, and bask in the sun during the day. Their weapons generally consist of a long seventeen-feet spear, a matchlock, sabre, and pistols. Their horses, also, are well trained and manageable; but, from a formidable foe they will run like cowards, and hide themselves till the danger is over. Should they be surprised by any British force, they will run, and on the road plunder one another; which sometimes is attended with bloodshed. These people seldom marry, but live together as long as they like one another, and no longer. From the debauched habits of both sexes, they are not long-lived. They make use of opium in large quantities. It is generally used by them as a stimulus to rouse their languid spirits to a state of hilarity. I have seen some of the women in a most piteous state, from having taken this drug too freely; so stupefied that they could not articulate a word.

These were the people that the government of India wisely annihilated, in the years 1817 and 1818. "In the destruction," says Sir John Malcolm, "of this predatory system, which was converting the finest provinces into a wilderness, the British government has performed a splendid act of justice, policy, and humanity, which fairly entitles it to be regarded as a conservative and beneficent power, whose supremacy has been the deliverance of the people. That system was the baleful dregs of the exhausted military establishment of the Mohammedan dynasties; and it succeeded to the wars of Aurungzebe, like pestilence after famine, rioting in the exhaustion of the country."

After a long and tedious march, we reached the fort of Dhamoony. The rightful and proper owner of this extraordinary fort was the *rajah* of Nagpore. He had, but a short period before, been placed on the throne—so termed by the Indians—that is, in possession of his inheritance, and acknowledged by the British government as the rightful possessor, and their ally, and protected and guarded in quiet dominion, when he suddenly entered into a league with the *peishwah* of Poonah, to destroy the English, in violation of good faith, and to the disregard of a most solemn treaty. When the Company were guarding and protecting this treacherous *rajah*, he was harbouring in his bosom a plot of the most base ingratitude. Such had been the secrecy with which he carried on his intrigues with the *peishwah*, that a little band of British troops was completely surrounded by fifty or sixty thousand horse, before the Company were aware of his diabolical treachery. Our troops, in this desperate situation, consisted of one regiment of native infantry, and a few troops of the 5th regiment of Bengal native cavalry, in all not seven hundred men, with, I believe, two six-pounders, against fifty or sixty thousand! What was to be done? To stand and be shot at would have been the height of folly and madness; nor could they, under such heavy fire and force, hope to reach any other place of safety. Captain Fitzgerald, commanding, or second in command of the 6th cavalry, proposed charging the enemy, and selling their lives as dearly as possible, declaring that, if he could gain a small eminence on which they had a few guns, he should not despair of keeping them off and saving their lives. In this proposal he was seconded by Mr. Jenkins, the British resident at the court of Nagpore. The brave soldiers one and all consented, and, sword in hand, on they galloped, and actually cut their way through that immense mass of horsemen; in time gained the hill; took their guns, and turned them upon the enemy; and there maintained their post till reinforcements arrived. This piece of gallantry saved the lives of all the party, and places on the brows of that brave corps laurels that never can fade—honours of which the iron hand of time cannot rob them. I have frequently met the officer who commanded on this occasion (Captain Fitzgerald) in company, and it is difficult to offend him more than by mentioning this Nagpore affair, or attaching to him any peculiar praise or merit. I once heard him say, very angrily, "D—n the place—I wish I had never seen it; it's more plague to me, and oftener sounded in my ears, than if I had turned coward and run away. If I am to be pestered thus for having merely done my duty, the devil may fight next time, for I won't." It is true that a soldier cannot do more than his duty; every effort that he can make is due to his country, and every nerve should be exerted to promote its glory. From my own career, I am convinced that, where the danger is most imminent, the soul rises in proportion in energy and courage to meet it. I have invariably found it so myself, and I dare say that my feelings on these occasions are similar to those of most other soldiers.

The fort of Dhamoony is built of stone, and is situated in a most extraordinary place, and, as the people relate, was built on account of the following remarkable circumstance. Some *rajah* was hunting in its vicinity, when a hare got up and afforded excellent sport for a considerable time, and ultimately attacked and killed one of the *rajah's* bloodhounds. This singular circumstance induced him to erect the present fort of Dhamoony. It literally stands in a hole, surrounded by a wild and inaccessible jungle, and two of its sides resting on the steep banks, or rocky heads, of a tremendous ditch or ravine, in some places a hundred feet deep. Upon this stands the wall, some thirty or forty feet high; and, to view one of the bastions from this excavation is really terrific. On the front and other side there is scarcely any ditch; but the entrance is through five gateways, each of these commanded by small guns, and having small loop-holes for matchlocks.

The occupants of this fort actually fired at our advance, when nearly three miles off; I suppose to let us know that they were resolved to fight. We encamped about two miles from the small ridge of hills on which we afterwards erected our breaching-battery. In three days everything was ready, when the usual offer was made to them, as we did not wish wantonly to spill human blood. They spurned the proffered mercy; so to show them that we were in earnest, we commenced by giving them a salvo from our twenty-four pounders, accompanied with three cheers. They manfully returned both; and, from the show of heads upon the wall, we imagined we should have a tough job, and began to think the *rajah*'s boast, that his fort was impregnable, not unfounded, for our shots rebounded some hundred feet; at which the garrison laughed and cheered most heartily. They little imagined what was in preparation for them, and was soon to follow. In about an hour, we effectually disturbed their merriment, and their turbans were seen flying in all directions from our little whistling shrapnells. In five minutes not a soul could be seen; but the screaming of women and children was dreadful. The first day our balls seemed to have made little or no impression upon the wall; but, on the following day, some large stones in the centre of the bastion seemed tired of being battered, and began to shake, and in the course of the morning two of them tumbled out, when an Irish sergeant of the Company's Bengal Foot Artillery exclaimed to a corporal, "Corporal Hogan! come here, joy; sure, we have knocked two of her teeth out at last, and we'll soon bother her wig for her." The corporal replied, "Ah, Paddy, that bastion comes down like sin."

"How is that, Hogan?" asked the sergeant. "By degrees, to be sure," replied the corporal; "for, when that once begins to come, faith! it tumbles on one by the hundreds." Some of the enemy having heard the noise of the stones falling, a few of them peeped their noses out to see what was the matter, and soon retired again, impressed with a conviction that the prophecies of the superstitious builder, as well as his boasted fort, would soon be without a foundation. These fears were rational enough, for the bastion began to give way in all directions. About one o'clock we expected our grand shelling-battery to open, which must certainly have completed the demolition of the fort, for our shells were of enormous calibre. About this time we generally broke off firing, for the purpose of the men getting their dinners; and this was the only time that the inmates of the fort dared to show their noses. Many were now gazing on the falling and dilapidated tower. Its top had giving warning of its being tired of the contest, having found out that iron is harder than stone. I thought I should like to take a nearer peep; so I asked Captain Cruikshank if he would accompany me to take a nearer view of the fort, that we might know what kind of ground we had to go over. I would advise all young soldiers to ascertain this grand point, whenever they can do so without risk of discovery or personal danger, that, when storming on dark nights, they may know where to run, and where to walk. I need not say that Captain Cruikshank, who was a most gallant officer, readily assented to my proposal. We crept down within a hundred yards of the bastion, and were so close, that we were observed peeping by those upon the wall. One of them said, "Come on; do not be afraid; we will not fire on you." This was repeated by several others, who stood on the walls. We asked them what they wanted by inviting us to go nearer; and they told us that, if we would cease firing, they would give up the fort. We replied that, if they were really inclined to do so, we would come nearer, and listen to their proposals and wishes. They swore most positively it was the wish of the *keeledar* and garrison. For myself, I scarcely thought that their oaths were to be trusted; but Captain Cruikshank said, if I would go, he would; so I had no alternative left, as, of course, after such an invitation, I could not say no. We accordingly approached close to the bastion, and they faithfully promised to surrender the fort, if we would cease firing. As we now felt assured that they were in earnest, their wishes were promptly communicated to the commander; and Brigadier-General Watson came down to where we had been standing, when it was settled, that all the occupants of the fort should be permitted to march out, with their families and private property, but that they should lay down their arms. This they readily assented to, and, as a pledge of their good faith, they undertook to send out the *keeledar* immediately. Our occupying-party was in readiness in the trenches. We, therefore, with the general, quarter-master-general, and several others, with about twenty soldiers, waited at the outer gate for the *keeledar*, who at last arrived, a poor hoary-headed old man, who had been bound for proposing to give up the fort before we commenced the siege. For having given utterance to such a proposal, his mutinous troops had kept him confined till that moment. When he was liberated, he looked the picture of misery and despair. His white beard was clotted together from weeping, and he seemed almost starved. We had given the garrison to understand that, if any treachery was attempted, the governor's life should be the forfeit. At this juncture, a most untoward circumstance occurred. An eight-mortar battery erected in the village, being uninformed of this parley, opened their new shelling fortification, to try the distance. The first shell fell within five yards of General Watson's feet, and exploded; but, strange to say, we all escaped. Another fell on the tree under which we were standing, and another burst over our heads; but it miraculously happened that no one was hurt. All was consternation. The poor old *keeledar* cried out "Treachery!" and some few shots were fired from the garrison. I was immediately dispatched towards our mortar-battery to stop their proceedings; but I had not gone ten yards before a shell fell within five paces of me. I immediately threw myself on my face, and hugged the ground, and thus escaped. I am persuaded that, when the shell bursts, it ascends a little, for I could hear the pieces buzzing over my head. The danger being over, I again made the best use of my legs, when I met the artillery-officer coming to see the effect of the shots which had been fired, to judge of the distance for the next eight, which were all ready. I was so completely out of breath that I could only say, "For God's sake, stop your firing!"

The officer, alarmed at my appearance and manner, said, "What the devil is the matter with you, Shipp?"

"Matter! my dear fellow," I replied; "why, you have, I suppose, by this time killed the general, quartermaster-general, and half the officers in camp."

Hearing this he set off at a gallop towards the fort, to see the extent of the mischief he had done from his ignorance of the parley. I followed at a slow trot, and was delighted to find that none of the shells, although eight had been thrown, had done any other injury than frightening those whom they came near. I can speak for myself, at all events; and I protest I did not at all relish the idea of being shot by the shells of our own batteries. There was something unnatural in this mode of making one's exit; and, to tell the candid truth, I was terribly scared, and the captain of the battery and I never got on such terms of intimacy again as to be within shelling distance, as I was not fond of such combustible acquaintances.

After I had stopped the shelling from our battery, and was thinking of my miraculous escape, I was interrupted by an inquisitive sergeant; and, as I always made it a point of attending civilly to every man who spoke to me, I permitted him to go on. He addressed me as follows:

"Pray, was your honour there when the first shell fell, for I was after laying that self-same mortar?"

"Yes," said I, "and you nearly laid me in the grave."

"By the powers, but I should have been mighty sorry for that, your honour."

I thanked him for his sorrow, but he continued following me towards the scene of action, and at last again broke silence.

"Is all the fight over, your honour?"

I said, I hoped so.

"I hope not," replied he.

I told him I was pretty confident of it, as the enemy were willing to give up the fort.

Hearing this, he coolly replied, "Then bad luck to them, after all the trouble we have had in building and completing that sweet eight-gun battery forenent yonder."

"Well, but my good fellow," I replied, "you cannot expect with reason more than they have to give."

"I don't mane that, your honour; it's only so much time thrown away for nothing, without getting any satisfaction for it; besides, your honour, it is quite tantalizing to one's feelings; and a great big fight would have been some kind of compensation."

"Supposing that, in that great big fight, you or I should have been killed, sergeant?"

"By my conscience," said he, laughing loudly, "but that would have been rather unpleasant, certainly."

"That would have been but a poor compensation for your trouble. What do you think, sergeant?"

"Faith! your honour, I like short reckonings, and I do not like to work for nothing."

Here we rejoined the party; he mixed in the general bustle, and I lost sight of him. I afterwards saw the same man in the fort, and I pointed out to him a poor woman whose legs had been shot off, but who still carried her babe in her arms, saying, "Well, sergeant, I hope you are now compensated for your trouble in the erection of your battery." He turned his head to where I pointed, and said (I shall never forget his pathetic manner), "By my conscience, your honour, if I had thought I should ever have seen such a murderous sight, I would not have come near the place." I saw him wipe the tear of sympathy from his eye with the back of his hand, and he continued, "Shall I take the poor creature to the hospital?"

"No, sergeant," replied I, "you would only increase her pain."

Almost immediately after this, the poor woman breathed her last sigh. In her last struggle she grasped her child, and, even after death, her cold eye rested on the features of her unconscious babe. We induced another woman, whose child had been killed, to take charge of this. She cheerfully consented; but whether the poor child really found in her a second mother, I had no means of knowing.

All the outer gates of the fort were barricaded with huge piles of stones, which we were obliged to remove before we could enter, and which took up a considerable time. We had prepared everything, in case of treachery, and we therefore marched in as if proceeding to storm.

As we entered, they threw open the gates; but there was a degree of expressive fear on the face of every man in the fort, for they were strangers to the principles of Europeans, and they judged them by their own. Every man was ready, with his match lighted, resolved, as we were afterwards given to understand, to sell their lives dearly, should we prove treacherous. No sooner did we enter, than the eye instinctively closed, on beholding the appalling scene before us. Terrified and decrepit old men and women were in great numbers; and agonized mothers were seen hugging their lifeless babes to their bosoms. Far and wide lay strewed bodies and parts of bodies. Some young women bared their bosoms to the pointed bayonets, calling upon our men either to kill them or return their murdered babes and husbands. One young maiden screamed bitterly for her father, who had been killed; and her last breath died upon the breeze, for she fell, and expired in the arms of her aged mother.

Having observed that we acted on the defensive only, and seemed rather to sympathize with them in their griefs, the enemy gained confidence, and left their elevated posts with apparent faith. They moved gradually and slowly out, taking with them their little property unmolested. They were pictures of the most abject misery and want. They had not received any pay from their master, the *rajah* of Nagpore, for the long period of two years, during which they had lived upon the produce of their exactions from the villagers of the surrounding country. I would venture to say that, out of fifteen hundred people, they had not a hundred *rupees* amongst them; but, had they millions, it was guaranteed to them by the word of faith which Britons had never broken in India. They quietly grounded their arms as they came out one by one, accompanied by their families. Some of them cast a last fond look at their sabres, probably some family relic, and heaved a parting sigh. The surrounding country being in a state of commotion, created by small parties of the Pindarees flying towards their long-forsaken homes, and purloining everything they came near on the road, our humane general permitted every tenth man to keep his matchlock and sword, for self-preservation. Under the dusk of the evening they moved towards their homes, and we took possession of the fort, having lost but very few men during the whole siege.

CHAPTER 20

Against the Nagpore Rajah

The property in the fort of Dhamoony was literally nothing. The whole consisted of some five or six small guns, principally iron, and a considerable quantity of grain; the produce of which, as well as what was found in other forts taken during the campaign, was thrown into the general fund. Here, for a time, a small detachment was left; but they soon became so sickly, and died so fast, that we were obliged to dismantle the place, and leave it to the ravages of time.

The poor *keeledar* was alone detained and held responsible for the rebellion of his garrison. He was punished in a most exemplary manner by our government, by being placed on eight *rupees* per diem, as a prisoner; quite as much, I should imagine, as he got in a whole month as *keeledar* of the fort of Dhamoony. The unbounded liberality of the East India Company is quite unknown in England, and, indeed, in the more remote parts even of Hindostan. Their munificence is proverbial among the whole of the native powers with whom they have ever been concerned. Their extreme liberality, and their good faith in all treaties, which has never been tarnished, establish them in India on a rock which no power can shake. Whatever treaty, whether commercial or political, is entered into by them, it is as sure as that the sun will rise and the moon will shine, that its terms will be strictly fulfilled. Whatever may be the loss of such a treaty or bargain, its stipulations are adhered to to the very letter. These are principles that have established the Company's possessions in India on the firmest basis; and, aided by Old England, she may now defy the combined power of all Europe. Her native troops are good soldiers, and loyal and faithful subjects; but they certainly require a little humouring. There are certain indulgences which must be granted to them: the free exercise of their religious rites; certain comforts, such as additional clothing, &c., during the several seasons of the year; and by no means to attempt to induce them to wear anything that is objected to by their several castes. However absurd their habits may appear to a person unacquainted with Indian affairs, they must be, to some extent, sanctioned. I am speaking, of course, of things reasonable. I do not mean to say that, if a Hindoo priest fancied himself a greater man than the bishop of Calcutta, his lordship should resign his office in his favour; but simply that they should be indulged in every way not inconsistent with prudence and justice. I am persuaded that two or three millions of native troops could, in the course of one year, be organized and fit for the field; and I do not hesitate to affirm that, when headed by brave European officers, and encouraged by the example of British gallantry, they would be found equal to any troops in the world. I speak this from my own experience in India, and from being constantly engaged on active service with these troops. The Company have ever been justly conscious of the importance of attending to the different sects of men admitted as soldiers, selecting those of the higher class of Hindoos for their infantry, and of the Mahometan castes for their cavalry. Whenever men of inferior caste have crept in, little rebellions have been traced to that source. I do not mean to say, that men of an inferior caste are not equally brave soldiers; but I do maintain, the higher the caste or sect of the native, the more he may be trusted, and the more likely he will be to prove himself a faithful subject, as well as a good soldier.

Our division was now directed to proceed against another fort of the Nagpore *rajah*'s, called Gurrah Mundellah, to which we had to march some two or three hundred miles, over hill and dale, cutting down mountains and filling up rivers. Our march was, therefore, of course very tedious. The government political agent, Major O'Brien, joined us at Jubblepore, and we proceeded slowly towards the place of our destination. In some parts of this country we were obliged to cut nearly our whole day's march through underwood and ravines; and, in some places, such was the impossibility of ascent over many of the hills, that it took a whole day to cut a road so as to accomplish the next day's march through this wild and desolate country; but some of the views in the openings were truly splendid and beautiful. Everything that could please the eye or delight the senses was to be found in this spot—the haunt of beasts of prey. One of these little valleys reminded me of a scene in the *Arabian Nights' Entertainments*; it was indeed a fairy land, to describe which I am quite incompetent.

In this valley I arose about the hour of midnight, to view the enchanting scene. The moon was of unclouded brightness, and far on its western journey. Close beneath my tent was a clear and sweetly murmuring stream, in which the moon dipped its silver wings, and its brilliant rays shed so clear a light through the trees that I could see every white tent around. Their inmates were all slumbering, lulled by the gentle moaning of the lofty pine. Hushed was every tongue, calm was every bosom, save those of one solitary mendicant priest at his midnight prostrations. His little tinkling bell disturbed the serenity of the night, and grated on my ear with discordance.

In three days more, after most tedious marches, we began to inhale the same atmosphere as our enemy, and we were obliged to approach the several *ghauts* with caution. The country that surrounded the large town and fort against which we were advancing was terrifically wild; and, in some parts, deep-sunk dells and excavations in the earth told us that caution alone would insure success. In this fort, we had been given to understand, a considerable body of the flying Pindarees had been enlisted, to assist in defending the fort against the English, their hated enemies. These we were resolved to make an example of; consequently, a strict investment of the fort was our primary object, to prevent their escape. For this purpose, Brigadier-General Watson, C. B., was dispatched with the cavalry and some few infantry. I accompanied this party, and we commenced our march in the afternoon, working our way through rivers, jungles, and over immense hills. A little after dark, on passing a small hill a little on our left flank, two shots were fired at us. The general dispatched a company of infantry to reconnoitre the spot from whence the shots had proceeded. On examination, it proved to be a small look-out of the enemy. We found several small cots or bedsteads here, and their fires were still burning; but, after firing their two shots, they must have immediately fled; and we were extremely obliged to them for their hint, which reminded us of the necessity for caution.

We had gained information from our spies, that our road lay over a high *ghaut*, on which the enemy had a strong piquet; that, when we had surmounted that *ghaut*, the road to the fort of Gurrah Mundellah was over lowlands interspersed with water; and that we should have to cross the Nerbuddah, where we might expect to be opposed, as that river was wide, deep, and stony. Acting upon this information, our brave brigadier accompanied a small party, for the purpose of dislodging this piquet, without giving them a shot at the whole division. We were a long time ascending; so that, by the time we got up, the residue of the army were at the bottom. The enemy heard them by the neighing of the horses and the confounded clatter of our dragoons' swords, which may be heard for miles. It would be much more musical if they would tie bells round the horses' necks, than to tolerate this abominable noise. The moment the piquet heard them, they fired, their long *ginjalls*, which kill a mile off. The first shot wounded a poor grass-cutter of the 8th Native Cavalry through the leg. At this time our detachment, which was stealing up the side of the hill, was so close upon the enemy, that they had not time to fire many more shots. They then ran off, leaving eight or ten of their *ginjalls* suspended from branches of trees. At this place were ten or twelve fires, and about twenty cots. Some of their rice was cooking; but, for fear they might have poisoned it, we broke the utensils. The *ginjalls* we also broke, not being able to carry them with us. We then descended the hill; when the moon rose, and diffused her bright rays over the distant plain. The sight was enchanting, in comparison with prowling about in the pitchy darkness of the night, not knowing the moment we might be saluted with a pound ball from one of their long *ginjalls*. The corn-fields, the crops of which were then in a state of maturity, looked silvery bright, and it was a great relief to the eye that had been intensely watching in dreary darkness. Lighted torches, or fires, could be seen on the distant hills, and those in the intermediate space were, no doubt, indications to the fort, of our approach.

We halted on the banks of a sweet crystal brook, and drank of its renovating stream. In about an hour we resumed our march on a tolerably good road, but crossed by little rippling rills almost every half-mile, which kept our feet continually damp and cold. We passed through many rice-fields, and the country seemed fertile and cheerful, but not a man, or even a solitary hut, could we discover. We at last saw a light, apparently about a mile ahead of us. As we advanced, the light still appeared in the same situation. Sometimes we imagined that it was borne by some of the flying enemy, who had good reasons for keeping that distance ahead of us; but we soon discovered the fallacious light to be nothing more than the *ignis fatuus* on its midnight rambles. Shortly afterwards we came to a small village, consisting of about twenty huts; but nothing was to be found here except a few Pariah dogs, and some wandering cattle. Here we halted for the night, and handed round biscuits and grog to those who had not had the precaution to provide themselves with some refreshment. On similar occasions I had formerly been negligent, and had often suffered the pangs of hunger through my own neglect; but this evening, foreseeing, from the nature of the country, that our supplies could not reach us, I had provided myself with a whole bottle of brandy and a considerable quantity of biscuit, which went freely round. The morning was very chilly, and we had no covering; but, notwithstanding this, the weary bodies of the men soon sank to sleep. My favourite mare had a blanket, which I would not deprive her of, as she would not drink brandy. Her portion of biscuit she had. When I awoke, what was my astonishment to see my groom wrapped up in my mare's blanket, and snoring like a pig, while the poor mare stood shrivelled up, and looking almost frozen to death. At this piece of consummate impudence on the part of the groom, I lost my temper, which nothing could restore but the satisfaction of giving the fellow a good horsewhipping. Besides this, I made him forfeit one *rupee* of his pay to purchase sweetmeats for the mare, to which she was exceedingly partial. I made the groom feed her himself with this remunerative luxury, and, to give the poor fellow his due, he did it good-naturedly enough.

Soon after daybreak we again got on our way, but found that we were a much greater distance from the fort than we had been led by our spies to suppose. We now marched in full preparation to meet the enemy, assured that they would not lose the fair opportunity of stopping our progress, which was now afforded them. On our arrival at the spot where we expected to meet with resistance, to view the wide roaring river, the Nerbuddah, majestically rolling over its rocky bed, would alone have been sufficient to stop the progress of soldiers less inured to difficulties than we were. Had that river been defended, the forcing of the passage would have cost us dearly in lives. The banks on the opposite side were bold and abrupt; and the only accessible part for wheel-carriages was a roadway that had been excavated from the sides of the river. Had this ford been defended, or the road stopped, our passage would have been attended with immense difficulty and danger; but we did not see a single man, and we could form no other conclusion from such apparent indifference to so advantageous a position, than that they had occupied, and were resolved to defend, some place which they deemed more suitable to their purpose. About a mile farther, we saw some unarmed stragglers on the edge or margin of a wood, peeping at us. I rode after one of this party, whom, when I came up, I found to be a woman. She immediately threw herself on her knees, and begged for mercy, saying she was a poor villager. When she saw that I had not the remotest intention of injuring her, she afforded me every information I required; stating that all the soldiers were in the fort and town, and that, until we got there, we should fall in with none but poor and inoffensive people, who were leaving the fort for their native homes. With a large party of this kind we fell in, almost immediately afterwards. They were armed, and drawn up in battle array; and nothing but the appearance of women and children among them would have prevented our advance from firing on them. From the fortunate circumstance that the poor woman with whom I had fallen in, had informed me that some of the people that did not wish to serve the rebel *rajah* had left the fort, the whole of this party was permitted to pass without molestation, with commendations on their faith to the British government. They departed, and we proceeded towards the fort.

About a mile further on, from an eminence we could distinctly see the town, with its thick and high walls, inside of which was a strong-built stone fort. With a glass we could see people on the walls and bastions in great numbers, and guns peeping from the embrasures, of enormous size. When we were in complete view, they indulged us with a few sixty-four pounders; so that we were obliged to give them a much wider field. One of our guides stated that he had been in the fort, as a mendicant priest, and we had no reason to question his veracity. He produced a long sketch of the fortifications, strength, number of troops, &c., that induced some timid ones to make their last wills, and even impressed the more resolute with the idea that they had not a light job before them. Guns were new-flinted, pistols reloaded, swords fresh-pointed, and preparations were busily making on all sides, while searching for a place called the Home Doongra, which was an eminence that looked into the fort, at a distance of about two miles from their centre bastion, and near which we intended to encamp. Whenever the enemy saw our men collected on this height, they saluted us with long shots from a gun of enormous size. Several smaller ones were also thrown, and some of them were well directed. This is easily accounted for. I have frequently found that, wherever there was good cannonading, the *golundauze* gunners had been taught in the Company's army. I have no doubt that many of our native gunners enter the Company's service in those situations, as a preparatory step to entering the service of a native prince or *rajah* in the same capacity. The gunners are the only class of men in the service of these rajahs that are regularly paid. In the Company's army, a *sepoy*, or other servant, can always leave, by expressing his disinclination to continue in the service; and this great indulgence is very often taken advantage of by well-drilled men, who have been taught all the minutia of military evolutions, and are probably proficients in gunnery. It is not an uncommon thing in native armies, for persons of this description to get fifty or sixty *rupees* per month, when other soldiers are glad to get four. In this fort were three or four men, who had, in the manner I have described, acquired a complete knowledge of gunnery, and were good shots. These men are so highly extolled among their caste, that they will madly throw themselves upon the bayonet, rather than desert the gun which they command. Two of the *golundauze* in this fort were killed during the siege; the other returned to his home, which was Allahabad.

This fort of the Nagpore *rajah* had rebelled. The *rajah* himself had violated his treaty, and broken off his alliance with the Company. The inhabitants of this fortress, a short period before we encamped before it, had been summoned to evince their loyalty to the Company, to which they readily consented. For this purpose, a small force consisting of one regiment of Native Infantry, and some part of the 8th regiment of Bengal Native Cavalry, under the command of Major O'Brien, of the latter corps (then political agent for the arrangement of the country belonging to the rebel and treacherous *rajah* of Nagpore), marched to occupy the fort of Mundellah, which the governor had consented to give up. As soon, however, as the garrison saw the detachment (a mere handful of men) under the major, within gunshot of the fort, they fired on the party, who were, of course, obliged to make a precipitate retreat.

Before this affair of Major O'Brien's, the moment the treacherous intentions of the *rajah* had been detected, the British resident of Nagpore ordered his person to be seized. For this purpose, Captain Brown, of the Bengal Native Infantry, was dispatched, with troops, to seize him. On the approach of this force, the *rajah* flew to his *zenanah*, and sought protection amongst his concubines. At any other time, and under any other circumstances, respect would have been shown to this sanctum of illicit pleasure; but, under the present circumstances of the case, delicacy was quite out of the question, and the party rushed in and seized him. The women in the *zenanah*, in their impotent rage, flew at Captain Brown, who came off minus a considerable quantity of skin from his face, of some hair from his head and whiskers, and of one wing of his military full-dress coat; but he succeeded in securing his man, and dragging him from his screaming women. The *rajah*, being now a prisoner, was, a short time after this, sent under a strong escort towards the frontiers of our provinces, under the special charge of Captain Brown; but he escaped from him in the following extraordinary manner. I believe he was not disgraced by having his person fettered, or divested of its treasures; but he was permitted to be at large in his tent. His seemingly placid and penitential manner lulled his captors into the belief that he bitterly lamented his former treachery; but, had their vigilance been ever so exemplary, his escape would have been accomplished, for a conspiracy was formed—no doubt with a view to gain—by some *sepoys* of his guard, and of those forming his escort, to facilitate his escape under cover of the night. The conspirators so managed, as to get on sentry at the same time, or relieve each other; but the officer on the night-duty had positive orders to see the *rajah*, and did see him, every relief, which I believed was hourly. He had, in the course of the day, feigned ill, and wrapped himself up in his bed-covering; and the officer was naturally satisfied on seeing him, as he supposed, as usual, enveloped in his bed-clothes; but the cunning *rajah*, instead of being penitent for his crimes, had, under the garb of sickness, actually planned and made his escape: and several of our native soldiers (the conspirators) had flown with him. Some time after he was gone, they discovered that the object whom the officer of the night supposed to be the sick *rajah* wrapped up in his bed-clothes, was nothing more than a large pillow. When the last officer went his rounds, he was satisfied, from appearances, that his charge was secure. This hint ought to be a warning to young soldiers, not to trust to others what they ought to do themselves. The neglect of the inferior officer fell upon the commanding officer in charge, and he was brought to general court martial, but acquitted, on the ground of the conspiracy of his detachment. There could have been no necessity for such a trial, had the visiting officer detected the escape at the prescribed time of his visiting, and not been satisfied with the appearance instead of the reality. What could be expected from such a character—from one who had planned the destruction of those very people who so basely aided and abetted his escape? Of the *sepoys* who thus broke their allegiance to the government, all who were taken suffered the heavy penalty of their crime—death. This should ever be the result of conspiracy. There can be no question that the *rajah* had bribed them with some valuable jewels at the time, or held out to these infatuated and mercenary traitors golden promises of future aggrandizement. His escape was in the very heart of his own country; but who would admit a traitor? He could not procure an asylum, even in the midst of his own territory. He was hunted from fort to fort, and literally from door to door, execrated and despised; and he was, at last, found dead somewhere in Scindia's country—the just reward of his unprovoked, treasonable, and treacherous conduct. He justly forfeited his throne, and merited his fall.

We took up our quarters for the night in a small tope of trees, near the Home Doongra, the eminence which I have before spoken of. The night being sultry and hot, I slept on the outside of my tent. Close to my feet ran a little rippling stream, the banks of which were thick and bushy. I had not reclined long on my couch, before I heard a rustling noise among the bushes, and the cries of so many animals, that I began to think I was in rather a dangerous neighbourhood, and got my pistols ready, in case a tiger or other beast of prey should have taken a fancy to the body of the baggage-master, in preference to that of some more comely person. I listened attentively for a considerable time, when I heard imitations of the sounds of birds. I then knew I was in the vicinity of thieves, and kept my pistol on the cock. At last, I distinctly heard a low voice say, "He wakes—squat down." I instantly jumped off my cot, and ran towards the place; but they were off, and, from the darkness of the night, I could not see them, or they were so close it was quite impossible they could have escaped. From the noise they made in scampering off, there must have been some five or six of them. I should have changed my quarters after this, but the moon at this time stole from behind a cloud, and illumined all around, and I slept peaceably till the morning dawned. We then commenced our reconnoitring, during which we were frequently saluted with a sixty-four pounder, but escaped unhurt.

The remainder of the division arrived this morning, and in the course of the day we completely invested the town and fort. We took up our position on the east side of the fort, having the river Nerbuddah, with a large village and tope of trees, in our front, which completely screened us from view. The information brought into camp by the spy spoken of, with his plans and drawings of the fort, were found, on a minute examination, to be utterly false. It turned out that he had never been near the fort, but loitered about in the woods and villages in its vicinity, and there gained the information from which he drew his plans. The integrity and faith of this native had been such, that his master would have trusted his life on his veracity. For the long period of more than twenty years had this spy borne the toils and risks of his perilous occupation, without once having been detected in a falsehood; but his grey hairs were now, at a late period of his life, disgraced. For his long services, however, he was pensioned off, and placed in a solitary hut in his old age, to repent of this one act of deception. He confessed that his old tottering frame had refused to bear him as heretofore, and that fear had caused him to commit this his first transgression.

We had gained unquestionable information that a large body of our old friends, the Pindarees, had found an asylum in this fort, to the number of five hundred men, to assist in its defence. The place was so closely invested by us, that a man could not possibly escape; and we, one and all, were determined to chastise the garrison for their base treachery, and the Pindarees for their impudence. Although this town and fort occupied more than three miles in circumference, yet, at night, such was our care of their precious inmates, we formed a complete and close chain of sentinels around the whole of the space; and every quarter of a mile we had posted strong mounted and dismounted piquets, whose horses were constantly on the bit. The primary object of our brave general was to avoid any unnecessary effusion of blood; and, consequently, mercy was tendered to the occupants of the fort, provided they would give it up. Every base stratagem was resorted to, as usual, to gain time to reinforce and strengthen the fort, under the plea of taking time to think of the proffered terms of reconciliation. All this while we could see every hand employed in building new fortifications, under the delusion that our guns were only intended to intimidate them into compliance. They were confirmed in this opinion, not only by the predictions of their priests, but from the supposed impossibility of getting any guns of a large size over the gigantic mountains we had traversed; and, indeed, to view the lofty mountains, to use the words of the natives, "It was difficult for the sharp-eyed hawk to find his way over such precipices, for they were as stupendous as the midnight moon, or the morning light peeping from the newly-lighted chambers of the East." This delusion lulled them into fancied security, and their hardened hearts became steeled to the advice of reason, and our offers of compassion in favour of their mothers, wives, and babes. We soon convinced them that our guns were not so much to be despised as they imagined; but, before we opened our batteries on them, one effort more was made by us to prevent the destruction of life, by another offer of mercy, accompanied by the most earnest entreaties that, if their own hearts still continued hardened and obdurate, and they were resolved to resist the dictates of reason, they would, at least, not imbrue their hands in the blood of their families. These messages of mercy were treated with contempt, and spurned with indignation. Every effort that the feeling mind could suggest, or humanity dictate, was resorted to, to induce these deluded people to listen to our proposals; and every kind of forbearance was shown to them, up to the last moment. On the following morning our guns opened, which drove their priests early to the temple, to solicit protection and aid from the dumb objects of their idolatrous worship. The warrior was now seen putting on his coat of mail; all was bustle, consternation, and confusion. When our cannonading commenced, the birds, scared, soon got on the rapid wing, and sought shelter in the distant woods, and the deer fled with the quickness of lightning across the plain, bending their way towards the dreary forest. The enemy returned our fire, and hoisted their colours as a proof of earnest and total defiance of our power. We had not as yet completed our shelling-batteries, and therefore, before these magazines of death were finished, we once more called upon the inmates of the fort to send their families out, with an assurance that we would guarantee their protection and safety; that they should have a safeguard to whatever part of the country they wished to proceed; and that they should not be deprived of any of their private property. We could not make up our minds to fight against women and children. Our humane general begged most earnestly, that this, his last entreaty, might be attended to, as he should, on their refusal, commence his shelling, which would bereave them of many of those dear objects whom he now, for the last time, gave them an opportunity to save. A certain time was given for an answer. They knew that the guarantee proffered for the safety of their families was inviolable. On this point they were fully satisfied, and our continued solicitations at length melted their hearts. They consented; and the following morning, at ten o'clock, was fixed for their coming out. At this prospect we all felt much delighted, for it deadens the heart of a brave man to hear the cries and wailings of inoffensive women and innocent children. Every bosom panted at the happy event, as some great calamity removed from our own hearts.

In the morning, the sun rose in all his majesty, and his bright beams seemed to shine with approbation on our act of mercy. We had selected a large mango tope as the place of rendezvous. The appointed hour arrived, and we were delighted to see an immense number of people issuing from the fort, and bending their slow and gloomy steps towards the tope. It seemed like some funeral procession following some dear relative to the tomb. Some wept aloud and some in silence; some pressed their little offspring to their anguished bosoms; and others cast a lingering eye on the distant tower, where stood the objects of their love. Yet there seemed a confidence of safety beaming from every eye. A few men accompanied them, but without arms; and the bastion and walls were lined with soldiers, to witness the scene. There came grey-headed mothers, young wives, and numbers of children, from ten and twelve years old, to the fondling at the mother's breast. What a group of mortal creatures rescued from the tomb of destruction! The total number was about one thousand. Some of the women were truly beautiful, and very elegantly attired. Having made known their places of abode, they were dispatched under a safeguard. The procession moved slowly on. At about four hundred yards from the fort, the eyes of most of the party were turned towards the objects of their love, whom they were about to leave in danger; and many did bid farewell, and for the last time—for many of their husbands fell victims to their infatuated and blindfold zeal. When they had proceeded about a mile from the fort, we gave the enemy three cheers, testifying that we had strictly fulfilled the duties of the trust confided to us. The garrison returned our cheers; and, having now performed the duties of humanity, our next duty was due to our country. In mercy to their families we did not commence shelling till the doleful sounds could not reach their ears. We opened them about noon, and our first shell fell about midway, which created a shout on the part of the enemy; but the next started them from their hiding-places, and they could be seen running in all directions.

Having thrown about a dozen, the *rajah* mounted the *shawbroodge* (king's bastion) attended in state, to see the fun. We could recognise him by his glittering *chattah* (state umbrella). In the bastion I suppose there could not be less than twenty or thirty persons, nor could the distance be less than a mile and a half. The captain of the artillery, determined to regain his credit for his first bad shot, laid on a special one for the bastion, and, wonderful to say, it lodged on its very top. In an instant, even before the smoke cleared, the state *chattah* and every soul disappeared, and the shouting in our batteries was terrific. Not a word was returned from the fort; all seemed gloom and despair; and self-preservation seemed to be thought of most by them, from the general movement of the garrison. When the effect of the shell was seen, an Irish sergeant of the artillery bellowed out, "By my conscience, captain, but that was after picking some of their teeth for them, for I saw one of the spalpeens scratching his head."

The captain replied, "You must have capital eyes, sergeant, to see a man scratch his head at this distance."

"By the powers, your honour, I did see it, because I happened to be looking at the very time, or I should not perhaps have seen him."

"Well, sergeant, I have no reason to doubt your word; will you try a shell?"

"I should have no objection, but I have no chance of driving them away, because they are all gone; but I should like to try one, and see if I could hit something."

He fired, and immediately cried out, "By St. Patrick, but that's amongst them, if they should happen to be there." This blunder caused a general laugh at poor Paddy's expense, who seemed a little nettled, and peevishly replied, "Fait! you may laugh, but that's more than those will who were kilt by that shell just now."

We could distinctly hear the moanings of the wounded; and sad must have been the fate of those poor fellows whose gaping wounds were left bleeding, the shattered bones protruding through the lacerated flesh. The very idea makes the sympathetic mind shudder; but the hearts of these unfortunate creatures were as impenetrable as the stubborn rock on which their fort was erected. Yet, this very fact serves but to increase our sorrow for their benighted souls, influenced and guided by some hypocritical priest or mendicant impostor, who leads them blindfold to destruction.

The firing from the fort was good and steady, and some of their long shots would have been no disgrace to a European gunner. I was, during this siege, as before, baggage-master and acting aid-de-camp to Brigadier-General Watson, C. B., who invested this fort in person, and saw hourly the operations carried on under his own eye, being constantly riding round the chain of posts, or in the breaching and other batteries, always seeing things done, and strictly watching the progress of the siege.

Our principal breaching-battery was on the east side of the fort, keeping the pure stream of the sweet Nerbuddah running between ourselves and the foe. Many of the enemy, when sipping of its crystal water, were killed in the attempt to moisten their parched lips. I have more than once nearly quarrelled with my brother officers on the following subject, nor can I ever reconcile to my bosom, that the act is fair or right. The question to which I alluded is this, whether it is fair that I should secrete myself in a hole, or behind a wall, with a rifle, and thus, unseen, shoot every poor creature who shows his nose, without my own person being in the slightest danger. It is true, it is an enemy whom you thus treat, but I do consider the act of placing one's self in security, and from the hiding-place dealing out death, treads close upon the heels of cowardice, if it does not come under the designation of actual murder. Give me man to man, and sword to sword. I hate unfairness in anything; and I do not think this practice, though often adopted, will stand the test of scrutiny in the eye of justice.

We breached a corner bastion of the town, the base of which ran down into the river, on the banks of which we could approach the breach out of sight, and pounce upon it unobserved, and out of the reach of their cannon and small arms. All was impatience to get to work. The breach seemed fit for storming. Various were the opinions of the impetuous soldiers relative to its practicability. Some said they could ride up it, others that they could drive a gig up. Thus went round the thoughtless opinions of rash youth, ever willing to run headstrong into danger; but our prudent engineer, Captain Tickell, smiled on their hasty opinions, and sarcastically replied, "Whenever you do storm, rest assured you will not find the ascent of that breach a light job. To satisfy myself," he continued, "I will go. It is better to sacrifice one life than a hundred." Saying this, he immediately crossed the river, about a quarter of a mile lower down, and stole along the banks of the Nerbuddah unobserved, having given previous instructions to the whole of the batteries to keep their fire for the top of the breach, should he be attacked. He seemed to ascend with difficulty. Every heart trembled for his safety, for he was a brave officer, and one of our best engineers. He at last mounted the summit of the breach, and waved his hat. At that moment several of the enemy rushed out, but he jumped down the breach. They came to the very verge of it; but no sooner were their bodies seen, and the engineer safe from its top, than the whole of our guns, with shot and shells, were opened, and those who rushed out for his destruction met their own. Not one of them returned to tell the tale.

On the return of the engineer to the battery, he said nothing to any one, having been before much annoyed by the speculative opinions of those who stood about him. He, however, after his return, altered the direction of the firing of the breaching-battery to a large tree which had been shot down, and which must necessarily impede our ascent. This, he afterwards said, completely blocked up the footing of the breach; and, had we stormed according to the opinions and ardent wishes of many of the inexperienced, we must have suffered considerably in the loss of lives. He afterwards said, that he thought it a providential thing that such opinions, however foolish, had been expressed, for it was the cause of his being able to remedy an evil he could not for a moment have foreseen. On the contrary, it had before been his opinion, that the fallen tree would have facilitated our progress rather than impeded it. He thought we should be able to storm in the afternoon. A howitzer was immediately laid for the removal of this obstacle, and the shell fired from it lodged in the very centre of the rooty part of the tree, and when it burst blew it to pieces. This drew upon the artillery-officer who laid it the eulogiums of the spectators. Amongst the number was the Irish sergeant, who cried out, "By the powers, captain, but that's what I call a moving shot."

"Yes," replied the captain, "a remover, certainly, for I see the stump of the tree is gone. I wish you would remove the other large bough that hangs on the side of the bastion."

"I will try, if your honour pleases; but I should rather see your honour do it, to finish the work you are just after completing, and I will try and do the rest."

Thus went round the merry joke, and we were all laughing heartily at poor Pat's bulls and drollery, when a whisper was heard running the lines, "Fall in, storming-party!" On went the pointed bayonet; in went the new flint. Everybody was busy in an instant, and naught was heard save the hammering of flints and the fixing of bayonets. This was about three o'clock in the afternoon. We crossed the Nerbuddah, and marched along the bed of the river to our other breaching-battery, and there rendezvoused for a time, till all was ready.

The gallant general on whose staff I had acted had volunteered to lead the storming-party in person, as it was supposed we had a sharp job before us. I, as part of his staff, did not of course remain behind, but had the honour to participate with the general in the toils and glory of the day. Our situations, I assure the reader, were no sinecures; for we fought and fagged hard for nearly three hours.

About four o'clock the party moved on, led by the brave general and his suite. The storming-party consisted of two companies of the Bengal 14th regiment Native Infantry, supported by the 13th regiment. We stole slowly on along the bank, every tongue as still as the midnight thief. About ten or twenty paces before we got to the breach, the column was visible to a projecting bastion of the fort, from which a strong party of Arabs was dispatched, to stay our progress and oppose our entrance. These for a considerable time disputed our entry, but our brave native troops, inspired by the cheering of their gallant leader, soon beat them from their posts. They then took possession of some huts that had escaped being burnt, and fired through loop-holes; but they soon burnt themselves out, by setting fire, either by intention or accident, to these huts. This for a moment stopped our further progress, as we could not pass the flaming huts. Here we lost some few men; and, seeing that the destruction of numbers of our brave *sepoys* was inevitable, if we remained long in this position, we rushed through the flames, and on the opposite side found a large body of men drawn up to oppose us. For a short time the struggle was hard; but our brave little general soon gave the word, "Charge!" It was then that the butchery commenced. For a time our brave opponents would not give way, but rushed upon the bayonet's point, and fought sword in hand; but, when they did begin to run, the carnage was truly dreadful. I saw one grey-headed old Arab, notwithstanding that he had two bayonets through his body, and was lying on his back, cutting away in a most resolute and heroic manner. The third wound which he received was a shot through his head, which settled him. We followed close on the heels of the fugitives, who fell in all directions. They branched off towards the left, in the hope of getting off in that quarter, but we had previously sent a strong party of infantry and cavalry to prevent their escape. They were now completely hemmed in, and fight they must, or die. They did fight, and I never saw men fall so fast. They were in such numbers that every shot told. Hundreds of them threw down their arms and took to the water. These were for the most part drowned, and those who reached the opposite shore were made prisoners; but these were comparatively few to the number who met a watery grave. Some few escaped into the fort; and others threw down their arms, and begged for mercy.

In a deep ravine were about a hundred women and children. These poor creatures had been detained as corn-grinders, and our shells, unfortunately, had made sad destruction amongst them. Many of their children had their legs and arms shot off, and I saw one with its entrails protruding, a ball having gone completely through its body. We left a guard over this wretched party, to prevent them from being fired on. At this point we were exposed to a smart fire from the fort, which took off our attention from these women, and we pushed on, and in an hour had completely cleared the town of its fighting men. The fire from the fort became warmer; and it was therefore requisite that we should maintain what we had got, for night now began to cast a gloom on the scene below. It was now necessary to establish ourselves for the night, under cover from the shots of the fort; which we did by occupying temples and other buildings, as also the principal entrances to the main streets. In a couple of hours we were secure and safe, and not a single shot was fired. All was calm and quiet, save the distressing moanings of the wounded and the dying, whose cries and groans were truly touching to the heart. We grieved that we could not relieve them; but all that we could do was to take care that none of our troops or followers ventured to add to, or aggravate their pains, by rifling their persons, or by any taunting triumph. It would have been a mercy to have hidden from the human eye such a sight as was then before us, and we hailed with joy the closing of day, which shut from our view the distorted features of dying men, and the gushing streams of the wounded. The night set in, in dreary darkness, and the clouds seemed thick and gloomy; and in an instant all was hidden from short-sighted man, and seen alone to Him to whose care and protection we will leave the sufferers.

CHAPTER 21

Gurra Khootah

After we had taken full possession of the town of Gurrah Mundellah, I was directed, at about ten o'clock at night, to proceed alone and examine a distant temple, to ascertain if it was a safe asylum to lodge men in for the night. This temple stood at the end of a long street, to which I was obliged to grope my way, guided only by the distant fired hut, or a peeping star. Why did the general send me alone? Because he knew I would go, and it was better to risk the life of one man than five hundred. I cannot say that I had any great penchant for this job; but off I marched without a murmur. It was the general's part to order, and my duty promptly and cheerfully to obey. The night being dark, and the dead and the dying lying in all directions, it was no very enviable trip; but duty led me through every difficulty. My pace was slow and cautious; not quite so slow as the goose-step, but something near it. In each hand I had a pistol, and I kept one eye turned to the right and the other to the left, now and then stealing a glimpse to the front, but could not spare time to look behind me. Occasionally my pointed toe would come in contact with a dead body or wounded man. This created sensations by no means agreeable. I had not proceeded far, when some person seized my leg, and said, "Who are you?" This a little startled me; I suddenly drew it away, and said I was his friend. "Then give me some water," said he, "for I am wounded." I felt every inclination to render the poor creature this service, but it was quite impossible; so I passed on, but had hardly recovered my fright, when a large beam that was on fire fell with a tremendous crash, and several voices were heard, and the sound of persons running from the place where the beam fell. I stopped for a moment to listen, but all was again quiet, and I moved on slowly till I reached the foot or steps of the temple, when I heard the tinkling of a small bell. I ascended the steps and reached the door, when I heard some person murmuring out his midnight prayers. I at last peeped in, and discerned an aged priest prostrating himself on the ground before one of his gods. A small lamp was suspended from the ceiling. I entered and gave him the customary salute of the evening, but he had not the politeness to return my salute, but blew out the light and ran out precipitately, and I followed him, having first minutely surveyed the temple. What the priest took me for I know not, but probably for a ghost, for he was out of the temple in a moment. I returned by the same streets I came down, but a little faster. When about half-way, I heard voices; then horses' feet; and, at last, I could see several men on horseback approaching, and soon found, by their conversation, that they were some men from our camp, belonging to our ally, Scindia, who had got in for the purpose of plundering. I slunk behind a hut till they had passed, as I knew well that these marauders would have cut my throat for the sake of the buttons on my coat; so I permitted them to pass on, and I had hardly emerged from my hiding-place, when a huge Pariah dog set up a tremendous howling. He was sitting down close by a dead man, no doubt his master, for on the following morning he was still there, and howled piteously when any one approached the body. The poor animal was shot, and thus put out of his misery.

I at last reached the general, and made my report; after which I had the honour of escorting two companies to the temple; but the old priest had not returned. I then had to return alone; and, having established the troops, the general and suite, myself among the number, returned to camp, and, after a good dinner, retired to bed and slept soundly.

We recommenced our work on the following morning. On our arrival in the town, we were informed that a Captain B. and about fifty men had been in the fort the greater part of the night. On receiving this information, the general could hardly credit the assertion; but, on approaching the fort, he found it was true. The gate of the fort was thrown open, and we entered; and, never did human eye look on more accumulated woe and misery than the scene before us presented. The carnage far exceeded that of Hattrass, or of any of the other storms I have had the unpleasant task to narrate. I shall not attempt to describe the scene; and, should these memoirs ever meet the eye of any of my fair countrywomen, I am confident they will thank me for the omission. Suffice that upwards of five hundred bodies were, in the course of the day, committed to a large well, into which the enemy had thrown many of the dead during the siege. This well was closed up; and a man of the artillery sculptured on a stone, with his bayonet,

The Soldier's Grave
There let them rest in peace!

We had scarcely proceeded one hundred yards when we met Captain B. and his men, with the *keeledar* and another person in custody. The general thus addressed him, "Captain B., by what authority have you acted as you have done, and thus, without orders or instruction, permitted your men to enter the fort?" The captain told a lame story, to the effect that the *keeledar* had offered him a bribe to permit him to escape through the limits of his post; and that, having refused this, he received information that, if he wished, he might march his men into the fort. There was evidently a mystery in all this, and the ill-natured world said many unkind things on the subject; but how far these may have been true I cannot pretend to say. Certain it is, however, that there was something that came out a short time afterwards, that would have brought the affair under the investigation of a general court-martial; but the individual died, and the affair died with him, and he was buried on the spot. He was an officer of unblemished character; and little did he think that the spot where he was accused of committing his first offence would be his grave. The *keeledar* was a most respectable-looking man, and elegantly dressed; but I do not think I ever saw a more careworn and dejected face than his in my life-time. He seemed weighed down with woe.

He salaamed to the general in a most respectful and humble manner, and said, "Do what you please with me," at the same time offering his head.

I was desired to inform him that he must answer for his rebellion before a court-martial, and that his life would be the forfeit if he could not state satisfactory reasons for his treachery and rebellion, and satisfy the government that this act of disaffection was not his own. He replied, "I am as willing to meet death as I am to meet you here." He was placed in security, and our next object was to dispose of the prisoners. These were in number about two thousand, and more than one-third of them were wounded. They were allowed their option, either to return to their homes, or remain in the town. The greater part of them availed themselves of the former offer; and, having been deprived of their arms, they went off to join their families, and bear the sad tidings to many an anxious wife of her husband's death, and to many a fond mother the bitter news of her son having been shot.

Having arranged everything for the protection of the property, I was appointed a prize agent for headquarters, and we immediately commenced collecting the property to one spot. My first care was to put double sentinels on the entrance to the *zenanah*, till I could, with the other two prize-agents, search that place; but, as they were busy in another place, I took a peep at my double sentinels, and found one of them had left his post, and gone inside. I met him coming towards me with two large boxes, about two feet by three. I asked him what he had got there, and he said that they contained nothing but *paun*. I told him to give them to me. He did so, and I found them of an enormous weight. They contained, in fact, the whole of the jewellery of the *zenanah*. In the veranda were large bales of shawls and silks, sewn together like quilts, and in an inner room was the family of the *keeledar*, consisting of his wife and two daughters, who, on beholding me, threw themselves at my feet, and begged for mercy in the most beseeching manner.

I could as soon have laid the finger of harm on the author of my being; indeed, the duties of my present situation were repugnant and uncongenial to my feelings; but, whatever situation I was appointed to, or entrusted with, I always made it my primary object to fulfil the several branches of it in the most rigid manner, consistent with the rules of the service and usages of war; and, therefore, the more sympathetic feelings were absorbed in those of duty. I, however, consoled these poor weeping creatures with the full assurance of their safety and protection against harm or pollution, of which they expressed the most dreadful fears. This privileged right of war, so esteemed by the native powers, has in no instance ever stained the victorious banners of the East India Company; but these females had wrought their anguished minds on this subject to a pitch of frenzy and distraction, and all I could do and say could not drive from their fear-distorted features the evident dread under which they laboured. When, at length, I called God to witness the sincerity of my assurances, I could see a ray of hope beam and shine through their tears of apprehension, and their tempestuous bosoms became comparatively quieted and calmed. The thanks and prayers of the elder daughter would have affected with pity and commiseration the most tyrannic heart. She was, I think, the most perfect beauty I had ever seen. Her form was sylph-like and elegant; her features regular and beautifully shaped; and her eyes were of a jet black, and peeped from under her dark eyebrows like stars stealing from behind the murky clouds of night. Her voice, when she spoke, was extremely sweet, and the words of consolation which she addressed to her aged mother, would have drawn tears of pity from the most obdurate heart. When she threw herself at my feet, and supplicated for mercy, her piercing and anguished looks stole drops of pity from my eyes; and the conjuring expression of her beautiful countenance would have won the most savage bosom to commiseration. She seized my sabre, which was suspended from my side, and grasped it with both her hands, till I solemnly pledged myself for her protection and safety. When I did this, her beautiful eyes beamed forth that gratitude which she could not find words to express. I assisted her to rise, and then placed the three ladies in a room upstairs, till they could, with propriety, be made over to the *keeledar*, who was at present in custody, and must meet the sentence of a general court-martial. It was supposed that nothing could save him from the heavy penalty of his rebellion.

We were the whole day getting together the prize property—elephants, camels, horses, bullocks, &c. During the day, the general visited the *keeledar*'s afflicted family. He assured them of their protection and safety, and ordered that every requisite for their use should be given them, more especially their clothes, which were splendid indeed! They were protected, consoled, and sympathized with. It is the boast and pride of the brave to administer succour to the afflicted, and wipe away the tear of sorrow.

Our brave general was humane as he was brave; and when he visited this weeping family, he said, "Shipp, this is a sad sight; what can possibly be done to relieve their distress?"

He desired me to inform them of his inclination to alleviate their sufferings; that they should, in the course of the day, see their father; and that, should they wish it, they might be permitted to see him every day, but that, for the present, he must live separate from them. The general desired me to say everything that could console them. The elder daughter threw herself at his feet, and thanked him for his kindness. I saw the tear stealing down the gallant general's cheek as he turned his head from her; and for a time he was so overpowered by his feelings that he could not speak.

In the course of the day the ladies were permitted to visit the *keeledar*. They proceeded, veiled, to the room in which he was confined; and the meeting was truly distressing. The daughter whispered words of comfort into her father's ear, and did her utmost to console and support him; begging him not to be so dejected, and assuring him that they had fallen into the hands of merciful and humane persons, whose general had himself assured her of her safety and protection from all harm. She continued, "Come, dear father, cheer up;" and she kissed away his tears, and wiped his eyes with the end of her white muslin dress. The old man cried and sobbed most piteously; but, having given full vent to his tears, he was more cheerful. They remained with him about a couple of hours, and then returned to their apartments in the *zenanah*, greatly composed and comforted.

The prize property was removed to camp, and sold by public auction, which lasted a whole day. It realized a very large sum of money. The general court-martial for the trial of the rebel *keeledar* now assembled, composed entirely of native commissioned officers, the senior officer acting as president. A warrant had been granted by the governor-general in council of Fort William, for the convening of native general courts-martial, for the trial of all such persons as might rebel against the government. This man now stood arraigned before a tribunal thus constituted, charged with treachery and rebellion against the government. Forty years' service crowned the brow of the venerable *soubahdar* who presided on this occasion, and he was a very shrewd clever fellow. The proceedings were conducted by a European officer, through an interpreter, and committed to paper in English. The crime with which the prisoner stood charged was read to him by the interpreter. He seemed perfectly to comprehend the charge against him, and he pleaded "Guilty." This he pronounced in a manly and firm voice, stating, that he fought entirely irresponsibly, and that he was ready and willing to meet the penalty of the law, and atone for his disobedience with his life. Here he struck his bosom, and seemed to wait the order for his execution.

The president turned round to him, and said, in a most pathetic manner, "Keeledar, you have now put your seal to your own death by that confession; but have you not got a wife and children? If you have no value for your own life, will you also murder them?"

This appeal, urged in the most impressive manner, roused the *keeledar* from his lethargy. He started, looked wild, paused; his lips seemed to quiver; and his head dropped on his heaving bosom. There seemed to be an innate working of the soul—a dreadful struggle between two contending feelings.

The good and humane president soothingly said, "Take your time, ere you pronounce the sad doom of your wife and children—your time is ours."

The whole court, and the numerous spectators, now waited with breathless impatience and anxiety, to hear the *keeledar*'s reply. At last he said, "Your observation relative to my wife and children is just. I will not be the means of agonizing their feelings; but," continued he, "what will the *rajah* say, should I deceive him?"

The *rajah*'s treachery and rebellion were explained to him, and he was apprised of his elopement, and the probability there was that he was dead. Upon hearing this, his feelings seemed to undergo another struggle, and, after a short pause, he drew from his bosom a long roll of paper, which contained the most peremptory instructions from the *rajah*, to fight the English, *"as long as one stone of Gurrah Mundellah stood upon another, and as long as one drop of water remained in the Nerbuddah, to wash away their blood."* This letter was received the very day he had promised to give up the fort to Major O'Brien. Other documents fully proved that his resistance to the government was in fulfilment of the positive orders of his master. He was consequently fully acquitted, but kept in custody for some time. He was afterwards pensioned by the Company. Had this man been hanged, it would have cast a gloom over our victory. He afterwards confessed to me, that the difficulty he had experienced in resolving upon the course which he at last was induced to pursue on his trial, arose from his doubts whether it was more honourable to sacrifice his own life, or eternally to offend his tyrannic master. He expressed himself as being very grateful to the court for their great care and anxiety about him, more especially to the good *soubahdar*.

I immediately communicated the fact of his acquittal to his agonized family, who prostrated themselves on the earth, and said, "Bless the humane English! may they long live and prosper in this land!" Immediately after his acquittal he was permitted to live with his wife and daughters, and he was received by them with feelings that would have done credit and honour to a more enlightened family. From that moment his beautiful daughter was no more visible; but they all proceeded with us towards the small fort of Huttra, until the turbulence of the country in which the *keeledar* resided had in some measure subsided, when he was permitted to return to his home.

Having left a regiment for the protection of the fort of Huttra, we proceeded towards Saugar. On our way we had to call on several smaller forts, the occupants of which gave them up without a murmur; and in a short time we reached our cantonments: but scarcely had we had time to cool ourselves, when we were again put in requisition, and directed to proceed against the strong stone fort of Gurrah Khootah. Towards this fort we moved some time in the month of March, 1819; and we were not displeased with the news, as we were indebted to the *keeledar* of that fort an old grudge, for his impudence when we passed it some few months before. The garrison was overbearing, and it was high time to bring them to their senses. This fort belonged to

Scindia, one of our allies, but had been sold by the garrison, for their ten months' arrears of pay, to a neighbouring *rajah*, who could not or would not give it up without a fight for it. The circumstances of the purchase are these:—

Some years before that period, the fort of Gurrah Khootah was besieged by a considerable force from the Deccan, and they persisted in the siege for some eighteen months, but could not take it. The *rajah*, then its owner, not being able to drive the invading force away, solicited Jean Baptiste, a bastard Frenchman in Scindia's service, to disperse the besiegers, with a promise that he would reward him for so doing with some land in the vicinity of the fort. This was accepted by the Frenchman, who, with a considerable force, succeeded in driving the besiegers to their own country. This accomplished, he took up his ground on the place the besiegers had left; and, a day having been appointed for the arrangement of the promised reward, the hypocritical Jean Baptiste marched into the fort in the greatest splendour and magnificence, with colours flying, drums beating, war-trumpets screeching, &c. His forces were permitted to enter indiscriminately, and no treachery was even dreamed of. When the usual greetings and congratulations were over, shoulder to shoulder, and breast to breast, at a preconcerted signal, the unsuspecting and unarmed garrison were pounced upon, and driven out of the fort, and deprived of their wives and daughters. Jean Baptiste then gave, or sold, the said fort to Scindia, who placed in charge of it one Harratoone, an Armenian.

The garrison, under this man's command, sold the fort for their arrears of pay, and the purchaser was the grandson of him whom Jean Baptiste had so treacherously deceived; and, if every one had his right, it was legally his own without paying for it.

This grandson of the original owner of the fort paid up the arrears of the garrison—eighty thousand *rupees*—the old garrison walked out, and he walked in. Scindia, however, still considered this fort to be his; but, as he could not take it, he called upon us, his allies, to take it for him. Had it been the old garrison, we should have been better pleased; but it was our duty to obey orders; so to work we went, the garrison having positively refused to give it up without a struggle.

This fort stands on the river Scend; and two sides of it are protected and guarded by that river, which is deep. The other two faces are protected by a strong stone wall thrown round the fort, on the banks of a branch of the same river. It was, therefore, necessary that we should make ourselves masters of this outwork, before we commenced breaching the fort. For this purpose a corner bastion was selected, where the water of the river was not more than three feet deep. In a few hours the breach was ready, and the moon's rising was the time appointed for the storming of this bastion. The ascent was high and difficult. The general was in the battery when the storming party moved out, and I was rather surprised to see him proceed with them down to the river. I, of course, stuck close to his elbow. The enemy soon observed us, and commenced a heavy fire, but too high. Our brave *sepoys* mounted the breach like heroes; but at the top the fight seemed desperate on both sides, and at one time we thought our men were giving way. Impressed with this notion, our brave little general dashed through the water, and was on the top of the bastion in a moment, and soon cheered his men in. The enemy fled towards the fort, and left us in quiet possession of the outer fortification. There was a large house, about two hundred paces from this corner, which our men occupied during the night, and we returned to the camp pleased with our day's exploit, and that we had not stained Old England's banner.

On the following morning the engineer fixed on a place for the batteries on the opposite side of the river, and breached an enormous bastion, which, like that of the fort of Mundellah, ran down to the water's edge. In four-and-twenty hours the heavy guns were moved down and put into their places for work, establishing our grand magazine in a village immediately behind them, to which a road had been dug for the purpose of conveying the ammunition, without being exposed to the firing from the fort. The general gave most positive orders, before he left the battery, that no ammunition should, on any account, be lodged in the magazine, but that it should be kept behind the village. These orders having been given, we rode home to breakfast. I had scarcely swallowed a mouthful when the general seemed restless, and presently said, "Shipp, saddle your horse immediately, and ride at speed to the grand battery. I have a strange presentiment that all is not right there." My horse was saddled in a moment, and I galloped down with all possible speed. When I arrived at the battery I really thought I should have fallen off my horse, for the first things that met my eye were the whole of the tumbrels, with shots and shells, and some thousands of rounds of gunpowder. These were all drawn up in the battery, and a single shot from the fort would have blown them all up. I ordered them to be removed instantly behind the village; and this we completed without the enemy's firing one shot. I found, on inquiry, that the captain to whom the general's command was given, delivered his orders to his subaltern—the subaltern to the sergeant—

the sergeant to the corporal—and so on to the poor stupid driver of the bullocks. I hope this circumstance may meet the eye of the young soldier, and teach him the absolute necessity of the strictest obedience to orders, and impress upon his mind that, whatever may be his rank, it does not place him above seeing things executed himself. Had those tumbrels, through the neglect which occurred, been blown up, many lives must have been destroyed, and the loss of the contents of the *tumbrels* would have obliged us to have raised the siege, and given the enemy time to fortify their fort. All this mischief would have fallen on him whose imperative duty it was to have seen the general's orders obeyed, and not to have entrusted their execution to others. Crimes out of number would have been framed against him: such as utter contempt of orders—pointed neglect of duty—wantonly destroying the lives of his soldiers, and the property of the government with which he had been entrusted. Nothing could have saved his commission; and, if the accident had happened, what could have soothed his feelings? As it was, the escape was quite providential; for, scarcely had the last *tumbrel* got round the corner of the village, before the enemy commenced a heavy cannonade on the very spot from which the ammunition *tumbrels* had been removed. On my return towards camp I met the general riding towards the fort at speed, still imagining that something was not right. When I reported to him the circumstances just described, he rode on and admonished the captain in most severe terms; but his heart was as humane as it was brave, and he soon pardoned the neglect, and forgot all about it.

We then went round the other works, to see that everything was safe and in obedience to his orders. In the mortar-battery, the general observed to the captain of the artillery, that he thought the magazine was too close to the battery; but the officer explained the nature of its construction, which satisfied him of its security, and we rode home again.

We were in hopes of opening our breaching-guns on the following morning, for which purpose we all rode down to see them commence. The shelling-battery had commenced the day before, and did wonderful execution. The guns were loaded; the match was lit; when, on a sudden, our attention was drawn from the contemplation of this view to one of a less pleasant nature—an awful explosion in our mortar-battery, the shells from which were ascending some yards above the heads of the artillery-men, and then exploding. I was immediately dispatched to ascertain the cause of this unfortunate occurrence. I rode within a hundred and eighty yards of the fort, but I was not conscious that I was so near, till their balls roused me from my reverie. Something still kept blowing up in our mortar-battery, so that I had not time to go further round. I continued my course, therefore, as hard as my horse would go, till I arrived at the river. The crossing, at this part of the river, was completely commanded by three guns, which the good-natured souls in the fort had laid for me when I should get in the middle of the said crossing. The water was about four feet deep; consequently, my progress was slow. The first shot went about twenty yards over me; the next fell short; but the third struck the water so close to me, that the spray covered both myself and my horse, and I was wet through. In this state I dismounted, keeping my horse between me and the fort, for I had still the worst part to go over. The moment they saw me dismount, there was a general shout from the bastion, conceiving that the last shot had killed me. This shouting and taunting roused the indignation of the aid-de-camp, and, to check their mirth, he mounted again, and took off his hat and waved it in defiance of them. Upon this they sent three messengers at once, but not one came to me. Before I reached the battery the enemy were, naturally enough, very busy in availing themselves of the general panic caused by our mortar magazine having blown up. Near the battery, the first object that met my sight was a native gunner literally skinned from head to foot, crying most piteously for a drink of water. Nearer the battery lay several European and native soldiers dead. Everything was in the greatest confusion, and consternation was on every countenance. The dreadful catastrophe happened in the following manner:

Behind the mortars lay some hundreds of shells, ready loaded, to be used as they might be required; a shell, fired from one of the centre mortars, burst in the muzzle; the fusee recoiled and fell on the loaded shells; these exploded, and communicated with the magazine, which, at that moment, a person had entered for the purpose of bringing out some requisite. The explosion blew up this poor man, the unfortunate native gunner before spoken of. It was more than twenty paces between the magazine and the spot where this poor creature was found. In two days after, he died. The melancholy event could not have been foreseen or prevented; but the consequences were serious—sixteen men suffered, four of them Europeans. Three of the victims were lying in the battery, without their bodies having been even touched with gunpowder. They died from concussion of the brain. One European was blown some yards into the river, without the slightest injury. Conductor Glassop, of the Bengal Foot Artillery, a man of upwards of twenty stone, was standing amidst the shells when they blew up, and, strange to say, escaped uninjured. Circumstances like these are the inscrutable doings of Providence, and far beyond man's poor and narrow comprehension. At this time the general had himself arrived, and having ascertained the cause of the sad catastrophe, could only add his moiety of commiseration for the poor sufferers. Blame could not be attached to anyone. The affair was one of the unavoidable accidents of war, which no human foresight could have guarded against or prevented.

The enemy, availing themselves of the calamity, rushed to that side of the fort in great numbers, and brought every moveable gun and matchlock to bear on the scene of woe. Having removed the dead and wounded to camp, we reloaded the whole of the mortars and howitzers in the two batteries, and levelled them at the multitude of people that had collected on the fort. They were fired in quick succession, when a general flight took place, and many of them ran their last race. Nearly sixty shells, with some few shots, were fired in a few minutes, and not a soul could for some time afterwards be seen at the same side of the fort, save some few bearing away the dead and the wounded. We then gave them three cheers, but they returned not the greeting.

At this moment our breaching-battery opened with a salvo, accompanied with three hearty cheers, which that side of the garrison returned. After this we went on coolly and systematically, and we returned home again, visiting the several posts and batteries. In the evening, the European soldiers were committed to the grave, followed by their comrades, who dropped a tear to their memory.

The following morning I went to breakfast with Captain Daggalier, of the old 13th regiment Bengal Native Infantry, in the large house occupied by our men, about five hundred yards from the fort. We were busily engaged upstairs securing a hearty meal, when a large three-pound shot found its way through the window of the room in which we sat, and passed under the table between my legs and those of Captain Daggalier. This convinced me that there is some advantage in having long legs. Mine were so excessively lanky, that I could only just screw them under the edge of the little camp-table; from which fact only I can still boast of having two legs. I need not say that the tea-things, breakfast, &c., were broken and upset. I joined another party, and, having finished my breakfast, I proceeded to meet the general, who had arrived to examine our approaches in this direction.

CHAPTER 22

Asseerghur

The breached bastion was found to be a tough piece of masonry, extremely thick and well put together; so we pegged away at its foundation. At last some of the stones began to give warning that they were tired of the fun, and would not stand it any longer—so down they came; and those on the top, wishing to show their attachment, soon followed, and by the following day, the breach looked ascendable.

When I went down to the breaching-battery, I saw my old friend, the Irish sergeant, busy laying a gun. "Well, sergeant," said I, "what do you think of the breach?"

He replied, "The divel a better within a day's march."

"Do you think we shall get in, sergeant?"

"The divel a fear of that, for there is not a living soul but what our shells have kilt and destroyed; so that when you are in, you will have nothing to do but shoot the remainder, and take the place in a moment."

"I am afraid you are too sanguine, sergeant," said I.

"Not at all, your honour: you will not find ten living men in the whole fort that our shells have not destroyed. If you do, call Paddy Dogan a *spalpeen*."

"Well," I answered, "we shall see, sergeant."

"Fait!" said he, "that's more than they will; it would do their dead eyes good to take a peep at our brave boys getting up the breach."

Here was a general titter at the expense of poor Pat; and he exclaimed, "Fait! you may laugh, but it's no laughing matter; how would you like to be kilt yourselves? Answer me that question."

At the back of the breach stood the once splendid palace of its rightful owner, but now one general mass of ruins. The breach was reported practicable, and the storming ordered for the following morning, giving time to knock off all defences behind which the enemy could secrete and hide themselves, so as to annoy the storming party; but the *keeledar* of the fort, seeing his haughty tower tumbling to the ground, his soldiers falling victims to our shells wherever they showed themselves, and that several fatal explosions had already occurred during the siege, began to think seriously of giving up the fort, rather than stand the storm. He had, indeed, lost a great number of his best men. A messenger was therefore dispatched from the fort, stating that, if the general would permit them to march out with their arms and private property, they would give up the fort. The proposal stood on these grounds: their arms were not worth ten pounds, and the whole of their property consisted of what they stood in. Need there be a scruple in granting such a proposition? Was there anything dishonourable in meeting such a proposal, if only in mercy for human lives? Certainly not. The breach was a most difficult one, and there is no question that, if they had defended it, we should have lost fifty or more men; and it was by no means clear to me, or any man who knew what a breach was, that our success would have been at all a certain thing. Our brave and humane general agreed at once to the terms proposed, much against the will of some of the Company's officers, who attempted to attach some degree of blame to his permitting them to march out with their arms. Our general, however, by his own nice judgment, and the advice of his staff-officers, some of whom had been years in the Company's army, overruled the opinions of the firebrand sub in search of promotion, and the following morning was appointed for their marching out. On viewing the garrison the next morning, it was found to consist of fifteen hundred fine men, well armed and equipped; so that we had no reason to regret that we had not wantonly sacrificed men's lives. The garrison had been originally two thousand strong, but was now reduced to about fifteen hundred, the others having been killed and wounded. When we marched down, the gates of the fort were closed, and the men had manned the ramparts. I was desired to inform them, that the time for giving the fort up had expired; and, if not at once complied with, the general must instantly order the storming-party to proceed, for which purpose they had been drawn up near the breach. At last the gates were thrown open, and the *keeledar*, at the head of his men, marched out in column, with a firm steady pace. He was a fine-looking man, and, indeed, so were all his soldiers. Their wounded men were brought out by their comrades on cots. These poor fellows we begged might be sent to our hospital, for the purpose of being dressed. On passing the general, the *keeledar* saluted. The general coolly returned; they marched out, and we marched in. The inside of the gate was covered with dead bodies of men, horses, bullocks, &c.; many of the houses were torn up by the roots, and the smell was beyond anything dreadful. The palace had been torn to pieces, and under its gigantic pillars protruded legs and arms of men and women. The sight was truly horrifying, and I will hasten over it as fast as possible. In the centre of the fort was found the old Armenian governor, who had, during the siege, been confined in a cell, and almost starved to death. I never in my life saw such a picture of woe as this poor creature. He was about sixty years of age; his hair quite white. He was the son of an Armenian by a native woman, and, consequently, of fair complexion, which his confinement caused to look cadaverous. You could almost have laid your finger in the furrows of his careworn cheek, and his little black eyes were sunk deep into his head. He was permitted to join his family, which had been sent to a small village during the siege.

The fort presented one mass of desolation and poverty, the old garrison having taken care of everything of value before they sold it. I had been appointed, on this occasion, prize-agent for the staff of the army, and commenced my search. It was rumoured that Jean Baptiste had in this fort secreted thirty *lacs* of *rupees*, which we were resolved to find, if possible. We dug up large pigs of lead, bars of iron, sheets of copper, pits of grain, vats of *ghee* (a kind of butter), but no money. If perseverance could discover this hidden treasure, we were resolved to find it. After digging above twenty feet, and working our way under the palace, we discovered a dungeon, or cell. Into this we descended, at the risk of treading on reptiles. From this dungeon we traced several rooms or cells, no doubt formerly the prisons of some captive beauties, till they were reconciled to an illicit intercourse with their tyrants. Searching every hole, and digging in every corner, we came at last to a kind of wall, newly built up, through the top of which we could see a door. This wall and door we soon forced to obedience, and we entered a large room, recently cleaned and whitewashed. In the centre of this room was a trap-door, with a large lock. Our hearts beat high with expectation; but what was our surprise, when we found this tomb contained the body of some poor murdered person, who had been buried here! Thus ended our search; and the whole captured property sold for fifteen hundred *rupees*, which we were obliged to hand over to Scindia some time afterwards. Our next duty was to commit the dead to the earth. In the performance of this unpleasant task, I had to follow one of the Company's artillery to his last home. Observing one of the funeral party lagging behind the rest, I asked him why he did not keep up. He answered, that "He had had a great big fight with the deceased a short time before he went dead, and he did not think the man had forgiven him."

"Poh! poh!" replied I, "the man cannot hurt you now he is dead."

"Och, fait!" said he, "I beg your honour's pardon. I once knew a man that was as dead as Barney Flynn's great-grandmother, come to life; besides, the deceased said he would never rest, dead or no dead, till he gave me a great big bating; and I should not like to provoke him."

"Do not talk such nonsense to me," said I.

"Nonsense! your honour; it's no such thing at all, at all; he was a mighty cunning chap when alive, and who knows what he has learned since he went dead?" All I could say I could not induce this man to approach till the corpse was lowered into the grave, and that half filled, when he at last ventured to look in, and said, "Fait! I believe you are snug enough now, joy."

"Throw in a piece of earth as a signal that you part friends," said one of the men; but Paddy quickly replied, "No, no; that would be striking the first blow;" and he went away immediately, no doubt full of apprehensions that he should some time or other receive a nocturnal visit from his comrade, who now slumbered in peace, secure in the cold grave from war's alarms. So much for superstition!

Having buried our dead, we left one regiment of native infantry till Scindia should send a more loyal garrison. We were afterwards given to understand, that his highness was not at all obliged to us for knocking his fort to pieces. We then turned towards home, and in a few days reached Saugar to rest our weary limbs.

After the toils of war, and seeing no prospect of having anything more to do, I obtained permission to visit my wife at Cawnpore, some four hundred miles from Saugar. This was readily granted: I reached Cawnpore in the space of fourteen days; and, in the embraces of an affectionate wife, I forgot, for a time, the "pride, pomp, and circumstance of glorious war." I remained in Cawnpore about eight or ten days, and the place was at that time the seat of festivity and splendour. Dinners, balls, and routs, followed each other in quick succession, so that, at the end of the ten days, I was completely exhausted by dissipation. On the eleventh day, I again bent my way to Saugar, to join the division. My affectionate little partner accompanied me some miles on the road, and would willingly have followed me to the field; but there are scenes even on the line of march that must ever offend the eye of delicacy; and I have always condemned the folly of those wives who have followed their husbands to the field of battle. However ardent may be the affections of such wives, the very act attaches to them want of delicacy: but what will not woman do for the man she loves; she will even share with him the cup of dishonour, and linger in his sight a short moment ere he is plunged into eternity, to satisfy the offended laws of his country. Pity it is either that women love so much, or that men deserve their love so little! Dearly as I loved my wife, I could not expose her to the scenes incident to an Indian encampment.

Having bidden her farewell, I started at speed, that I might not see her again; yet I could not help stealing another last look, when I saw her head was still turned towards me. I, would sooner go through the toils of a campaign than suffer the heaviness I always experience at parting with my family; but duty was my passport, and surmounted every difficulty and obstacle, and in thirteen days I reached Saugar; but, from being exposed to incessant rain, and afterwards to the scorching sun, I had sown the seeds of a disease which nearly cost me my life, though it was some time before it burst forth. It was supposed that the division of the army to which I was attached, would be continued at this station, for the purpose of watching the new-conquered provinces of Saugar and Candish; so we began to build huts or asylums against the winter, and we agreed to send for our wives—for what is man's life debarred the pleasure of female society? Men are little better than monsters without it. Wherever modest women are, there will always be a becoming decorum and decency; but men, when long estranged from their society, dwindle into gross habits; and the hilarity of an immodest song, and the cup of inebriety, form their pleasures, and the summit of their felicity. Our wives having been invited to join us, mine was the first to set the example; and, although the journey was attended with considerable danger, she reached me in four days, at the fort of Huttra, whither I had proceeded to meet her. This personal risk, on her part, to join me, could not but gratify my feelings and increase my love. In the course of a month, ten ladies had arrived, and the little station was the gayest of the gay. We generally met every day, either at dinner, ball, or supper, and our hearts were as light as our pockets.

While we were at this station, there was a large monkey that was a general nuisance, from the numerous robberies which he committed under the dark mantle of night. He would pounce into shops, and would run off with silks, satins, silver, gold, and indeed anything within his reach. On one of these excursions, having taken a fancy to a shawl, he rushed into the shop and grasped it; but the shawl being rather heavy and long, it retarded his progress, and the master of the shop seized him by the tail. He held fast, the monkey pulled; he called for help, the monkey screamed; he kicked, the monkey bit. At last the owner of the shawl seized the animal's tail with his grinders, and poor Jacko went off with his prize, but minus some six inches of his tail. By the blood they traced his steps to an old dilapidated mosque, where he was shot. Here were found the spoils of many a midnight ramble, and which many an honest neighbour laid under the stigma of having stolen. Such was the power of this monkey, that he would have mastered many a man. These animals, in India, I think are very sagacious and cunning, being petted and fed by men, and frequently living in the houses of the Hindoos. I recollect a young man, a cadet, who was proceeding up the river, and was not accustomed to these creatures, incautiously shot one of the older gentlemen out of several whom he saw. Even amongst these animals age is honourable; they one, and all sallied out upon him, and he took to his heels fast, throwing away his pouch, which was full of balls, shot, &c. These they seized, and still pursued him, until he parted with his shot-belt, and at last threw away his gun. As soon as they saw him unarmed, they bit him terribly, and he escaped merely with life. The boats to which he belonged were fortunately not far distant from him, and from these a party was formed, who sallied out against his pursuers. The first sight that presented itself was about a dozen hoary gentlemen examining the contents of the shot-belt and pouch. Seeing themselves overpowered, they wisely ran into the adjoining woods, taking with them the pouch and shot-belt. The gun they declined having anything to do with. I would caution young men proceeding up the river, to steer clear of these artful and mischievous creatures.

In the midst of all our gaiety our little division was again put in requisition, to proceed against the strong hill-fort of Asseerghur, some three hundred miles from Saugar. The monsoons or rains had commenced, and this sudden news distressed all the ladies exceedingly; but no faint-hearted husband shammed sick to remain behind. In two or three days we bade farewell to our fair spouses, and bent our way towards Asseerghur. The weather was intensely hot, so much so, that in a large double pool-tent, with *tatties*, or mats, suspended all round, made of grass, and continually kept wet, the glass stood at mid-day, at 120 and 130, and, after a shower of rain, the earth was like a hotbed. Notwithstanding this, we were obliged to proceed by forced marches, to reach Asseerghur as soon as possible. Our force was not very large, but our battering-train was considerable. The country in the immediate vicinity of this fort is barren and desolate, infested

Madras, Bengal and Bombay Native Troops of Shipp's Day

with wild beasts of every description, and many of our smaller cattle were carried away at night by them. The forces of the other two Presidencies, Madras and Bombay, had arrived before us, leaving a space for the Bengal division; and a most dreary and barren spot it was. The earth was dried and parched up, and nothing like vegetation could be seen except some prickly bushes. Not a leaf or blade of grass condescended to smile upon this spot. It was about a mile and a half from the fort, the gigantic sides of which seemed, even at this distance, to hang over us. They were really terrific even to look at; and, how we were to ascend such a precipice would puzzle a wiser head than mine. We that morning breakfasted with Major-General Doveton, commanding the whole of the forces before Asseerghur; but, not having the least fancy to their insipid dried fish and meats, we saved our appetites for our Bengal luxuries, and made a hearty second breakfast on our return to our tents.

The fort had been the property of Scindia, who had agreed to cede it to the Company for some equivalent; but the governor had the impudence to refuse to obey the orders of his master and the summons of the Company, and to fire on the troops of both whenever they passed. This fellow trusted, no doubt, to the supposed impracticability of the fort, and therefore came to the resolution of keeping possession of it for himself. The great natural strength of this hill seemed to defy the combined power of the world. Human art and labour had also added to its strength. The idea of ever being able to ascend such a place seemed absurd and romantic, and to effect a breach would have been equally impracticable. To mine it was beyond the power of human skill. From its base to its summit was about two miles high, and, on a perpendicular rock, from a hundred and fifty to two hundred feet high, stood strong fortifications, with some very heavy cannon and *ginjalls*. In the centre stood their grand mosque, with its two sharp spires pricking holes in the clouds. At a considerable distance from this temple was a large sheet of water, fed by a beautiful spring; and the troops could shelter themselves from our shells in excavated rocks. The fort was about two miles long, by three-quarters broad. On the south side was their *cuttrah*, or walled town, and at the principal entrance above the town innumerable underworks and bastions had been erected for its defence. When the sun shed its bright beams on its gigantic and variegated sides, it was truly beautiful. On the following morning I rose early to accompany the general, who commenced his inspection of the spots pointed out for our batteries. The top of the fort seemed entombed in the slumbering clouds, and it was some time before they dispersed. The position pointed out by the engineer, was upon a hill about two-thirds of the way up the ascent to the perpendicular rock, and then our guns were so elevated that we were obliged to sink the trail in the ground, and, having but little or no room to recoil, they were much injured, and we could do but little, if any good, except by knocking off the defences. Indeed, success seemed out of the question, and the only prospect we could foresee was to shell them into obedience. Our shelling, therefore, went on systematically, and with great vigour.

One night, having dined with an officer of the Madras army, during the time that we were before this place, and partaken rather too freely of the Tuscan grape, I started towards home on my favourite mare, whose speed not a horse in camp could equal, and lost my way. There was a considerable space between the camp where I dined, and our own encampment, the lights of which I thought I was standing fair for; but, after riding a much greater distance than that between the two encampments, and being in a thick jungle infested with tigers, I began to reflect seriously on my situation, and for a moment I paused to consider, under such circumstances, what was best to be done. How short-sighted is mortal man! That brief moment had nearly been my last! I had laid the reins of my mare over her neck, when in an instant she gathered herself up, snorted, and wheeled right round. Fortunately for me, I seized the mane, and, in an instant after, I saw, squatted down and crouching to the ground, a huge tiger. To have run from him would have been inevitable destruction. I therefore wheeled my mare round, and pressed her on towards him, but she would not approach him. I had a pair of loaded pistols in my holster-pipes. One of these I drew out, resolving, however, not to throw away my fire. While endeavouring to spur my mare on, and making all the noise I could, the ferocious animal slunk off, to the great joy of both my mare and myself, and I was not long before I reached my own tent.

I had some recollection of the place where this happened, as I always made a point of making myself acquainted with the localities of the encampment and its vicinity; so early the following morning I rode towards the spot, which was not far from the road, and where I found that the said tiger had feasted on a more delicious morsel—a nice little *ghinee* (a small cow).

I would recommend to those who may chance to get into the vicinity of such bad neighbours, never to run from them, but, if sufficient courage can possibly be mustered, to run at them, or to stand and stare them full in the face. A captain in the Company's service once told me, when speaking of these savage beasts, that he was out shooting in some part near Loodianah alone, and he had just discharged his last barrel at some wild ducks, when a large tiger made his appearance. He had not time to load again, but, for a time, stood his ground. He stared—the tiger grinned, but did not seem inclined to come to the scratch. This said captain, being a funny fellow, at last thought of a stratagem that was likely to put his grinning neighbour to flight, which was by turning his back to the animal, looking at him through his legs, and thus running off backwards. He positively declared that, the moment the tiger saw this strange metamorphosis, he took to his heels, and was out of sight in an instant. I will not vouch for the verity of this tale, but I have heard, since my arrival in England, that the same trick was actually played on a savage mastiff belonging to a tan-yard, that would not permit a stranger near the premises without tearing him to pieces, but the moment he saw this curious figure he took refuge in a drying-house, and for some time after on the least noise he would hide himself, thinking, no doubt, it was his friend with his head between his legs again. The reason on account of which I cannot take upon myself to vouch for the veracity of my friend the captain, is this: I once *tiffed* in company where this brave son of Mars was one of the party. The conversation turned on the privations which soldiers and sailors are frequently called on to endure. Some of the company said that, in the course of their services, they had not tasted food for three days; some mentioned a longer period. I said I did not believe that the system could be sustained for more than seven days, if so long, without food or some kind of sustenance. The captain, however, thought otherwise; and, begging my pardon most politely, he protested that he had often, when in the West Indies, lived himself for weeks without food; and that once, for six months, he had nothing to eat but Cayenne pepper! This was likely to be a hot man in dispute, so we left him in possession of the field as well as of his story; and this is the reason why I would not take upon me to vouch for the authenticity of his tiger adventure.

 A few days after we had commenced the siege against this strong fort, General Watson, commanding the Bengal division, came into my tent, and, by the smile on his countenance, I could see he was much pleased. At last he said, "Shipp, I have got some good news for you, which I am sure will please you much." I replied, "General, good news is acceptable at all times; what is it?"

 "I have at last obtained permission," said the general, "to lead in person my own column to the storm; and I am sure you and Knollis will support me with your lives." I replied, "Whenever my duty calls me, Sir, my life will be willingly risked in the service of my country."

"I know it," said the general; "and, ere this day week, I hope to plant Old England's banner higher on the tower of glory than it ever has been. This fortification is, I believe, the highest in the world, some fifteen hundred feet above the level of the plain." Some short time after this the fort was surrendered, and the gallant general, fortunately, still lives in the bosom of domestic bliss in his native land. I say "fortunately," because, after the surrender of this strong and impregnable fortress, it was deemed, by one and all, that it was beyond the power of mortal ascent, and our beloved general must infallibly have fallen a victim to his zeal. Many deeds of high daring had marked the long and glorious career of this respected officer. He had been in one corps (the 14th regiment) as subaltern and commander, for the long period of three-and-thirty or four-and-thirty years, without being a day absent from his duty; and he was universally beloved for his urbanity and affability of manners. I should justly be accused of ingratitude did I not take this opportunity of returning him my most heartfelt thanks for his uniform generosity and disinterested friendship to me, displayed on numberless occasions.

After shelling almost incessantly for several days, a great number of the men in the fort were killed in going for water, which was about a hundred yards from their hiding-places, and these became so offensive that the garrison persuaded the *keeledar* to give up the fort as a hopeless business. To this the *keeledar*, who was a most dastardly coward, readily consented; for which purpose he dispatched a messenger to say, that if he would cease shelling he would come to some amicable arrangement. Our officers, foreseeing the total impossibility of our success, complied in some slight degree, stipulating that they would cease firing for a few hours. This was calculated to impress the garrison with a conviction, that a further resistance on their part in withholding the fort, would be only seeking their own destruction, and imbruing their hands in their own blood; and that, as the English were now inclined to be merciful, under the supposition that the garrison had been seduced to disaffection by some artful rebel, it would be better for them at once to surrender. The message returned by our commander was that if they were sincere in their wish to give up the fort unconditionally, firing for the present, from the shelling-batteries only, would cease; and that, if the terms were not accepted, they would recommence with redoubled force. It was further agreed that one more parley would be attended to. The messenger departed, and orders were dispatched to the shelling-batteries to cease till further orders.

Natives, speaking of the height of this place, say that "none but the crafty hawk, high lingering over his prey, or the morning lark, sweetly soaring and singing over its young, could ever see the inside of Asseerghur."

Some few days before our arrival, the *cuttrah* had been stormed and taken by a division of the Bombay army, under the command of Colonel Frazer, of the Royal Scots; but they found the detention of their little conquered town warm work, it being so completely commanded, that every street could be raked by the firing from the fort. Some part of the upper-works of the fort were within three hundred yards of the town. Our soldiers were obliged, therefore, to seek shelter in the temples and huts. If they had not had the opportunity of retiring to these places, the town would not have been tenable. Those who were obliged, in the course of duty, to run from one place to another, had, the moment they were observed, a hundred shots at them. The enemy, with some reason, conceived that this occupation of the town was but a preparatory step to an entry by escalade into their fort. They, therefore, had a strong party constantly on the look-out for the opportunity of destroying all whom they could attack, either by surprise or stratagem. Soldiers are prone to look about them, and many of them will, in spite of all risks, go in search of plunder. Some of our troops, on this occasion, paid dearly for their disobedience of orders and violation of military laws. The principal post held by our troops in this town, was a large mosque or temple, of which the officers occupied one side, and the soldiers the other. One by one the men stole off in search of plunder. The enemy, having observed this, rushed on the remaining few, and the brave colonel was killed in defending himself against unequal numbers. On the return of these soldiers to their deserted post, what must have been their mortification and panic to find their brave colonel butchered, through their neglect and disobedience of all orders, and their poor wounded comrades, who but an hour before had shared with them in glory, weltering in their blood! What could have equalled their anguish, if their minds had not sunk below the ebb of feeling? Young soldiers, let this be a warning to you. It is but one instance, out of a great number within my own knowledge, of the fatal effects of breach of discipline. Whatever may be your prospect of gain, never be seduced to leave your post. You are, by such transgression, guilty of three prominent offences against the Articles of War: leaving your post before an enemy—death; abandoning your officer—death; plundering—death. There is scarcely a section in the Articles of War that does not touch this crime.

Chapter 23

The End of the Campaign

Ten o'clock came, but no messenger from the fort. A little time was given, and the shelling-batteries did not re-commence till nearly eleven o'clock; but when they did the top of the hill became one entire mass of smoke and fire, and thus it continued till the afternoon, when a messenger at length made his appearance, and informed the general that the *keeledar* would be down immediately to ratify the treaty and give up the fort. For this purpose the shelling was again stopped, and at about two o'clock the *keeledar* began to descend in a palanquin, with three or four followers. All the general and staff-officers in camp were directed to assemble for the purpose of meeting this rebellious chief. General Doveton's tent was the place of rendezvous. On the way to this tent the people appointed to escort the *keeledar* took him through our park of artillery, where there were some fifty guns, besides those then in use. This *keeledar* was a most unseemly-looking man; a great fat buffalo of a fellow, with enormous flitches of fat hanging over his hips. He was also excessively dirty in his person and dress, and looked as if he had just been turned out of an oil-shop. He entered the tent with all the impudence of a *nawab*, chewing *paun*, and as though he was fully prepared to receive a welcome greeting. In this he was disappointed. He was desired to be seated, but his reception was cool and distant, and the knitted brow of Major-General Sir John Malcolm, the political agent for the government, portended no very flattering entertainment. When the whole were seated, Sir John broke silence, by stating "that the British army had no time to lose in unnecessary parley, and that, therefore, any argument of his would be waste of words, and unavailing, as nothing would suffice but the unconditional surrender of the fort to the troops of his government, and that he should, in his person, answer to his master, Scindia, for his rebellion and disloyalty." Here the fat *keeledar* began to gather himself up into speaking order, and at last mumbled out, that he was surprised that a person so well conversant with the Eastern customs and usages of war should propose such a thing as laying down their arms, as Sir John must know, that a *rajah-poot* would sooner suffer ten thousand deaths than be deprived of his arms. He concluded by protesting that for him to attempt to enforce such a thing would be endangering his own life. Sir John replied that he did well know the customs of the country and the characters of *rajah-poot* soldiers; but the *keeledar* must keep in view that these were terms offered to rebels, whose heads were the just forfeit of their disobedience and rebellion, and that, therefore, if they persisted in their rebellion, he should not advise the government to mitigate the penalty a single jot, but to hang every one of them. This was pronounced with some degree of displeasure, and the man of fat, not doubting in the least that of course he was included in the number to be hanged, began to quake for fear. He turned round and reflected for some time, his eye fixed on the dark and displeased countenance of Sir John Malcolm. At last he repeated that he dared not propose such terms to the garrison. "But," added he with the greatest effrontery and impudence, his villainy suddenly bursting forth, while he at the same time "grinned horribly a ghastly smile,"

"could you not *promise* them their arms and property, and, when they are fairly out, pounce upon them and take them from them?"

General Doveton, Sir John Malcolm, and half-a-dozen brigadiers, at this diabolical proposition rose simultaneously, and I really thought Sir John would have jumped down the rascal's throat, or have cut him to pieces on the spot, as he warmly replied, "Rebel! what grounds have you for supposing that the English could ever stoop to commit such an act of infamy? Can you, or any native of India, adduce a single instance of our government's having ever acted so treacherous and cowardly a part? No, miscreant; were your fort ten thousand times as strong, and ten thousand times as high as it is, we will either take it or level it with the plain. I cannot imagine how you have dared to make such an offer before these gentlemen. It would serve you right to cleave you to the ground for such an insult, and we can only treat such a proposition as arising from the baseness of your own heart. I desire that you will this moment return to your fort, and dare not again to insult this assembly with your vile propositions. Go and fight your fort, and we will soon force you to do what we now in pity offer. Go this moment, or I will give directions for the shelling to commence."

Upon this the man of Lambertian breed began to shake in a frightful manner; but at last he said, "I am out of danger, and will keep so; I will not return to the fort to be killed." Sir John replied, "But you shall, if I am obliged to carry you on my back." One of the officers present—I think General Watson—observed, "Then, Sir John, you would indeed have a load of infamy on your shoulders, that you could not easily shake off."

The *keeledar*, finding that he had gone his length, began now to smooth a little, and said that he would endeavour to induce the garrison to give up their arms, but that he dreaded the result. I caught his deep sunk eye, which beamed forth the most malevolent malice and hatred. I could see an innate working of revenge in his soul; but he at last said he would guarantee to give up the fort by ten o'clock the following day, upon the terms of unconditional surrender. To this he pledged his word, and offered to ratify the treaty under his hand and seal.

After much consultation, and apparent reluctance on our part, it was agreed that we would accept of the surrender, but with this proviso—that, if they did not march out by the hour agreed on, the negotiation should be considered as entirely closed, and that no further proposition would be listened to.

The *keeledar* then left the tent in sore displeasure, and rolled into his palanquin. Sir John Malcolm was as good as his word, for he saw him to the very entrance of his fort. Multitudes assembled to meet their infamous and treacherous governor; but what could they possibly expect from such a man? If he would rebel against his government, would he not deceive his garrison? A soldier doing the former is capable of committing any other crime, however enormous it may be. This fellow returned to his garrison and told them that he had frightened the English to grant them their arms, their property, and everything they wished. Under these terms the whole garrison actually marched out with their property, arms, &c, and rendezvoused under the hill, where we had a strong party ready to march in. They were in number about seven or eight hundred, poor half-starved-looking creatures, and some of them almost naked. Sir John, having severely admonished them for their rebellious conduct, desired them to ground their arms and property. The infamy of the *keeledar* then came out; and, but for the interference of our troops, his men would have torn him to pieces. When he was asked if he had really held out those promises as from us, he laughingly replied, "I had no other method of getting them out, and I was not fool enough to remain in that fort to have my brains blown out. They are now in your power; do what you please with them. I have done my part; now do yours." The *keeledar* was immediately placed in confinement, and Sir John thus addressed the wretched-looking creatures who had constituted the garrison:

"I have every reason to believe that you came out under the idea that you should keep your arms and little property, and with the understanding that this indulgence had been granted by the English. No such thing was ever promised by us, nor could a rebellious garrison expect such an indulgence from the government, when death alone was the penalty of such conduct; but as you have been deceived by your base *keeledar*, into a belief that such terms were offered by us, and have surrendered the fort under this confident expectation, we will not enforce the terms insisted on through your treacherous *keeledar*, but permit you to depart as you are. You may therefore go, and I would advise you to retire quietly to your homes, and there to make your peace with your justly-offended master, Scindia."

This party was escorted some miles from camp, and the *keeledar* was sent a prisoner to his master; but what became of him I never heard. There can be little doubt, however, that his refusing to give up this fort was by positive instructions received from Scindia himself, who was closely connected with the conspiracy formed against the British government, during the Pindaree campaign; but the presence of the Marquis of Hastings, with the centre division of the grand army, under the very walls of his capital, kept that combined conspiracy from breaking forth.

From the tremendous height of this fort, the shelling at night was truly splendid and magnificent. I have seen ten and fifteen shells soaring in the air together, and, from the extreme height from which they were obliged to be thrown, they looked like falling stars. When they burst, the report below was like thunder.

Thus ended the campaign of 1818-19, and we had no occasion to complain of not having had the honour of storming the fort of Asseerghur, as all the guns in the world could never have effected a breach. Where we did attempt a breach, our twenty-four-pound balls only served to knock off little bits of the more prominent and projecting rocks, and to make the ascent more difficult and formidable, by removing the very pieces of rock by which we had a chance of ascent. The part which we attempted to breach was a kind of nook, which had the appearance of once having been a waterfall. I am confident, if we had battered at it till doomsday, we never could get up; and, even if we could, a dozen old women might have killed us every one by rolling down stones upon us. I therefore think it a most fortunate event that this fort was given up without being stormed, and I certainly may be considered as speaking feelingly on this subject, for, my gallant general having volunteered (being the oldest colonel in camp) to lead in his own column, it is not very probable that I should have left him alone to find his way to the breach. Often when I viewed this spot, did I think, "Here ends my career;" and so strong was this impression on my mind, that I began to fix my eye on some little romantic spot where I should like to be interred, should I have here ended my days; for I was convinced of the total impossibility of success. I began to arrange my papers, and had fully made up my mind to end my career, as I had commenced it, in the field of glory. But I had a wife—ay, and a fond wife too, which reflection much embittered the prospect before me. Had I been without this tie, it would have been my heart's first choice to have ended my days in the service of my country. When I say this, I am far from pretending that I had any particular wish to die; but had it been my fate, I would, from choice, sooner have made my exit fighting for my country's liberty and glory, than on the downy bed; but Providence has ordered it otherwise.

In the afternoon we went to examine the fort; and every step I took more thoroughly convinced me of the utter impossibility of any earthly power ever taking it by storm. I was obliged to halt a dozen times in ascending, quite at my leisure, towards the grand entrance. By the time I reached the gate I was completely exhausted, and I was ten minutes in getting to the top. If we had stormed this place, it would, beyond question, have been the grave of hundreds. On the walls were huge stones, piled up for our destruction, some of them weighing two or three hundred-weight, which a child might have pushed off. When once up, the eye extended along a considerable level plain, on which were fields, woods, and gardens. In the centre was a large tank of water, as clear as crystal, but purple streams of blood lingered on its margins and banks. Many dead bodies lay by the side of this tank. Some of them must have been shot in the very act of drinking. The stench was dreadful. Their sacred temple was contaminated and defiled with every kind of dirt and filth, and their gods wore marks of disfigurement from our shells. One had lost a head, but which, by the by, he could well spare, as he had a dozen. In one of the excavations of the rock was discovered a woman lying dead, with a dead infant in her arms. She was seated on a large stone, with her right side reclining on another rock or side of the excavation. Her left hand grasped the child round the body, and on her right reclined her head. The head of the infant, which I should suppose was about a year old, hung over her right knee. The woman had not a bruise about her; but it was supposed she had fled there from those destructive instruments of death, the shells. Near her lay several dead and mutilated bodies, in a state of putrefaction. She was a young woman about twenty, and well dressed. On inquiry among the prisoners, we learned that her husband had been killed by one of our first shells, and thrown into the very hole near which she was found, but it was not known whether she had followed him there, or whether she died before him; for the soldiers were so panic-struck that they could not directly answer the most simple question. Behind the temple lay a headless trunk. We understood that this was the body of the head priest of the said temple; that he was boasting of his being proof against anything that could be hurled against him by his hated foe; and, as we were informed by a surviving mendicant, scarcely had the superstitious words escaped his mouth, than he fell, a headless body, to the ground. His head, we were told, was found some yards from the spot where he lay. We immediately went in search of it, and found it eleven paces from the body, but not a human feature was left. The face was literally torn to pieces. To sketch the horrible scenes that presented themselves would fill a volume. I shall mention but one more; a shell had burst between a man's legs, and had literally split him up to the neck.

The large masses of congealed blood, seen at almost every step between the temple and tank, were convincing proofs that the loss of life must have been very great; but most of the dead bodies had been thrown over the walls, to find their way to the bottom of some excavated rock or tiger's den. The place altogether exhibited nothing but signs of poverty and distress, and they must have been, after the loss of the town, literally in a state of starvation. From this eminence the prospect was extensive and truly beautiful. The city of Borhanpore was plainly visible; and, although fourteen miles distant, such was the height of this place, that it seemed almost to hang over it. Men in the several encampments looked like babes. When the evening closed in, I found the atmosphere chilly and cold. This soon sent us down to the warmer regions below, where the glass, at the cool of eve, stood at eighty-five, and sometimes at ninety. The height of the thermometer at that hour, when the evening breeze is cool and salubrious, was no doubt occasioned by the great heat absorbed by the earth during the day. In India, it is quite common to inhale the sweet and refreshing breeze of eve, when, under foot, the ground is like a hotbed. The soil here was a kind of glittering red sand, and in some places rocky; and we were not at all sorry that we were about to leave it.

CHAPTER 24

Ill Fortune

The combined army was now on the point of marching from Asseerghur, after the cession of that fortress.

We bent our way once more towards cantonments, accompanying Sir John Malcolm to his new station of Mhow, for the purpose of visiting the celebrated cities of Indore and Ougein. This was some miles out of our direct route; but no traveller ought to pass such places without viewing the splendour and magnificence of ancient architecture for which those two cities are celebrated. A careful survey of such places will well compensate the traveller for going out of his way; feed his astonished mind with contemplation for years to come; and impress him with the conviction, that the system of architecture in Europe, in comparison with that of the East, is but in its infancy.

The approach towards Mhow is very difficult and fatiguing. One *ghaut* which we were necessarily obliged to ascend was frightful even to look at. The road had been scooped out from the side of the hill, which from its base was almost perpendicular, and seemed to defy mortal ascent. When I arrived at the bottom, I saw elephants, camels, and horses, men, women, and children, that seemed hanging on the projecting bosom of the flinty rock, or suspended from the clouds. When the elephants had reached the summit, they looked like small ponies, and the men like little dark specks in the sky. About two hundred yards from the top was a strong gateway, and two large bastions, for the protection of this pass into Holkar's provinces. Upon the hill was a strong stone-built fort, belonging to that chieftain, which was well filled with guns and men. This hill, from its base to its summit, is more than two miles. There are several wells during the ascent, for the accommodation of travellers, fed by springs hewn out of the solid rock. It is a good day's march to complete the ascent of this hill; and how cattle get up, with their enormous loads on their backs, is to the spectator wonderful to behold. Nothing of moment occurred on the journey, save some broken shins and knees; and, for three days after this trip, I was so stiff that I could scarcely move. We encamped on the top of this hill, and the view from its summit comprised an extent of at least fifty miles. The people below seemed of another world. In the lowlands the atmosphere was intensely hot and sultry; but upon the hill it was pure, cool, and salubrious, so that we seemed quite in another country. When we again set out on our journey, we travelled about a hundred miles without again descending. The whole of this distance the country was one general flat, and we did not find any descent till we got near Callenger, where the *ghaut* is nearly as high.

In two days more we reached the new station of Mhow, the residence of Sir John Malcolm, with whom we spent two pleasant days. Sir John was as hospitable as he was brave, and his tables groaned under the luxuries of the season. He possesses a profundity of wit; so that, wherever he is, the whole company are sure to be on the broad grin. I should recommend all people subject to liver complaints to pay Sir John a visit, if opportunity favours them, and I would wager ten to one that, in one month, he would laugh most of them out of their complaints. I was myself suffering under a violent attack when I was his guest, and the smallest motion, more particularly that caused by laughter, was attended with most excruciating pain; but our host could almost make a dead man laugh. The consequence was, that I laughed to some purpose, for I actually got rid of my complaint. Sir John generally made it a point of getting me close to him. He said to me one morning, "Shipp, did I ever tell you the story of my being invited to breakfast off a dead colonel?" I answered, "No, Sir John; nor are my poor sides in a state to hear it."

"Oh, but I must tell you: it's rather a serious story than otherwise." Finding there was no escape, I put both my hands to my sides (a necessary precaution to prevent them from bursting) and listened attentively. Sir John had a peculiar manner of relating anecdotes, which, for effect, I have never seen equalled; and a sort of squeaking voice, in which he generally spoke, especially when pleased, added greatly to the drollery of his stories. "I was invited to breakfast," said Sir John, "with a queer old colonel of the Bombay Artillery. This colonel was famous for giving good breakfasts, so I accepted his invitation, and went to his residence rather early, where I walked without ceremony into the breakfast-room. It is customary in India, when breakfast-things are laid, to throw a table-cloth over the whole, to keep the flies off. I thought it strange that I did not see a single servant; but I walked up and down the room, very contentedly, for nearly a quarter of an hour. At last I got quite hungry, so I thought I would help myself to a biscuit. For this purpose, I lifted the end of the cloth, and the first object that met my eye was—the colonel's head!" Just at this instant Sir John Malcolm struck me a violent blow on the shoulders, which so startled me, that I really thought the dead colonel was on my back. From that time, however, I lost all symptoms of the liver complaint.

After a short time our generous entertainer good-naturedly accompanied us to Indore, where the British resident, Mr. Wellesley, treated us in a most splendid and hospitable manner. He took us to visit the court of young Holkar, who, a short time before, had rebelled against the government, in consequence of which his troops had been dreadfully cut up at Mahidpoor, so that we could not expect a very cordial greeting. We, however, all proceeded thither, mounted on elephants, and we were received at the outer gates, by the junior officers of Holkar's court, rather coolly. Here we dismounted, and in the inner court we were met by some officers of higher rank, by whom we were conducted to a long room, on which was spread a clean white cloth, with innumerable pillows and cushions for the purpose of lounging on. Young Holkar rose on the entrance of the resident, and we all in our turn had a hug at him. He was a dirty-looking boy, about thirteen years of age, shabbily dressed, and who, it was said, has never been known to laugh out. After the usual greeting, and sprinkling of scents, we could see his rancour working within him. It was Sir John who had given his troops such a drubbing, and he could not, even on this occasion, conceal the hatred that rankled in his heart towards the English. The recollection of the disastrous defeat of his troops rushed across his mind, no doubt, the moment he saw Sir John Malcolm, and it left evident traces on his features, that indicated the most malevolent feelings towards his visitors. It appeared to be with difficulty that he could behave with decent civility; but, from fear of offending the British resident, he was compelled, with his courtiers and ministers, to affect a cordiality which he did not feel. Sir John Malcolm, however, soon disturbed their ceremonious gravity, which he converted into peals of laughter, so that the room resounded with shouts of merriment; and the before frowning *rajah*, who was reputed unable to laugh, actually threw himself on his back, and laughed most lustily. It was a considerable time before we could re-establish order; after which, an interesting conversation took place, which was followed by the distribution of presents, in which the young *rajah* was liberal, and we broke up much more friendly than we had met. We all returned to the resident's house, to a most splendid dinner.

On the following morning we bade farewell to our hospitable friends, Sir John Malcolm and Mr. Wellesley, and bent our way towards Ougein by forced marches, to make up for the time we had spent at Mhow and Indore. The Bengal division did not return with us, but went the direct road to Saugar, where they arrived some days before us. In two days we reached Ougein, and encamped in a small tope of trees, about a mile from the city, which is situated on the banks of the river Scend, opposite to which are the beautiful and extensive gardens, once the favourite resort of Scindia, but which, of late years, he has not visited. The once splendid palace of this ancient city has been actually permitted to tumble to pieces, and this seat of oriental magnificence may now be said to be the habitation of snakes, scorpions, and every kind of reptiles. The beautiful pleasure-grounds are still kept in some kind of order, as they are the haunts of mendicant priests, who willingly sojourn here, and by whom these gardens are considered as a holy place of worship. In the morning the rippling stream of the Scend is crowded with these Brahmin priests, sanctifying their hoary heads, as they suppose, with the pure waters of this fair and sparkling stream, and offering worship to their gods.

In the course of the afternoon we visited the old city, that had been buried by an earthquake. We could distinctly see tops of temples, trees, and houses, and there are still many wide and yawning excavations in the earth. At the extreme end of this old town stands the palace, in a state of dilapidation and decay. Some few priests reside in what was once the *zenanah*, the lower apartments of which run into the gliding stream of the Scend, and are washed by this beautiful river passing through them. Here we bathed, to the great annoyance and mortification of the priests who resided there, who did not fail to tell us in plain terms, that we had contaminated and polluted the sacred stream.

We next visited the subterraneous passage which was reported to reach from Ougein to the city of Benares, some two thousand miles! We commenced our exploration of this place by candle-light, and every ten yards descended into rooms almost square, till the place became so damp and chilly, that we were induced to return; but, even from the short distance we had accomplished, we could easily discover that it led to the palace, which stood about a quarter of a mile from it, and had no doubt been a secret passage to the *zenanah*, for some nefarious purpose. These subterraneous passages to the palaces of the great must have been designed for purposes dark as they are mysterious; and, could these dark and lonely cells but speak, I fear they would tell many a woeful tale. Over the mouth, or entrance, of this subterraneous passage, was a kind of old gateway, and on its still tottering towers were sculptured many tales of wonder, as false as they were strange. Wishing to see everything worth beholding, we commenced our march, by descending three or four steps into a square room, that was perfectly green from the damp vapour rising from the ground. In one corner of this room, which was about six feet square, we discovered a wrinkled old man reposing on some ashes, his hair white and his beard of great length. He viewed us with the eye of a lynx, and, having bid us the usual greeting of the morning, he at the same time sat up, and, assuming a considerable degree of self-consequence, he demanded where we were going, from whence we came, and what were our intentions. I was appointed interpreter, and I replied that we wished to see this wonderful subterraneous passage. He replied, "Yes, wonderful indeed! two thousand miles dug out of the bowels of the earth by manual labour, and which cost as much money as would purchase another world; but," continued he, "where are your provisions—your oil—your Koran? If you wish to explore this great wonder of man's power, you surely would not attempt it without first invoking Almighty aid! The journey is long, dangerous, and tedious."

"How far, then," said I, "does the excavation extend, that so many precautions are required?"

"To the famous city of Benares," replied he. "There may be found, though scarcely known to mortal man, the other entrance. This is as true as it appears wonderful to you who are unacquainted with these hidden mysteries. If you doubt my assertion, go on, and your own eyes will convince you of the truth of what I have told you."

We proceeded through some three or four rooms, descending two or three steps down to each, till a chilly dampness told us to return. We did so, and, not wishing to offend old grey-beard by evincing any disbelief of what we had heard, we gave him a few *rupees*, which he seized with all the avidity of a miser. His cunning eye sparkled again when he found the *rupees* within his grasp, and he bowed to the ground in token of thanks. He told us many stories, as wonderful as they were false: amongst the rest, the following:—That some of his holy sect (Brahmins) had, a short period before, attempted to explore this passage; but, when they had proceeded about half way, some of them died. The others consulted whether it was more prudent to proceed to the accomplishment of their design, or at once return, while it was certain that their oil and provisions would last them. They agreed to return, and they reached the spot from which they had first started, after an absence of some months. The hoary-headed mendicant told this barefaced falsehood with all the solemnity of truth, and confirmed it by emphatically calling on his Maker to witness his assertion. We did not think it prudent to dispute his word till we were fairly out of his clutches; but, just as we were about to take our departure, I told him that what he had asserted was nothing but a delusion to exact money from the English traveller, and that we could plainly see, from the nature of the passage, that it was a secret inlet to the great palace, for some dark and murderous purpose. This he denied with all the effrontery of which these people are capable, and we parted on no very friendly terms. This same old fellow accounted for the earthquake having visited the city of Ougein in the following happy manner. He said that a white man had sojourned there some three or four years, subsisting on the gifts of the benevolent.

"He spoke fluently all the Oriental tongues, was affable, and became generally esteemed. Having accumulated some money, he built a little temple, and, in two or three years, gained a considerable number of converts to his religion, and became so powerful in his arguments, and so persuasive in his discourses, that the Brahmin priests held a consultation. The result of this meeting was never published, for it was on that day—that long-to-be-remembered day—that the great visitation overtook this city, engulfing myriads of its inhabitants. This was a mark of their god's displeasure for permitting this ancient city to be defiled by the erection of a Christian temple. The temple was wholly swallowed up; but, Sir, strange to say, some one short minute before this, the white man had gone to a small school in a distant village, and escaped the catastrophe. On the same eve, however, he disappeared, and naught has been heard of him since that day—a day registered in blood in the annals of this ancient city."

We visited every place about Ougein worth seeing, and in the evening returned to our tents, where our hospitable general had, as usual, provided a sumptuous dinner, with every luxury of the season. On the following morning we stood towards Saugar, *via* Bopaul and Belsah, old Pindaree haunts; but nothing of moment occurred on the road, save that some of our servants lost their way in the night, and were never more heard of by us. There can be little doubt that they had fallen victims to banditti, for which this part of the country is notorious.

We soon arrived safe at Saugar, where we were met with open

arms by our affectionate wives. At this station all was now merriment and joy. Such is the life of a soldier! He no sooner furls his victorious banner, and sheaths his blood-stained sabre in the scabbard of peace, than, amid the revels of the fascinating and the gay, or in the more calm, but far sweeter enjoyment of domestic felicity, he loses all thought of "grim-visaged war."

I was blessed with a most affectionate partner, who shared in all my joys, and soothed me under all my sorrows. Her fond epistles to me, when in the field, were filled with expressions of pity for the poor deluded creatures with whom we were at war. She was the pillar of my best hopes; my bright star of happiness; my monitor in the hour of peril, and my sure refuge in distress. She had but one fault—that she doted where she should but have loved.

* * * * *

But, quitting recollections which, from subsequent events, have been rendered painful to me, perhaps the insertion of the following account of the extraordinary evidence given by an Irish sergeant before a court-martial may be tolerated, if only in consideration of its being the last of my Irish anecdotes.

President.—Well, sergeant, recollect you are upon your oath to speak the truth, and nothing but the truth, so help you God. State what you know touching the crime against the prisoner.

Sergeant.—I will, your honour. The other morning, when I was fast asleep on my cot, with my eyes open, I heard the prisoner there himself say to Patrick Gaffy, in a whisper—and sure I could tell his voice a mile off if I could hear him—that he would never rest day or night till he had kilt and murdered Corporal Ragon, becase he was always down upon him, and he would never let him alone besides.

President.—You have a strange way, sergeant, in giving your evidence: you say that you heard the prisoner, when you were asleep, tell Patrick Gaffy, in a whisper, that he would kill Corporal Ragon. Mind what you are about, Sir.

Sergeant.—A whisper, your honour! Fait, but it was such a whisper as you might have heard, if you had been on the look-out, all over the barrack, with your eyes shut.

President.—But you say that you were asleep?

Sergeant.—So I was, your honour; but the noise waked me; and I shut my eyes so that I might be sure I heard him.

President.—Can you hear in your sleep?

Sergeant.—Fait, can I. About a month ago, I was as sound as a mackerel, when, sure enough, I heard a man calling me by my name; and, when I opened my eyes, I saw him standing by my bedside, and he said he had been calling me for a long time.

President.—Perhaps you can see in your sleep also?

Sergeant.—By the powers, your honour, you may say that; for the other morning I catched myself at that self-same thing.

President.—How was that, sergeant?

Sergeant.—Fait! the other morning, when I was fast asleep, I felt my eyes, and found them wide awake.

President.—Probably you can always hear in your sleep?

Sergeant.—Not when my eyes are shut, your honour; for then I am quite deaf.

President.—Do you ever walk in your sleep?

Sergeant.—Never, your honour, after I lay down; but I did once, when a boy.

President.—Which you perfectly recollect, of course?

Sergeant.—Yes, your honour: I shall never forget it, because I have good cause to remember it.

President.—What may that be, sergeant?

Sergeant.—Why, your honour, I was about ten years old when I walked in my sleep, and I found myself wide awake in a horse-pond that stood near my father's house.

Member.—Well, but you said at the commencement of your evidence, that you were asleep, and heard the prisoner now before the court make use of the threat towards Corporal Ragon.

Sergeant.—Fait! did I, on my oath, and that's no lie, either.

Member.—Clearly and distinctly heard the identical words?

Sergeant.—Clear as mud, your honour.

Member.—Yet you say the words were given in a whisper?

Sergeant.—Yes, your honour, but it was so loud, there were several men besides me who heard it, that were asleep at the same time, and not so near as I was, becase they slept at the other side of the barrack.

President.—You must either be a confounded oaf, or you wish to impose upon the court. Take care you do not yourself become a prisoner and be tried before this very court for perjury. I suppose you mean to say that the prisoner's talking awoke you?

Sergeant.—Fait! that's the very thing.

President.—Then you heard the expressions after you awoke?

Sergeant.—Fait! I did.

President.—They were spoken quite loud?

Sergeant.—They were, your honour.

President.—Your evidence is most extraordinary. Prisoner, have you any questions to put to this witness?

Prisoner.—Yes, if you plase, your honour. Where was I standing when you heard me make use of the words you have been after mintioning to the court?

Sergeant.—Behind the pillar in the barrack.

Prisoner.—Did you see me at the time?

Sergeant.—Fait! did I, plain enough.

President.—What do you suppose was the distance of this pillar from you, sergeant?

Sergeant.—About twelve feet, your honour.

President.—You must have pretty good hearing, then, to hear a man whisper at that distance.

Sergeant.—The divel better hearing in the world.

President—How far, now, do you think you could hear a gunshot?

Sergeant.—Ten miles off, if I was near enough.

President.—You stupid fellow, if the sound reaches you, you must hear.

Sergeant.—Yes, your honour, but I meant that if I was wide awake I could hear a gun ten miles off, if the report was loud enough. I heard the guns at Vittoria when my eyes were shut and I was twenty miles off.

President.—If I could suppose for a moment that your extraordinary evidence proceeded from any other motive than utter ignorance, I would this moment try, break, and flog you; but granting that your testimony proceeds entirely from that channel, you are no longer fit for a non-commissioned officer, and I shall speak to the commanding-officer to reduce you.

The prisoner was released, and the proceedings terminated. It appeared afterwards, that all the witness meant to say was, that he was awake, but had his eyes shut, when the prisoner made use of the words alluded to.

*****

We did not remain at Saugar for above a month, after which the division of the army to which I was attached was ordered to be broken up, and I proceeded to rejoin my own corps at Cawnpore. This was in July, 1819; from which period to the beginning of the year 1821, my time was spent in domestic quiet, in the performance of the station-duties of my profession, and in social intercourse with my brother officers. About this period I was raised to the rank of lieutenant, and, to add to the happiness which I then enjoyed, on the 22nd of March, 1821, I became a father by the birth of a little boy. Little did I then think that this blessing was the forerunner of much evil to me and mine; but just at this crisis I entered into an agreement with the late Lieutenant-Colonel, then Major, Browne, to run, in partnership with him, at the ensuing Cawnpore races. My father-in-law being then in a bad state of health, and just about to leave India, I obtained leave of absence for six months, and accompanied him to Calcutta. Here I was to purchase certain horses, &c., for the races; and the circumstances connected with this unfortunate racing transaction led ultimately to a court-martial, the sentence of which was as follows:

> The court, having maturely weighed and considered the evidence for and against the prisoner, together with what he has urged in his defence, is of opinion that he is guilty of both the charges preferred against him, which being in breach of the Articles of War, it does sentence him, Lieutenant John Shipp, of his majesty's 87th regiment, to be discharged his majesty's service.
> Approved and confirmed,
> *Edward Paget*
> General, Commander-in-Chief

Attached to the sentence was the following recommendation of the court:

> The court having performed a painful but imperative duty, in finding the prisoner guilty, beg respectfully, though earnestly, to recommend him to the clemency of his excellency the commander-in-chief. In presuming to express a wish that mercy may be extended to the present case, the court are impressed with a hope that the gallantry so frequently displayed by the prisoner, the numerous wounds he has received, and the high and apparently merited character which he has hitherto borne, will appear to his excellency sufficient grounds for the court's thus warmly interesting themselves in the prisoner's fate, and urging with anxious solicitude the present recommendation.
>
> Before closing their proceedings, the court deem it a justice due to Lieutenant-Colonel Browne, to express their opinion that his conduct, as far as it has come before them, has been honourable to himself and indulgent towards the prisoner.

Remarks by the Commander-in-Chief:

Lieutenant Shipp has thus, by his persevering resistance to the advice of his late most respected commanding-officer, of the general of his division, and of the commander-in-chief, brought upon himself the heavy penalty of the forfeiture of his commission. Although these are circumstances calculated greatly to aggravate the offences of this officer, still the commander-in-chief is willing to hope that, in yielding, as far as he feels it is consistent with his duty, to the earnest intercession of the court, he runs no risk of shaking the foundations of discipline and subordination. The sentence of the court is accordingly remitted; but as, under all the circumstances of the case, the commander-in-chief deems it quite impossible that Lieutenant Shipp should continue to do duty with the 87th regiment, he grants him leave of absence from it, and shall recommend that he be removed to the half-pay list.

The foregoing orders to be entered in the General Order-Book, and read at the head of every regiment in his majesty's service in India.

By order of his Excellency the Commander-in-Chief,
Thomas M'Mahon
Colonel, Adjutant-General
J Bowes
Lieutenant and Adjutant, 87th Regiment

On the tenth day of the proceedings, Colonel Browne, being examined on oath, is questioned by the court:

Question.—"How long have you known the prisoner, and what was your opinion of his character previous to the misunderstanding between you and him?"
Answer.—"I have known the prisoner since the year 1816. He was in the light company with me for a considerable time, and distinguished himself highly at Hattrass. I always considered him, and indeed know him to be, up to the present moment, one of the best officers in his majesty's service."[1]

CHAPTER 25

Comrades, Farewell

When an officer has been tried by an honourable military tribunal, composed of fifteen British officers, and the sentence of the court-martial has been sanctioned and approved by a most merciful and gracious sovereign, it were as fruitless, as it would be highly improper and presumptuous, for the sentenced individual to urge anything further in his defence. I, therefore, as a sincere admirer of my country's laws, bow most humbly to my fate; I love my country as truly as ever I did, and would as willingly as ever risk my life to support its laws and freedom.

During the trial, which lasted thirteen days, I was exceedingly harassed, and my feelings were worked up to a state bordering on frenzy. There was a host against me, and I had not a soul to advise me how to proceed. I stood alone and unaided, with a limited education, to rebut the whole mass of evidence adduced against me.

The time necessarily occupied in sending the proceedings of the court-martial to my native country, and the long period which elapsed before its return, were spent in the bosom of domestic bliss, where I found refuge from the storm. The contemplation of my recent fall would at times sink me in gloomy despair, and it was my wife only who could divert my mind from useless forebodings, and whisper in my ear sweet hopes of better days to come. I removed some miles from the regiment, as I could not bear the commiserating remarks of the soldiers as they passed me, which only served to plunge me deeper in the vortex of despondency. From these motives I was induced to remove from that station where my profession had been my pride and boast, to where I should not meet the pitying countenances of those brave fellows with whom I had often shared in glory, and where I could, unmolested and undisturbed, think of the future, and compose my feelings. On leaving the regiment, and passing by the houses of the officers, that hung on the rapid Ganges, my feelings can be better imagined than described. Need I be ashamed to confess that I felt the tear trickling down my cheek, and a weight at my heart that the utmost ingenuity of man cannot accurately describe. I could not help comparing my then forlorn situation with the day I looked back on the little white village spire out-topping the high poplars that reared their heads over the briar-woven grave of my mother, save that I had now one near and dear to me, and ever ready to share the cup of sorrow. Many of the men whom I had befriended and had got promoted, followed my boat on the banks of the river, wishing me every prosperity, till prudence bade them return to their lines. The feelings I experienced on this occasion are such as the tyrant soldier never knows, and never ought to know. These friendly greetings of the men gratified my pride, but only sunk my heart deeper in anguish. Scarcely were my feelings so composed as to reconcile me in some degree to my fate, when an event, the most dreadful and agonizing, and which of all others I was the least prepared for, happened to her on whom I had built my most felicitous hopes, when more halcyon days should visit our humble cot. I could have borne poverty with a smile of contentment; but this blow was vital, and at once dashed the flattering cup of hope from my lips. During my long and harassing trial, such was the anxiety of my wife, that a premature birth of a boy was the consequence. This had nearly deprived me of her who was my best friend and guide; but, by dint of great care and good nursing, she recovered, and was at this moment in all the health and beauty of twenty-two, and expected shortly to present me with another pledge of mutual love. A strange coincidence brought her good mother, brother, and sister to the station, neither of whom we could have expected, and we all waited the happy issue of this event. I cannot relate our preliminary proceedings and great anxiety. Suffice it that, on the following morning, having given birth, after twelve hours' protracted labour, to a beautiful boy, she was a corpse, having that morning completed her two-and-twentieth year. All my former misfortunes now rushed upon my distracted mind with tenfold force, and this last blow seemed to bereave me of all that on earth I could love; and my poor child, kissing the cold lips of his dead mother, and pathetically beseeching her to get up and speak to him, roused me to a full sense of my utter misery and woe. Neither his uncle nor his aunt could drag him from embracing the corpse of his dear mother; his cries were dreadful; and it was imagined, for some time after, that the dear boy's intellect had received a shock that was likely to prove lasting. He frequently wept bitterly, and would affectionately hug and kiss, a thousand times, any little thing that had been his mother's, preserving most carefully even little pieces of rag or paper that he knew had been hers. My poor mother-in-law scarcely ever spoke for the long period of six months, after this dreadful shock, but lay in a melancholy state of insensibility, not knowing even her little grandson, who would linger over her sick-bed for whole days together.

At this very crisis of my life the court-martial was communicated to me as having been confirmed in England, and I was directed to proceed to the Presidency of Fort William, preparatory to being sent home, to be placed on the half-pay.

This final sentence was communicated to me through the regiment, some few days after my wife's death, who was, therefore, spared this last pang. When the letter was delivered to me, I was sitting on a couch with my two motherless babes, one four years old, the other but a few days. On tracing the contents of the letter, when my eager eyes met the words "Dismissed the service," I could not repress the tear of anguish, nor refrain from indulging in the most unavailing grief. To wind up a military career like mine in this manner, was distressing indeed!

From the age of nine to forty-one, I had now been in the army—a period of thirty-two years. My services during that time are already before the reader. In the course of those services, I had received six matchlock-ball wounds:

One through the forehead, just above my eyes, which has so impaired my sight, that I have been obliged to use glasses for some years past.

Two on the top of my head, from which have, at different times, been extracted sixteen pieces of bone. These two wounds, at every change of the weather, cause a most excruciating headache.

One in the fleshy part of the right arm.

One through the forefinger of my left hand. Of this finger I have entirely lost the use, and I am still obliged to nurse it with great care, several pieces of bone having been extracted from it, and some splinters, as I fear, being still remaining.

One in the fleshy part of the right leg.

I had also received a flesh wound in my left shoulder, with several other slighter wounds not worth particularizing.

The above wounds, except one, having been received prior to the munificent grant of his present Majesty to wounded officers, I never received a farthing remuneration, except ninety-six pounds for the last—a year's pay as ensign.

GHAUT ON THE GANGES

I confess, then, I had entertained a sanguine hope, that the extent and nature of my services, and the number of wounds I had received, would have more than outweighed the offence of which I had been convicted, and I felt the disappointment most acutely, and could not avoid giving vent to my agonized feelings. I was aroused by the endearing behaviour of my child, whose arms had, on his observing my grief, encircled my neck. "What's the matter, father? you are always crying now, since mother is gone away," said he. This was touching a tenderer chord than the babe imagined, for he still supposed that his dear mother was gone for a time only, and his constant inquiries were when she would return. We were found in this state of woe by Captain Thomas Marshall, of the Bengal army, my neighbour. This officer was my neighbour indeed; for his kindness, and that of his amiable wife, towards me, were unabated and unceasing. In the affectionate bosom of this lady my orphan babe found a foster-mother, who shared with her infant, three days older than mine, the one half of its best comfort. Towards this dear and affectionate couple my heart will ever cherish the fond remembrance of gratitude, and I hope this humble declaration may meet them in the far-distant clime in which they sojourn. When Captain Marshall saw the sentence, he turned from me, and walked into another room—for what purpose, I leave the sympathizing reader to guess. He soon returned to me, and said, "Come, Shipp, you have often mounted the breach of danger—cheer up—and recollect you have those dear babes to clothe and feed." Here my little boy, supposing that this was meant as a kind of rebuke, said, "I don't want anything to eat, Captain Marshall; therefore, don't cry." These are touches which the feeling heart can alone appreciate. To prevent, for the time, any further indulgence in sorrow, I was prevailed on to accompany my kind neighbour to his hospitable house, where I spent the day with him, and where a little musical party assembled in the evening, to rouse me from the state of despondency into which this last blow had plunged me. But all attempts to divert me from the recollections of my misfortunes were fruitless. Music and society but added to my pain; and I found that I was never, for a length of time, so composed as in those days and nights which I spent free from all company but that of my two motherless babes, with whom only I could, if I may so express myself, luxuriate in grief.

In one month after the confirmed sentence of the court-martial had been made known to me, I was compelled to obey the orders which I had received to repair to Calcutta, previous to embarkation for England. To enable me to comply with these directions, I was obliged to sacrifice all my property for a mere nothing, and I set out for the Presidency with my little boy, now my only comfort, having made the little infant over to my brother-in-law, J. P. Mellaird, Esq., indigo-planter Tirhoot, where his grandmother, somewhat recovered, found refuge also.

The voyage down the lonely river Ganges was not calculated to soothe my sorrows or to cheer my prospects. I reached Calcutta in safety, and remained there a considerable time waiting for a ship, where, strange to say, I received an order to proceed home with invalids, and to place myself immediately under the command of Captain Mathers, of his majesty's 59th regiment. This order I was bound to obey; but it prevented me from bringing home my little boy, as every part of the ship was taken up for the troops, and the captain of the vessel would not accommodate me under a thousand *rupees*—a sum which I had not to give. A smaller foreign ship would have brought both myself and child home for what the Company allow for officers sent home—fifteen hundred *rupees*. By this I was deprived of the satisfaction of bringing home my child, who remains in India with my brother-in-law to this day.

In the beginning of the month of April, 1825, I embarked on board the free-trader, *Euphrates*, Captain Mead commanding, with an insufficient crew, as they did not exceed twenty-three hands in all, and winter was before us for the whole voyage. This would not have been a very pleasant prospect to the shattered nerves of an old Indian; but mine, although I had been so many years in that hot country, did not come under that description, and I had learnt long since to endure hardships. I was never much addicted to look on the dark side of things, but now it was impossible to refrain from thinking of the situation in which I stood. I was proceeding to a country, and that country my native home; but it was not endeared to me by a solitary relative that I knew of. I could not help comparing the close of my military career with its commencement. I was then friendless and isolated; and who had I now but those who mourned my departure from a land which I was compelled to quit for ever? I left England, when a child, without one friend or relative to bid me adieu, and I was now returning to it without one to bid me welcome! Yet there is something pleasing to every British bosom, in the anticipation of returning to the land of one's birth; and, although my prospects were anything but bright, I felt, notwithstanding, that I could be content to live in my native country, even in poverty. But the necessity which compelled me to leave behind me my two sweet babes distressed me exceedingly, and my eye seemed riveted on the arid sand along the banks of the river that had some few days before borne my boy from my sight. On the spot on which we parted I gazed with indescribable sensations, and I found that the more I gazed the dearer it grew in my estimation. There are few who have not experienced delight in revisiting, after many years' absence, the scenes of their childhood. When I returned to my native land from India, in the year 1807, after an absence of twelve years, I was proceeding home to visit my family; but when I reached Colchester (the place, as the reader will probably recollect, where I commenced "soldiering"), all the gambols and tricks I had played there when a boy, rushed upon my mind, and the place seemed endeared to me by a thousand recollections. Such was my wish to re-explore this place, that I forfeited my coach-hire for the rest of the journey, and stopped there that night. Early on the following morning I sauntered along to the lanes that stood in the vicinity of the barracks, and, on coming to a certain lane that ran behind them, where we went every day to practice, I found my name still on a stile. This had been cut by me when I frequented the place as a little fifer, twelve years before. Such were my feelings on this simple occasion, that I could scarcely restrain a tear, and I sat on the stile for an hour, looking on my own name a hundred times over. It will not, therefore, be wondered at, if the eye of a fond father should fondly linger on the spot where he took leave of, and last saw his motherless babe.

The scene before me in the vessel soon diverted me from the contemplation of all other subjects. I could have brooded over the fate of my dear little ones the whole night; but the din and tumult of more than two hundred soldiers, with their friends from shore, all rioting in the cup of inebriety, tumbling over each other, blaspheming, fighting, singing, fifing, and fiddling, and all huddled together in a confined space, with their beds, bedding, parrots, minors, and other birds, roused me to a lively sense of the scene before me.

On the following morning we bade farewell to Fort William, under whose proud battlements we had been lying. The wind was serene and fair, and the wave had scarcely a ripple on its silvery surface. Would that my bosom had been equally composed and tranquil; but my heart sickened within me when I felt the beautiful ship smoothly gliding down the rapid stream, and bearing me from that country and that service in which I had spent the prime of my life, and, I may say, the happiest of my days. The rapid Ganges soon bore me from the sight of the English flag, and I dropped a tear to the recollection of the many happy days I had spent at Fort William.

I soon found that I had a queer set to deal with, without the means of checking any indiscretion that drunkenness might drive them to commit. The captain commanding the detachment was in a dying state, and indeed did die on his passage home; consequently, all the trouble, anxiety, and care, fell upon me. I can venture to assert that, with the exception of about twenty men, a more disorderly and mutinous set than the fellows I had now under my charge, never disgraced the garb of soldiers.

An Eastern voyage, either home or out, is dull and monotonous enough, even with an agreeable party. Passengers we had none, save one lady and her little girl, her sick husband, the captain of the detachment, then lingering on the brink of the grave, and a young officer of the Company's Bengal Artillery, who survived but a few days the tossing of the ship, and was committed to a watery grave, ere the bloom of boyhood had left his cheek. We had one doctor on board, and a young officer of the Company's service, in charge of the Company's troops. Of the misery of the passage the reader may have some idea, when he is informed that we had upwards of two hundred men on board, some without legs, others without arms, and twenty of whom had been removed from hospital only a week or ten days before we sailed. Every man had a box or trunk, bed and bedding, with parrots, minors, and cockatoos, and all these poor creatures, with four women and four children, were huddled on one small deck, every one that could move endeavouring to seize the more secure spot, and tumbling over and treading on those who were unable, either from sickness or drunkenness, to move or assist themselves. The smell and heat below were beyond description. Added to all this, the men were, during the whole voyage, in a state of continual drunkenness, having means of procuring liquor privately, by some device which I never could discover. All my exertions were insufficient to check them in this practice, or indeed to keep them in any kind of order, from want of the usual means of enforcing obedience, there being neither a place of confinement, nor handcuffs, nor any other means of securing the ringleaders, in the ship. Nothing but the greatest personal risk on my part, and that of the Company's officer, Lieutenant Rock, prevented open mutiny among the troops; and I consider it a mercy that we were not both thrown overboard, which was more than once threatened.

Some of the more refractory among the soldiers soon discovered that my means to enforce obedience were limited; in consequence of which three-fourths of them set my orders at defiance, refusing in the most peremptory manner to obey me, even to clearing away their own filth and dirt; and I was ultimately obliged, rather than provoke that spirit of rebellion which I could evidently see only wanted some pretext to show itself, to pay a set of men daily, as a working party, to clear the deck, and keep off disease, so often occasioned on shipboard from a want of cleanliness. This I did by allowing those men two extra drams per day for their labour.

After a voyage of six months, spent in constant riot and anxiety, and the misery of the whole increased by scurvy, which prevailed on board, and the number of deaths which occurred during the passage, we at length reached our native land in safety, having, in the course of the voyage, thrown overboard the captain of the detachment, a lieutenant, who was a passenger, thirty-eight soldiers, and one child, all of whom had died in that short space of time. Most of the men fell victims to their intemperance in drink.

We reached England in the month of October, landed at Gravesend, and, on the following day, marched to the depot at Chatham, where the detachment was drawn up on parade, and I left them in charge of the staff-officer of Fort Pitt Barrack.

The parade on which I then stood finished my military career of upwards of thirty years—five-and-twenty of which I had spent on the burning soil of India. I had but little cause to feel regret in resigning my command over the turbulent and drunken set whom I now was about to quit; but, situated as I was myself, I could not even leave those poor creatures without a tear; and, when I reflected that I was no longer a soldier, I felt a weight at my heart that sunk me almost to the earth.

The public are now in possession of a faithful account of the vicissitudes which have marked the career of one who, in misfortune, can pride himself on having performed his duty to his country, loyally, faithfully, and, he trusts, bravely.

From my military readers I feel it impossible to part without a few valedictory words. Brothers in arms, farewell! May the bright star from heaven shine on your efforts, and may you be crowned with glory! May the banner of Albion be hoisted in victory wherever it goes! As long as my mortal sight will guide me along the annals of war, I will exult and triumph in your successes, and drop a tear of pity for those that fall. Comrades, farewell!

CHAPTER 26

Continuation of the Memoir Until the Death of Mr. Shipp

The military career, traced in the preceding pages, has probably never been surpassed either in homely, affecting narrative, or in thrilling scenes of war and strife, by that of any soldier of modern times. That Shipp did not rise more rapidly to the dizzy heights of a hero's ambition, in a much shorter time, may reasonably be attributed to the age in which he served, as well as to the peculiar regulations of our service, than to any deficiency of fitness, ability, courage, or even notoriety on his part. In the English army, all the avenues to preferment are generally so crowded by aspirants of merit and influence, and so jealously guarded by the legislature, that the best and most valuable soldiers—men whose services acquire a very early distinction—scarcely ever rise from the ranks to the elevation which Shipp twice attained by his gallantry and soldiership. And it was the consciousness of this fact, and the marked departure from the rigid rules of the service, in the instance of his individual promotion, that rendered him so resigned and submissive, under the heavy blow which his own temerity subsequently inflicted upon him. Had his destiny enabled him to steer past the siren pleasures that too often interrupt the path of men possessing power, distinction, and popularity, it is more than probable that, instead of being permitted to retire without any public brand of disgrace upon his brow, into the obscurity of a private station, he would have attained the highest rank in the British army, and have been conspicuous, like Collingwood, not only for winning victories more gloriously, but for describing them to his countrymen more perspicuously than any military man of the age he lived in. It is not in this little autobiography, written in so terse, agreeable, and piquant a manner, that the brilliant exploits of Shipp would have been sought for: the brightness of that page of history which recorded them, would alone have secured the publicity of his renown. Few ever possessed, more eminently, all the elements essential to success as a soldier. Unimpeachable bravery, unwavering perseverance, cool fortitude, and determined steadiness of purpose, were amongst the most conspicuous of his attributes; and to these we may add an inexhaustible energy of mind. Endowments of this nature are not often combined with clearness of judgment, or with that discretion which cautiously avoids the precipice. But if Shipp had not always his judgment entirely at command—which frequently results from a habit of decision and promptitude, mistaken by many for impetuosity—he was always fertile in resources, quick in expedients, and any errors arising from his first impulses were amply amended by the energy and skill with which he ultimately fulfilled every tittle of the duty entrusted to him.

When John Shipp stood upon the parade at Chatham, in the October of 1825, he was, as he has himself informed us, performing the last of his military duties. We have already seen with what feelings he bade adieu to "the plumed troop and the big war"—to the profession which had been the choice of his childhood and the pride of his riper years—amid which he had grown and flourished; and, when he had resigned his command to the officer of Fort Pitt Barrack, he wandered forth into the world a melancholy man, because no longer a soldier. His military career was thus finished, as he truly foreboded, for ever. That eventful and not inglorious campaign of his existence, of which he has given so vivid an account, was at an end, and he was now alone in the world, destitute of occupation, and without immediate aim or object. Hitherto, his life had been a romance, the various vicissitudes whereof forcibly verify the adage, that "truth is stranger than fiction." Though the reader will have henceforth to regard him as a mere civilian, his movements confined to his native island, where stirring incidents and dashing adventures are not rife, yet the details of his remaining years are not entirely destitute of interest and instruction.

Although the first and natural feeling of the gallant ex-lieutenant, at the contemplation of his position, was one of deep despondency, yet the manliness of his nature forbid a tame submission to vain and bootless melancholy. He had before risen superior to the oppression of that gloomy goddess. His energies soon rallied, and the innate fortitude of his character came to his aid. He was furnished with excellent credentials from those officers with whom he had served; and, having taken up his residence in the metropolis, he set himself sedulously to work to procure employment. At first he was elated with hope, from the numerous promises which he received, and the kindness and urbanity with which his pretensions were entertained. He soon found, however, that there was a difference between professions and practice—between hospitality and active benevolence.

Amongst the first applications which he made, was one to the Court of Directors of the East India Company, setting forth his services in India, the wounds which he had received, and his other claims on their favourable consideration. This application was successful; for, though the Directors were unable to confer on him any appointment, they generously granted him a pension of fifty pounds a year, for life, commencing from the preceding Christmas. This honourable allowance was sufficient to keep him above actual want; but, with the habits which he had imbibed in a land where extravagance and luxury are almost regarded as virtues, it was insufficient to keep him out of difficulties. He was himself well aware, and willing to allow on all occasions, that his chief failing was improvidence. Nor was he really extravagant; but he possessed little knowledge of the value of money, and was as prodigal of that essential commodity as if his supplies had been unlimited. His generosity was so unbounded, that he has often been known to recompense moderate services with a liberality wholly beyond his rank or means. The resources derived from the India House soon failing, he renewed his exertions to obtain employment, but still without success. Remembering that the story of his life was full of interest, and having determined upon telling it to the public, he turned himself with great perseverance to his new occupation, and in a short time became fired with all the ambition of an expectant author. As he was, however, naturally doubtful of his own powers, he submitted his manuscripts to the revision of a gentleman every way well qualified for the task, and who performed it with equal judgment, good taste, and ability. This sanguine temperament now led him to indulge in many a golden dream of the profits of authorship; an error that occasioned more profuse expenditure than he would, even with his acknowledged lack of worldly prudence, have deemed excusable.

It was while he was under the delusion of this phantom—the expectation of competent means from literary labours solely—that he thought of submitting a second time to the bonds of Hymen; and the interesting and amiable object of his affections has shown sufficiently the wisdom of his choice, by her exemplary conduct and virtuous life, when placed in circumstances painful, difficult, and trying. The only available means of support under the increased expenditure that attended his married state, was his pension from the India House—his chief prospective supply, the result of his publications. As an author he displayed invention and quickness; and the rapidity with which his works of fiction appeared, was not less extraordinary than the imagination which they displayed. In 1826 he published "The Shepherdess of Arranville; or, Father and Daughter;" a pathetic tale in three acts; and, in 1829, "The Maniac of the Pyrenees; or, the Heroic Soldier's Wife;" a melodrama in two acts, printed at Brentford. The success of these light works, however, was inferior to that of his memoirs, which soon became extensively popular, and have continued to gather favour with each added year. This reputation resulted, not more from the exciting nature of the details, than the freshness, rapidity, and air of candour, that pervades the whole. Shipp certainly derived advantage from the advice and assistance of an experienced and talented literary friend; but the vigour, playfulness, and peculiarity of style which characterize all his writings, were not infused by the pen of the ripe and ready writer—they were original qualities of the composition. Encouraged by the reception of his memoirs, and urged by pinching poverty to constant efforts for the improvement of his circumstances, he took advantage of his literary popularity, and sent into the world his "Military Bijou," and a pamphlet on military flogging. The latter, dedicated to Sir Francis Burdett, produced a decided sensation, and was so much approved of by the patriotic senator with whose name it was associated, that he generously presented the author with a cheque for sixty pounds. Such precarious supplies, however, could afford no permanent ease to a mind so energetic, so unbroken by reverses, so incapable of yielding to any untoward pressure of Providence: he applied himself, therefore, resolutely to the obtainment of an employment attended with a certain income, without regard to the amount of compensation, degree of humility, or difficulty of position. Confident of his powers, physical and intellectual; relying on the education derived from boundless experience of men and manners, and being a perfect master of the art of discipline, he very naturally concluded that his qualifications for the situation of a metropolitan police officer were unequalled. He had calculated rightly. Without a moment's hesitation—in fact accompanied by an expression of regret that no more lucrative or suitable appointment was vacant—the office of Inspector was stated to be at his service, and to await his acceptance.

Entering with alacrity on the duties of his new appointment, he had the good fortune to be introduced, by Colonel Rowan, to

Lieutenant W. Parlour, at that time superintendent of the Stepney division. This employment was not only particularly agreeable to Mr. Shipp, from the military rank of his superior in command, but laid the foundation of a steady friendship, which terminated only with his death. Mr. Shipp's talents and qualifications could not remain long unnoticed by the commissioners; indeed, they had evinced their perfect knowledge of both, and their desire to protect, encourage, and promote him, from the first moment of his presenting himself, by their placing him under the command of Lieutenant Parlour. A few months after Shipp's appointment, Lieutenant Parlour was made superintendent of the Liverpool constabulary force; and, on taking leave of his friend, assured him of his sincere determination to assist in restoring him to a situation of independence and respectful consideration. An opportunity soon presented itself. A superintendent for the night watch at Liverpool being required, Parlour sent an early communication to his friend Shipp, explaining all the advantages, the amount of salary (£200 per annum), and the respectable character of the employment; urging him to strain every nerve, turn every stone, ply every engine, to obtain the vacant place. The very conspicuous merits of Shipp soon distanced his numerous competitors, and procured for him the object of his ambition.

As superintendent of the night watch at Liverpool, Mr. Shipp proved himself a capable and efficient officer. By his intelligence, attention, excellent management, and gentlemanly manners, he gained the confidence and esteem, not only of the authorities, but of many individuals of wealth and consideration in that opulent community.

We have alluded to the fondness for scribbling which had been evinced by Mr. Shipp, from the period when he undertook the task of writing his memoirs. This propensity, so far from diminishing, seemed to gather strength, till at length it became one of his favourite occupations. On his first settlement in Liverpool, he contributed gratuitously, to several of the local papers, tales illustrative of the manners of the Hindoos. Shortly afterwards he published a rather ponderous volume, entitled "The Eastern Story Teller:" but it is somewhat remarkable that the real events of his own life surpassed in interest those which were the offspring of his imagination.

His propensity for literary composition never interfered with his responsible duties as an officer. Accustomed to command, and possessing, from long experience, a thorough knowledge of character, he had the force under his control in a state of admirable order and discipline. Nor were there wanting several occasions for the display of that natural intrepidity which was so striking a concomitant of his character. Though he had command of a civil force, a military disposition was not unfrequently required.

It was his duty to "set the watch" at a particular hour each evening—the time, of course, varying according to the season. After this it was his habit to take his round in the night, at some hour casually selected, in order to keep the men alert and vigilant. He resided in a district of the town called Toxteth Park, which was at that period infested by gangs of ruffians known by the designation of Park Bangers. Prior to the passing of the Municipal Act, Liverpool was not protected by the efficient day and night police that has since been established; and gangs of lawless individuals were in the habit of attacking pedestrians, male and female, sometimes for wanton mischief, and not unfrequently with the view of obtaining plunder. One winter's morning, Mr. Shipp, having performed a portion of his round, was returning home with the intention of taking a few hours' sleep, and then resuming his duty: as he was passing along one of the streets of the Park, his attention was attracted by a violent whirling of rattles, amid which he heard the shrieks of a female. He rushed forward in the direction of the sounds, and, on turning into a retired and respectable suburban street, saw two of his men fleeing with all the speed that their heavy habiliments would permit, before four fellows who brandished heavy bludgeons. A little further on lay a watchman, apparently insensible, while a couple of ruffians were kneeling over a prostrate figure on the footwalk. Leaning against the rails for support was a lady, whose shrieks had now subsided into heart-breaking sobs. Shipp saw in one instant how matters stood, and he hesitated not for a moment what course to take. Passing the fugitives and their pursuers, he rushed up to the fellows who were rifling the man on the footwalk, and, with the heavy stick which he always carried during his nocturnal perambulations, laid them both prostrate beside their victim. The remainder of the gang seeing this, turned from the pursuit of the watchmen, and rushed upon him; but, calling to the fugitives, he contrived to dart through his assailants, without receiving any injury save a contusion on the left shoulder. Another watchman who had heard the rattles, at this moment came; the two who were running off, hearing their superintendent's voice, had returned, and all four now faced the gang, who, however, fearing that the odds would soon be against them, fled, leaving one of their number a prisoner in the grasp of Mr. Shipp, in addition to the two whom he had prostrated, and who were then slowly recovering.

The victim of plunder had already recovered his legs. Mr. Shipp now learned that he was a respectable tradesman of the town, who was returning home from a Christmas festivity with his wife, when he was assailed by a gang of thieves, who, finding that he resisted stoutly, struck him to the ground. The cries of the lady brought the watchmen, one after another, to the spot. The first was knocked down, and the two others, after receiving a few blows, were running off in search of more assistance, when their superintendent arrived in time to prevent the villains from effecting their object.

Mr. Shipp was one evening taking a glass of wine with a few friends at the King's Arms, one of the principal inns in Liverpool, when suddenly a strange tumult was heard in the house, and sounds of feet passing rapidly along the floors. At first the party took no notice of the matter; but, a still more strange and unusual sound reaching their ears, they gazed at each other in silence and amazement. Suspense to Shipp being always intolerable, he rose at once, and, followed by his companions, rushed into the passage, which was a spacious apartment. Here they were met by vociferations of "Go back! go back! Mr. Shipp, and shut your door." The advice was instantly followed by every one, save Shipp alone, who, with that firm nerve that enabled him to face death in various shapes, remained outside, where a melancholy spectacle met his eyes. In the middle of the hall, just opposite the large window of the bar, where a crowd of servants had taken refuge, and from whence they called loudly for help, stood a grey-headed man, apparently about fifty years of age, who, from his dress, appeared to be a helper in the stable. In his right hand he grasped a carving-knife; and, while his face appeared convulsed with the fury of a maniac, he uttered the most fearful, though incoherent denunciations of vengeance, against any one who should approach him. At this instant a young woman belonging to the establishment came tripping down the stairs, whom the maniac perceiving, he repeated the same fearful cry which had so startled the company in the parlour, and, raising the knife, rushed at her. Shipp bounded after him like the lion from his lair, seized his uplifted arm, and, jamming the madman against the stairs with his knees, wrenched the weapon from his grasp. The terrified waiter now stepped forward, and assisted in securing the lunatic, who was immediately conveyed to Bridewell, and from thence to a proper asylum. He was an old servant of the establishment, who had on several occasions exhibited symptoms of mental derangement, which ultimately became confirmed by habits of intemperance. At length, on the evening in question, his malady had broken out into decided madness.

Shipp used himself to relate an incident, which has so much the character of romance, that it must not be omitted. He was seated one afternoon in an alcove on the green of the hotel at Birkenhead, when, in the adjoining recess, he overheard a deep masculine voice urging some tender proposal to a female: and he was about to depart, when he was struck by the extremely tremulous tones in which the girl refused compliance. "I cannot consent to go," said she; "it would not be proper."

"Well, but," replied the man, "I tell you your brother Tom is to go with us; he has consented to the whole arrangement; the sloop is in the river now, and we sail with the morning tide at five o'clock. We're all ready. Tom'll go on board this night; and, as he is fully expecting you, it will look foolish not to go. We can be married at Guernsey immediately, you know; and I shall have such a nice cottage for you; and we shall be as happy as possible."

"And why cannot I go on board when Tom does?" asked the girl. "Why, you know, dear," replied the man, with some hesitation, "the agents might board us this evening; and I should not like them to see us with a woman in the sloop. But come—I know you are not comfortable with that old aunt of yours; so just steal out of the house, and be on the watch for us at the slip, at half-past one. I shall have the boat waiting at one, close to the slip at George's Pier; the tide will be running in; I will pull over, and take you on board in a jiffy; and then away we go for beautiful Guernsey." A few more low sounds of tender entreaty followed, and then the girl seemed to yield a reluctant consent. The man, observing that she was faint, proposed that she should walk on the green and take the air. Shipp had then an opportunity of observing the pair. The girl was a pretty, graceful, innocent-looking creature, about twenty-two years of age. The man was a tall, swarthy, good-looking fellow, apparently a master in the merchant service. Shipp at once recognized him as an individual who had been, a few weeks before, convicted before the magistrates of Liverpool for smuggling, and heavily fined. By representation to the board, the fine had been considerably mitigated.

Shortly afterward, as Shipp was passing along the pier to the packet, he again passed the lovers, who were just separating. "Remember half-past one," said the man.

"I will," replied the girl, firmly; "tell brother Tom I shall scold him when I come on board, for not coming over to see me." The packet was moving from the pier, and the man stepped on board at the same moment as Mr. Shipp. The former was almost immediately accosted with great warmth by an individual, who pressed forward to meet him. The two shook hands familiarly, the friend exclaiming, "Ah! Captain, how are you? I haven't seen you this age. How's your wife?—is she in Liverpool?"

"No," replied the other, "I left her at home in Whitehaven three weeks ago, quite well and happy, thank you."

"And who is that pretty girl whom you've just parted with? I'll tell your wife, you rogue, the next time I see her. She ought to be jealous of you."

"Oh," replied the captain, "she is sister to a new acquaintance of mine; I've just been bidding her good-bye, as we sail to-morrow morning."

Shipp now became interested in the event, as he was convinced that some plot had been contrived, which would, in all probability, be fatal to the happiness of an innocent girl. When the passengers landed, he followed close to the man of whose proceedings he had become so strangely cognizant. As if fate had determined to let him into the whole secret, scarcely had the smuggler parted from the friend whom he had met in the packet, when he encountered a young man whom he addressed by the familiar appellation of Tom. "I've just left your sister," said he; "she's quite well—sends her love to you, and all that sort of thing, and wonders you have not been to see her. I told her you were going to Birmingham:—by the way, when do you start?"

"At five o'clock; but I wanted to see you before I went—how lucky I met you!"

Shipp heard no more, for he stood pondering on all that had passed under his notice, irresolute how to act. His first thought was to return immediately to Cheshire, and inform the young woman of the precipice on which she stood. A moment's reflection convinced him of the impracticability of this attempt, for he knew not her name or residence. His next impulse was to follow the brother, and inform him of the snare which had been laid for his sister. He turned, and followed in the direction which the pair had taken, but he was unable to find them. His next resolve, though not perhaps the most prudent that could have been adopted, was exceedingly accordant with his character and disposition.

It was his habit, when going his nightly rounds, to wear a rough overcoat of coarse blue cloth, and a broad-brimmed varnished hat, similar to those frequently worn by boatmen. Dressed in this guise, a few minutes before one o'clock, in the morning succeeding the afternoon just adverted to, he walked along George's Pier. The night was moonless, but not dark. The river was almost unruffled, though the faint light cast by the stars into the atmosphere was reflected in long lines upon the slight swell of the incoming tide. As he approached the steps, he discerned a boat in which four men were seated. His quick eye discovered that, as he had hoped, it was not a ship's boat, but one of the regular river craft. He began to descend the steps, when one of the boatmen exclaimed, "Is that you, Captain?"

"No," replied Shipp, coolly stepping into the boat, and seating himself in her bows, "but he'll be here immediately." The men, thinking he had been sent by the person who had employed them, made no remark. Presently footsteps were heard passing rapidly along the pier; the Captain, as the men called him, descended the steps, sprung into the boat, and, not observing Shipp, or, if he did so, thinking, from his position and appearance, that he was one of the regular crew, ordered the men to "push off, and pull away with a will." The men pulled with lusty sinews, and, in about half an hour, laid the boat alongside the pier at Birkenhead. "Holla!" exclaimed one of the boatmen, as their employer lifted a female into the boat, "is it a woman, Captain? this ought to be double pay, at least."

"Hold your tongue, man," replied the Captain, "and pull away for the sloop: I'll steer, for I know where she lies." The men again tugged hard at the oars, being as anxious as their employer to finish their job. Though the tide was now against them, another half hour of labour brought the boat alongside a small but handsome vessel, which was riding at anchor in the stream. "Hold fast, men," said the Captain, springing up the side of the sloop and gaining her deck; "stand by to help the lady, and then come on board and take a glass of grog, and be paid."

"Ay, ay, sir," was the ready response. It was now Shipp's turn to act. Stepping quickly to the stern of the boat he exclaimed loudly, "Let go, men, and pull ashore this instant. Young woman, you are deceived: this man is married: he has a wife at Whitehaven, and your brother is not on board his sloop."

"And who are you, Sir," exclaimed the master of the sloop, "that dare to interfere in my affairs?"

"I am one of the police-officers of Liverpool," replied Shipp, "and I take this lady under my protection."

"If she chooses to come into my vessel," said the master, in a voice hoarse with passion, "I presume your interference is cursed impertinent and uncalled for. You wish to come on board, Mary, don't you?"

"Not if this be true," sobbed the girl; "if you are not deceiving me, call brother Tom; you said he would be here."

"I tell you," said Shipp, "your brother has gone to Birmingham, and you were on the point of being ruined. Let go, men, or it will be worse for you!" Hearing this, the boat-hook was instantly loosed, and the tide swept the boat from the sloop's side in a moment. "And are we to lose our money?" said one of the boatmen, as he reluctantly put out his oar; "we were to have had thirty shillings for this job."

"I will pay you," said Shipp. "Huzza!" exclaimed the boatmen, "pull away, my hearties!" As they rowed to the pier, Shipp related to the girl all that he had witnessed and overheard on the preceding day. "God bless you, Sir!" said she; "from what misery you have saved me!" On the following day the girl returned to her aunt, and, shortly afterwards, her brother called upon Shipp, and thanked him fervently for the great service he had rendered.

In the month of May, 1833, the office of governor of the workhouse at Liverpool became vacant by the death of Mr. Hardman, who had for many years filled that situation. The special vestry, after mature deliberation, decided upon recommending Mr. Hewett, master of St. Andrew's, Holborn, London. The recommendation was, that Mr. Hewett and his wife should be governor and matron, at the joint salary of £300 per annum. As the situation was a very desirable one—a handsome residence, with all the necessaries, comforts, and even luxuries of life being provided, in addition to the salary—a host of candidates (no less than thirty-seven) were quickly in the field. Amongst those who sought the office was Mr. Shipp; and, though he came rather late to the goal, he pursued the contest with his accustomed energy and perseverance.

On the 23rd of May, 1833, a special vestry was held for the purpose of nominating candidates and electing a person to fill the office. Mr. Hewett, who was backed by the most influential men of the select vestry, was nominated by two of the members of that body, amid many expressions of disapprobation. Other individuals were nominated by their respective friends; but they were but coldly received. At length Mr. Venables, a barrister of high standing and respectability, proposed John Shipp, with a glowing eulogium on his character and qualifications. The nomination was received with loud and reiterated cheers. Mr. Hall, also an eminent barrister, afterwards a magistrate at Bow Street, seconded the nomination. The show of hands being greatly in favour of Mr. and Mrs. Shipp, a poll was demanded on behalf of the other individuals nominated.

On the following morning, at ten o'clock, the polling commenced at the Sessions House, in Chapel Street. It was soon evident that Mr. Hewett, the candidate recommended by the select vestry, had not the slightest chance of success; and that gentleman accordingly resigned, an hour or two after the opening of the poll. A contest unparalleled in elections of this description followed between Mr. Shipp and Mr. Haram, who, with a certain class, was the favourite candidate, though the popular voice was for Mr. Shipp. The town was canvassed in every quarter, and placards covered the walls in all directions, as at a parliamentary election. At the close of the first day, Haram was upwards of 140 ahead of his opponent. On the second day, Shipp brought up his lee-way, and at the close of the poll on Monday he was upwards of 300 ahead. On Tuesday morning Haram resigned the contest; and thus the election terminated in favour of Mr. Shipp, whose majority was 352.

We now find Mr. Shipp in a position of comparative affluence, which unfortunately he did not live long to enjoy. He was installed in his new office of governor of the workhouse, at the end of May, 1833. Soon after this he published a work called "The Private Soldier," a volume which did equal honour to his head and heart, and evinced his ardent love for that profession in which he had spent the best years of his life. He was still pressed by embarrassments, to the increase of which his literary speculations had in no slight degree contributed. The emoluments of his new situation, had he survived, would have enabled him to fulfil all his engagements, and make some provision for his family; but he enjoyed the comforts of the competency which had been bestowed upon him only a few months. In the February of 1834, he was suddenly seized with an attack of pleurisy, which terminated his existence after a few days of excruciating agony. He died on Thursday, the 27th of February, at the age of fifty-two, and was interred on the following Tuesday, in the chapel of St. Mary's cemetery. His funeral was attended by a vast number of his friends, as well as by all the inmates of the workhouse.

As Mr. Shipp had been greatly esteemed in Liverpool during his life, much sympathy was excited on behalf of his widow; and, as soon as it was known that her husband had died insolvent, a subscription was thought of for her relief. The gentleman who promoted, with the greatest zeal, the benevolent intentions of the public on behalf of the sorrowing widow, was Mr. William Parlour, whose name occurs in a former part of this Memoir. Through his instrumentality a meeting of Mr. Shipp's friends was called, at which it was resolved that a subscription should be opened; and in a few days £600 were collected. In addition to this liberal amount, a gentleman who held a bill of sale, including the chattel property of the deceased, made the widow a present of all the furniture which had reverted to him—a gift then valued at £200. This timely generosity—a tribute to the high character of her late husband, and to her own exemplary conduct—sustained the widow and her fatherless family, until that Providence, which never deserts the deserving, placed her in a situation less profitable, but not dissimilar to her former avocation.

Appendices

Appendix 1

CERTIFICATE OF MAJOR-GENERAL GREGORY, ATTESTING THAT LIEUTENANT SHIPP LED THE THREE FORLORN HOPES AGAINST BHURTPORE

I hereby certify that Lieutenant John Shipp served with me in the campaign of 1802, 3, 4, and 5, and that I was frequently an eyewitness to his heroic and gallant conduct, more particularly in leading the three forlorn hopes against Bhurtpore, in the year 1805.
J. S. Gregory
Major-General
Dinapore
16th Nov., 1824

Appendix 2

COPY OF A LETTER FROM THE COMMANDING-OFFICER OF THE 76TH REGIMENT, ADDRESSED TO LIEUTENANT SHIPP, ON HIS QUITTING THAT REGIMENT, IN 1808

Dear Sir,
I cannot permit you to leave the regiment without expressing my regret on your retiring from a service wherein you have acquitted yourself with so much benefit to your country, and honour to your own reflection. Your heroic conduct upon several trying occasions in India, but more particularly at Deig and Bhurtpore (the marks of which you bear), will long continue in the remembrance of your brother-officers.

Whatever may be your future pursuits in life, be assured you carry with you my best esteem, and I shall be proud and happy to hear of your welfare; and, should your restoration to health enable you again to assume the duties of a soldier, I am confident your zeal and spirit will add new laurels to the service of your country.

Wishing you every happiness, believe me to be, dear sir, most respectfully and truly yours,

John Covell
Major, commanding the 76th Regiment
Grouville, Jersey
14th March, 1808

Appendix 3

OFFICIAL CERTIFICATE, THAT LIEUTENANT SHIPP SERVED WITH THE 87TH REGIMENT DURING THE SECOND CAMPAIGN OF THE GOORKHA WAR, WHEN THE ENEMY'S POSITION AT CHIRECAH GHATTIE WAS TURNED, AND AFTERWARDS, WHEN THE ENEMY WAS DEFEATED ON THE HEIGHTS OF MUCKWANPORE. ALSO, THAT LIEUTENANT SHIPP SERVED WITH THE LEFT DIVISION OF THE GRAND ARMY DURING THE MAHRATTA AND PINDAREE WAR OF 1817-18

These are to certify, that Lieutenant John Shipp, of His majesty's 87th regiment of Foot, served with that corps during the second campaign of the Goorkha war, and was attached to the light company of his regiment, which formed part of the advanced-guard of the division under the command of Major-General Sir David Ochterlony, Bart., G. C. B., when the enemy's position, at the pass of Chirecah Ghattie, was turned; and afterwards, when the enemy was defeated in a general attack on the heights of Muckwanpore.

Lieutenant Shipp's conduct on the last occasion was much extolled, having, in personal conflict, with one of the enemy's *sirdars*, destroyed him, when charging the light company on its ascending the hill of Muckwanpore.

Lieutenant Shipp also served with his regiment at the siege of Hattrass; and, being one of the first to enter the gate of that fortress, in endeavouring to intercept the *rajah* and the garrison, then in the act of abandoning the place, he received a wound in the hand.

Lieutenant Shipp afterwards served with the left division of the grand army under the Marquis of Hastings, during the

Mahratta and Pindaree war of 1817-18, and was present at the several sieges in which the left division was employed, as well as in the pursuit of the Pindarees.
W. L. Watson
Major, Assistant-Adjutant-General with the Troops
on the occasions above cited
Calcutta, 6th Nov., 1824

Appendix 4

Attestation from Major-General Watson, in favour of Lieutenant Shipp's general conduct

I hereby certify that I knew Mr. Shipp when in the army in the year 1817, at which time he was on my staff, in the East Indies; that I had frequent opportunities of observing his character and conduct, and can with truth say, I never knew a more active or zealous officer. I always found him strictly honest, gentlemanlike, kind, and grateful, possessing docility of manners and nice feelings.
James Watson
Major-General
Denton, Whitby
March 14, 1827

Appendix 5

Certificate from Major-General Newberry, of Lieutenant Shipp's conduct during the Pindaree Campaign

Certified: that I have known Lieutenant Shipp since the year 1813. He was in the 24th Dragoons with me, and was baggage-master to the left division of the grand army during the Pindaree campaign. I always found him a most brave, active, and zealous officer. He was a volunteer on my staff when the left division fell in with an immense body of those marauders, on the 14th of March, 1818; on that occasion Lieutenant Shipp cut two of their men down.
J. Newberry
Major-General

Appendix 6

COPY OF A LETTER FROM THE HONOURABLE THE DIRECTORS OF THE EAST INDIA COMPANY, GRANTING LIEUTENANT SHIPP A PENSION, IN CONSIDERATION OF HIS SERVICES AND WOUNDS

East India House
27th January, 1826
Sir,
Your letter of the 4th November, 1825, has been laid before the Court of Directors of the East India Company, and I am commanded to acquaint you that, adverting to the circumstance of your not having derived the benefit of their resolution of the year 1809, to appoint you a cadet in the Company's service, and in consideration of the conspicuous gallantry which you have displayed on so many occasions, and of the wounds received by you in the course of your service in India, the Court have resolved that, as a mark of their favourable notice, you be granted a pension of fifty pounds per annum, commencing from Christmas last.
I am, &c.,
J. Dart,
Lieutenant John Shipp
Secretary
British Coffee-House
Cockspur Street

Appendix 7

EXTRACT OF A LETTER, WRITTEN BY CAPTAIN GULLY, 87TH REGIMENT, TO SIR ANTONY BUTTER, BART., LORD CHIEF JUSTICE OF CALCUTTA, RECOMMENDING LIEUTENANT SHIPP TO HIS LORDSHIP'S FAVOURABLE NOTICE

My dear Sir Antony,
From the very great regard I had for Lieutenant Shipp, formerly of the 87th regiment, who was unfortunately dismissed the service a short time since, but, in consequence of his general good conduct as an officer and a gentleman, was recommended for the half-pay, which was granted him, I hope you will excuse

the liberty I take in asking your assistance, should it be in your power, in getting him some situation which would contribute towards his maintenance.

He has left us much regretted by, I may say, all the officers of the corps. His conduct, previous to the unfortunate court-martial, was that of a brave soldier, a steady friend, and an upright, honest man; and I am convinced, should it be in your power to procure him a situation, that he will fill it with the greatest exactness.

Believe me to remain, &c. &c.,
W. L. Gully
Berhampore
16th Dec., 1824

ALSO FROM LEONAUR
AVAILABLE IN SOFTCOVER OR HARDCOVER WITH DUST JACKET

AFGHANISTAN: THE BELEAGUERED BRIGADE *by G. R. Gleig*—An Account of Sale's Brigade During the First Afghan War.

IN THE RANKS OF THE C. I. V *by Erskine Childers*—With the City Imperial Volunteer Battery (Honourable Artillery Company) in the Second Boer War.

THE BENGAL NATIVE ARMY *by F. G. Cardew*—An Invaluable Reference Resource.

THE 7TH (QUEEN'S OWN) HUSSARS: Volume 4—1688-1914 *by C. R. B. Barrett*—Uniforms, Equipment, Weapons, Traditions, the Services of Notable Officers and Men & the Appendices to All Volumes—Volume 4: 1688-1914.

THE SWORD OF THE CROWN *by Eric W. Sheppard*—A History of the British Army to 1914.

THE 7TH (QUEEN'S OWN) HUSSARS: Volume 3—1818-1914 *by C. R. B. Barrett*—On Campaign During the Canadian Rebellion, the Indian Mutiny, the Sudan, Matabeleland, Mashonaland and the Boer War Volume 3: 1818-1914.

THE KHARTOUM CAMPAIGN *by Bennet Burleigh*—A Special Correspondent's View of the Reconquest of the Sudan by British and Egyptian Forces under Kitchener—1898.

EL PUCHERO *by Richard McSherry*—The Letters of a Surgeon of Volunteers During Scott's Campaign of the American-Mexican War 1847-1848.

RIFLEMAN SAHIB *by E. Maude*—The Recollections of an Officer of the Bombay Rifles During the Southern Mahratta Campaign, Second Sikh War, Persian Campaign and Indian Mutiny.

THE KING'S HUSSAR *by Edwin Mole*—The Recollections of a 14th (King's) Hussar During the Victorian Era.

JOHN COMPANY'S CAVALRYMAN *by William Johnson*—The Experiences of a British Soldier in the Crimea, the Persian Campaign and the Indian Mutiny.

COLENSO & DURNFORD'S ZULU WAR *by Frances E. Colenso & Edward Durnford*—The first and possibly the most important history of the Zulu War.

U. S. DRAGOON *by Samuel E. Chamberlain*—Experiences in the Mexican War 1846-48 and on the South Western Frontier.

AVAILABLE ONLINE AT **www.leonaur.com**
AND FROM ALL GOOD BOOK STORES

ALSO FROM LEONAUR
AVAILABLE IN SOFTCOVER OR HARDCOVER WITH DUST JACKET

THE 2ND MAORI WAR: 1860-1861 *by Robert Carey*—The Second Maori War, or First Taranaki War, one more bloody instalment of the conflicts between European settlers and the indigenous Maori people.

A JOURNAL OF THE SECOND SIKH WAR *by Daniel A. Sandford*—The Experiences of an Ensign of the 2nd Bengal European Regiment During the Campaign in the Punjab, India, 1848-49.

THE LIGHT INFANTRY OFFICER *by John H. Cooke*—The Experiences of an Officer of the 43rd Light Infantry in America During the War of 1812.

BUSHVELDT CARBINEERS *by George Witton*—The War Against the Boers in South Africa and the 'Breaker' Morant Incident.

LAKE'S CAMPAIGNS IN INDIA *by Hugh Pearse*—The Second Anglo Maratha War, 1803-1807.

BRITAIN IN AFGHANISTAN 1: THE FIRST AFGHAN WAR 1839-42 *by Archibald Forbes*—From invasion to destruction-a British military disaster.

BRITAIN IN AFGHANISTAN 2: THE SECOND AFGHAN WAR 1878-80 *by Archibald Forbes*—This is the history of the Second Afghan War-another episode of British military history typified by savagery, massacre, siege and battles.

UP AMONG THE PANDIES *by Vivian Dering Majendie*—Experiences of a British Officer on Campaign During the Indian Mutiny, 1857-1858.

MUTINY: 1857 *by James Humphries*—Authentic Voices from the Indian Mutiny-First Hand Accounts of Battles, Sieges and Personal Hardships.

BLOW THE BUGLE, DRAW THE SWORD *by W. H. G. Kingston*—The Wars, Campaigns, Regiments and Soldiers of the British & Indian Armies During the Victorian Era, 1839-1898.

WAR BEYOND THE DRAGON PAGODA *by Major J. J. Snodgrass*—A Personal Narrative of the First Anglo-Burmese War 1824 - 1826.

THE HERO OF ALIWAL *by James Humphries*—The Campaigns of Sir Harry Smith in India, 1843-1846, During the Gwalior War & the First Sikh War.

ALL FOR A SHILLING A DAY *by Donald F. Featherstone*—The story of H.M. 16th, the Queen's Lancers During the first Sikh War 1845-1846.

AVAILABLE ONLINE AT **www.leonaur.com**
AND FROM ALL GOOD BOOK STORES

www.ingramcontent.com/pod-product-compliance
Lightning Source LLC
Chambersburg PA
CBHW031618160426
43196CB00006B/180